No Turning Back

Joanne Lees
No Turning Back

My Journey

HODDER &
STOUGHTON

First published in Great Britain in 2006 by Hodder & Stoughton
A division of Hodder Headline

A Hodder & Stoughton Book

1

A CIP catalogue record for this title is available from the British Library

Hardback ISBN 0 340 92441 1
978 0 340 92441 9
Trade Paperback ISBN 0 340 93285 6
978 0 340 93285 8

Printed and bound by Mackays of Chatham Ltd, Chatham, Kent

Hodder Headline's policy is to use papers that are natural, renewable and
recyclable products and made from wood grown in sustainable forests. The
logging and manufacturing processes are expected to conform to the
environmental regulations of the country of origin.

Hodder & Stoughton Ltd
A division of Hodder Headline
338 Euston Road
London NW1 3BH

For Pete

Contents

Contents

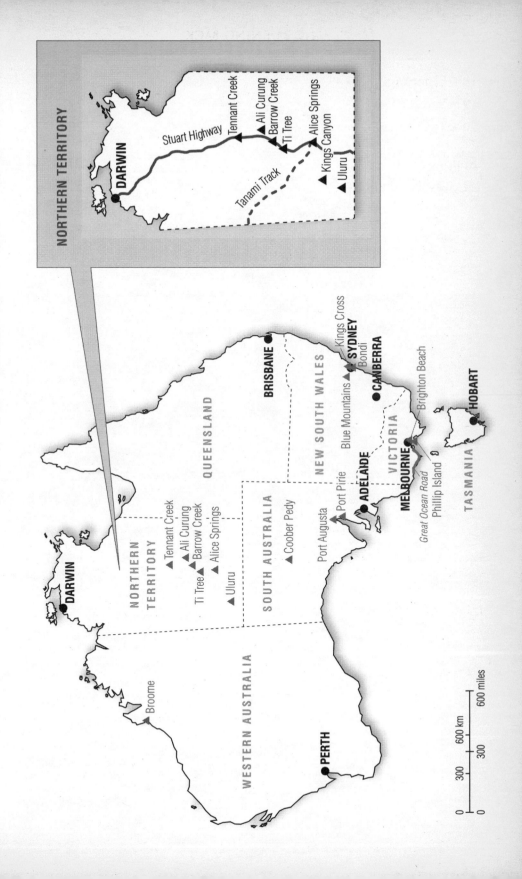

Preface

My name is Joanne Lees. On the 14th of July 2001 I was the victim of a serious crime. I was almost raped and murdered and the life that I thought I was going to have was stolen from me. On a lonely stretch of outback highway, a stranger murdered the man I loved and forever changed the way I would see the world. I then became the key witness in one of the most prominent criminal cases of recent times. As a result, for the last five years I have been the focus of intense public and media attention. People get murdered in Australia every day, but for some reason the murder of my boyfriend, Peter Falconio, generated massive and continuous interest. Others have their opinions about that night, about what happened, about what I did or didn't do. But they weren't there. They can never know what I saw, the terror I felt, or what Pete and I meant to each other.

No matter how much I would like to, I know there is no way of turning back time. I can't erase what happened and make things as they were. I hope no future survivor of such an incident will ever have to endure what I have, what the Falconio family has. Not just the shock and horror of the event itself, but the seemingly never-ending aftermath, which only ended recently with the conviction for murder of Bradley John Murdoch.

On my journey from that night to now, I have been spied on, lied to, and exploited by people pretending to have my best interests at heart; I have been portrayed in the most luridly negative way in the press, and all but accused of murder.

I have also met certain outstanding individuals – compassionate, caring human beings who have lifted my spirits and inspired me. They restored my faith in humanity and in myself.

The trial is now over. I hope to finally put those distressing times behind me. I would love to return to the life I once had. But I know I can never again be the person I once was. I've been exposed to a world of criminality and public scrutiny, and a media that cared only for getting the sensational story they wanted. I found myself criticised for wanting to grieve in private. It stunned me. While I maintained a necessary silence, my family, my friends and I endured a long list of upsetting untruths about me in the press. How could I speak openly and frankly when anything I said might be misconstrued or misreported and so jeopardise the trial? In the end the trial was all-important. It represented the hope of justice; justice for Pete, and for me.

That long-anticipated justice has now been served but I'm not the same person anymore and I can't go back.

I do realise that people have built up a deep curiosity about this case and my reticence has only served to intensify this. So I have decided to write this book to satisfy their curiosity. What chance do I have of a private life in the future if their questions remain unanswered?

But I have more important reasons for putting pen to paper.

Firstly, I am writing for Peter – who I loved, and who I shared a life with for five years. His name has been in constant use but most people have never stopped to consider the person he was. They have forgotten that the trial was about *his* murder and the seeking of justice for him.

This book is also written for other victims and their relatives. I would like them to see that it is worth the long wait and the tears and sleepless nights because, in the end, justice *can* be attained.

Many national newspapers were desperate for my story but I declined all offers, many of them substantial, because I wanted the public to have the full truth, not simply a journalistic take on what happened, glossed and distorted to make it as sensational as possible. In this book I will reclaim my life from other storytellers.

I know there are several books being published about what happened to me and Pete. It astonishes me that they could be written when none of the authors have ever spoken to me or even my close friends and family. I refuse to read these books but friends tell me that some accounts give the impression that they know what I felt and experienced. How could they possibly know that? The fact is they don't. The only person who can tell the authentic story, my story, is me. And that is why I am writing this book.

I hope that by the time you have read my story you will have all your questions answered; but to do that I have to go back to the beginning...

Joanne

1

It's all good

Writing my story is a strange process, I am not a writer and I don't pretend to be. But I do have a story and the only way I know to begin is to tell you about myself, things the headlines wouldn't ever have revealed.

I was born on the 25th of September 1973. For the first eleven years of my life it was just me and my Mum. I grew up in Huddersfield, Yorkshire, which is famous for being the birthplace of Rugby League. My Mum was everything to me and we were a team. We didn't have much money but she worked hard to make sure I had a happy childhood. There were times when I would catch my Mum sitting at the kitchen table crying, a pile of bills spread out in front of her. I was only a child but I would always try to make her feel better. Maybe that made me older than my years, but it was just how things were.

I spent years asking my Mum if I could get a dog and when I was eleven she finally gave in. Not long after, our family expanded again when she married. Now I had a dog, a stepfather, Vincent, and, pretty soon, a baby brother, Sam, who I adored and still do today.

The relationship between me and my Mum changed but the truth was, she was much happier. Now my Mum had an adult to confide in. I loved her and I wanted her to be happy so it was easy to accept the changes that Sam and Vincent's arrival meant for our relationship. My Mum was busy and I got on and did my own thing, safe in the knowledge that she was there if I needed her.

Because for so many years it had just been my Mum and me, and she was working to keep us both, I had always been very independent. I was not blessed with a large family, so I extended mine with a close circle of friends. I was happy with my family, my friends and the life I had.

As far back as I can remember I have been fascinated with different countries and faraway places. When I was a little girl my Mum couldn't afford expensive overseas holidays but she didn't let that stop us from getting away from home. We'd go on day trips to the seaside and weekends away to London. We would head off on outings to visit castles, museums, zoos and parks.

I think my desire to travel was genetic. In the seventies, when my Mum was in her early twenties, she hitchhiked throughout Europe with some friends. As I got older, she would often reminisce about her adventures. I'd listen intently while she described the places she'd been to and the people she had met.

As well as telling me her stories, my Mum gave me lots of keepsakes that she had collected on her travels. I particularly liked an unusual silver ring and a small doll, which looked like a troll. The doll was given to her by a Norwegian family and my Mum told me that as long as I had it I would never be without food or shelter. I still have them both and treasure the fact that my mother gave them to me and that they came from a time when she was so carefree.

After years of listening to my mother recount her travels it is probably not surprising that after leaving college I began working in a travel agency. Every day I was surrounded by holiday brochures, every day I would sell someone a holiday or book someone a flight. I enjoyed going to work and met interesting people from all walks of life. Everyone I dealt with had a story to tell. People travel for so many different reasons, some happy, some sad and some heartbreakingly tragic. I learnt to listen and let people tell me what they needed to.

Through my staff discounts and work trips I got to travel to many places. I was settled in my job, working hard and travelling whenever I could. I was twenty-two, single and having a great time hanging out with my friends. I felt secure within myself and though I would have liked a boyfriend I didn't *need* one. Up to that point I had never met anyone I wanted to be with.

Things changed on a summer evening in June 1996. I hadn't planned to go out that night but my friend Martin Jaffier (who I sometimes call Jaffa) invited me and a small group of friends round to his house for a few drinks. After a few hours, and a few beers, we decided to kick on at the local nightclub. We were dancing and laughing and having a great time when I locked eyes with a man across the dance floor and he gave me the most endearing smile. He was tall, with dark-brown hair and olive skin. It was strange. Without even speaking, some connection was made. I knew right then that I was going to be his girlfriend.

Time passed and as I chatted and danced I was always aware of where this man was in the room. When I looked at him, he would be looking back. It was electric and I felt my senses were heightened.

At the end of the night I started to leave and I felt a hand lightly touch my shoulder. I turned around and it was him. He introduced himself as Peter Falconio. He had a gorgeous smile and his dark-brown eyes twinkled when he looked at me. We chatted and I introduced Pete to my friends. Then I did something that shocked my friends and, if I am honest, probably myself. I left the nightclub with Pete. I had never gone off with a stranger before, but this was different. I just knew Pete was a good person and that I wanted to spend time with him. We went back to his parents' house and lay on his bed and talked softly until I fell asleep. I don't remember closing my eyes but when I woke Pete was looking into my eyes with a smile on his face and daylight was gently lightening the room. I couldn't help grinning back. I felt so comfortable with him from the first moment.

We sneaked out of his house quietly so we wouldn't wake his family and Pete drove me home. When we got to my place, we kissed goodbye in his car and then I dashed inside to get ready for work. After he'd driven off I realised that I hadn't given Pete my number, but I knew he'd be in touch.

* * *

From that first night Pete and I knew we wanted to be together and it happened very naturally. Over the summer of 1996, I got to know his family and friends and he got to know mine. Pete's parents, Joan and Luciano, welcomed me into their family. I got on well with them both and Pete and Luciano shared a cheekiness that I loved. The Falconios are a close-knit family and Pete is the third child of four brothers: Nicholas, Paul, Pete and Mark.

Pete loved travelling, too, and we would take off whenever we could. My favourite country that we visited was Italy. Pete's father, Luciano, was born in a small village in Italy, and some of my fondest memories are of the time Pete and I spent there. It is a special, secret place for me and it always will be.

The village is set on a sloping cliff edge. Villas line the winding cobbled streets and it is easier to find a church than a shop. The younger generations have all moved away to find work (like Luciano did) and so most of the year it is very quiet. Come August, holiday time, all the relatives return to visit. No tourists go there – it is all family. It is a place caught in time and when I am there I feel as though I am in another era. The houses are old and weathered, and even though it is not a wealthy area, all the houses are beautiful with huge oak doors, wooden shutters and marble floors.

Pete and I explored his family's house, from the wine cellars up through the many storeys. We would have a competition and race around the house trying to find the oldest thing we could. Pete and his family had been going there since he was a young boy, and there were drawings on the wall that were labelled 'Pete, five years old' and 'Nicholas, eight'.

One day I saw a group of nuns walking through the village in full habits. They fitted in perfectly. The older men and women of the village spend their days sitting in the local square, chatting, gossiping and watching the passers-by. The men sit in one group and the women in another. I am sure nothing went on in the community without them knowing about it. In fact, if you wrote to somebody you didn't even need to add an address and the letter would still find its way to the right person. Everyone I met in the village seemed to be related to Pete and people would stop us to chat. It made us both feel special to be connected to the place in some way.

* * *

At the end of that summer Pete left Huddersfield to study the second year of his construction planning degree at Brighton

University. Our relationship continued and, as often as we could, either Pete would return to Huddersfield or I would visit him in Brighton. Throughout that year we made plans to travel and work in New Zealand the following year, which would be Pete's gap year.

In the summer of 1997 I gave up my job, sold my car, and Pete and I paid a non-refundable deposit on our tickets to New Zealand. Shortly after I went on a holiday with some girlfriends, thinking it would be our last time together before I travelled to New Zealand for a year. When I got back Pete picked me up from the airport. I could tell he was nervous about something and he told me straightaway that he had been offered a year's employment with a construction company in Brighton. He was worried that I would be upset, but I knew it was an ideal opportunity for him to gain work experience and earn some money. I was pleased for him and touched that he had been so concerned about how this would affect me. We postponed our trip and Pete accepted the job offer. It was too good to refuse. I was a little disappointed but I knew we would get away one day. Pete invited me to move to Brighton to live with him. I did. Pete bought me a car (a very old one) and took me away on holiday to celebrate.

Brighton is on the south coast, sixty miles from London. I loved the city and have lived there ever since moving in with Pete. I like the period buildings, quirky cafes, bars, restaurants, marina and the beach being on my doorstep. I never tire of how Brighton Pier and the Grand Hotel look at night, illuminated by bright lights, and the mixture of people and different cultures. I made many friends, and Pete and I made a life together.

Pete enjoyed his one-year work experience with the construction company so much that when he was offered a permanent job he accepted and completed his degree part-time. I used to tease Pete about his interest in construction. Whenever I got any holiday photos developed I would inevitably find photographs of construction sites, scaffolding and cranes among our snapshots of beautiful beaches and exotic locations. It used to make me laugh.

* * *

In the summer of 2000, Pete graduated from Brighton University. We had been saving money and once he had his degree we decided it was the right time for us to travel. I was working in a travel agency so it made sense for me to plan and organise it all. On my birthday in September, as a present to myself, I confirmed our round-the-world tickets. We were to leave in just six weeks. I was working that day and couldn't stop singing and smiling. I kept telling all my customers where I was going. I must have been so annoying as I chatted about my round-the-world trip to people booking a package deal to Majorca. I wasn't being smug; I was just excited and wanted to share my news. One older Australian couple was in the office to work out some travel details and I told them my boyfriend and I were travelling there. They were very friendly and invited me to stay with them when I reached Australia. They wrote down their names and address on a piece of paper. I couldn't find one of my business cards so I gave them one of my colleague's, crossing out her name and writing in my name underneath. I could never have imagined that one day this kind couple would return this business card to me, enclosed in a letter of support, care of the Alice Springs Police Station.

Pete and I were a normal young couple. We were living together, saving for our big trip and getting on with life. I loved him and he loved me. We were happy. And, after four years together, we were about to set off on the adventure of a lifetime.

2

Many places,
Many faces

After months of preparing and saving, Pete and I flew from Heathrow airport to Kathmandu via Vienna on the 15th of November 2000. We were both excited to be heading off but almost straightaway we were reminded that the best-laid plans are easily disrupted when you are travelling. Our flight from Heathrow was delayed and so we had to rush to catch the flight from Vienna to Kathmandu. As we were passing through security I saw a young English couple of similar age to Pete and me. The man was frantically searching through his bag looking for their boarding passes. He was so focused on what he was looking for he wasn't being careful and he accidentally knocked his Discman out onto the floor where it broke. At that exact moment his girlfriend, who'd also been looking through her bag, straightened up and announced that she'd found their boarding passes. She'd had them all along. Naturally, the man wasn't happy and I heard him curse. I caught the girl's eye as Pete and I went past and gave her a knowing look.

We made the flight and arrived in Kathmandu the following morning. We had to queue for our visas and then wait to collect our rucksacks. We watched as passengers from the same flight gathered their luggage together and left. After a short while it was just me and Pete, the English couple that I'd seen earlier, and a few others left standing around the carousel. It became apparent after some enquiries that even though we'd made the flight our luggage hadn't. The only thing the Kathmandu airport officials could suggest was to come back in three days, when the next flight from Austria was due.

I was surprisingly calm, despite having just lost the bag I had packed so carefully on the very first leg of our journey. I felt optimistic that our luggage would turn up.

Pete and I spent our first three days in Kathmandu in the Thamel district. The place was a dusty, bustling maze of narrow winding streets lined with small shops and guesthouses. I wish I could describe the smell. It wasn't unpleasant, but a combination of incense, dust, traffic, food and garbage. It all combined to create some indefinable unique smell. One day, as I was standing negotiating a price with a rickshaw driver, I stopped for a moment to take in my surroundings. Someone was trying to polish my shoes; someone else was trying to sell me a chess set; yet another was selling tiger balm; a woman nearby started begging me for one hundred rupees; meanwhile a taxi driver pulled up and, leaning out of his window, told me he could offer me a better price than the rickshaw driver. It was chaotic and I loved it. Smiling, I jumped into the rickshaw.

Three days later, Pete and I went back to the airport and waited with the English couple, all hoping to be reunited with our rucksacks. We got chatting and I found out their names were Dan and Lisa and that they were also taking a year to go round the world. Their next stop was India. Our rucksacks finally appeared and after a small celebration we wished each other well and said goodbye.

As Pete and I explored Kathmandu we met two local boys called Ram and Prem. They were very friendly and were keen to practise their English skills on us. The boys spent a day with us and showed us around a number of temples and took us to traditional Nepalese places to eat. They said they wanted to spend time with Pete and me – to learn from us – but I am sure we learnt far more from them, as they taught us about the Nepalese way of life.

I enjoyed every moment we spent in Nepal. It was my first experience of being immersed in a completely different culture. I was touched at how proud, friendly and welcoming the Nepalese people were. Compared to what most people expect in the West, their lives were very simple and without the comforts we take for granted. It is easy to lose perspective in countries like England or Australia, where most basic needs are satisfied. Being in Nepal was a stark reminder that I was very lucky.

As Pete and I trekked through the Annapurna mountain range of the Himalayas, we met local Nepalese people and trekkers from all over the world. We never passed anyone without stopping to talk or at least share the greeting *Namaste*. 'Namaste' is both a spoken greeting and a gesture where you place your palms together (as in prayer) in front of your chest and nod your head forward as you speak.

We trekked through spectacular scenery which regularly took my breath away. Mountains surrounded us on all sides and their snow-capped summits were dazzling against the brilliant blue sky. Waterfalls flowed hundreds of metres into rivers below. The days were cool, bright and crisp. Each day we followed the Annapurna Trail and trekked for several hours before stopping to spend the night at small tea houses. I admit I found the first few days tough as we continually climbed upwards. On one occasion I stopped and dramatically told Pete that I would die if I had to climb anymore that day. Pete didn't say anything; he simply took my rucksack from me and carried it as well as his own for the rest of the day. I felt horribly guilty and kept asking for it back but Pete refused.

After we finished the trek, Pete and I went camping in the Royal Chitwan National Park for a few days. We stayed in a tent – by this time I'd become accustomed to living without electricity and hot water. Our days were spent with a small group of people and a local guide wandering through the jungle searching for wildlife, either on foot or on top of an elephant, which really is the ultimate four-wheel drive. Our guide gave us the following advice: 'If you have an encounter with a rhinoceros run away in a zigzag line; if it is with a tiger, stand still and stare it out. Alternatively, if you meet an aggressive sloth bear, act big.' At first I thought he was joking but I soon realised he was deadly serious.

Not long after he gave us this sage advice we were walking through the jungle and came across a rhinoceros and its baby. They were about three metres away. I excitedly turned round to tell our guide but he had already run off (I don't think he zigzagged!). Pete and I looked at each other and chased after him.

I adored the time we spent with the elephants. Each day I would ride an elephant into a river so it could bathe. The first time I did this I noticed leeches had attached themselves to my elephant. I was not concerned and started to pull them off, until I noticed that they were also on me. Pete ended up burning the ones on my legs off with his cigarette lighter.

After camping in the jungle Pete and I went back to Thamel and stayed at the Alice Hotel. All the staff who worked there were kind and friendly. We were only there a day or so when Pete started feeling very ill. He had caught a cold and couldn't get warm. I wasn't sure how to help him as I had no idea what Nepalese medication was like. I bought Pete a hot-water bottle and as it cooled I'd go out and ask the staff to refill it for me. After a while I didn't even need to ask, they would just turn up to refill it.

There was a young boy named Su who worked at the hotel. One evening he lit a bonfire up on the roof terrace so Pete could keep warm. As we sat quietly around the fire we were joined by an English couple, Isabella and Ben. We got talking and learnt that Ben had been an Olympic gold-medal winner at the Sydney Olympics for rowing. He was very modest about it. Later that same evening a group of Americans, who had escaped from a Buddhist monastery for the night, were attracted to the bonfire. We all talked about the things we had been doing and where we were off to next. It was what I liked most about travelling – meeting new people and learning about different ways of life.

I felt sad when we left Nepal. I had settled into the non-materialistic lifestyle and had become accustomed to seeing the world's highest mountains in the distance.

Our next stop was Singapore and it was a dramatic contrast to Nepal. The weather was hot and humid, the buildings tall and modern and the city very clean. Pete and I didn't find much to do in the way of adventure while we were there. We visited all the sights it had to offer, but it really seemed like a place to go shopping if you have lots of money to spend and we didn't.

Despite the fact we were backpackers, Pete and I always made sure we gave ourselves a treat now and then while travelling. After weeks of camping and exploring Nepal we were ready for some luxury, so Pete and I went and had cocktails in the most beautiful hotel I have ever seen called the Fullerton. Having seen pictures of luxury hotels in holiday brochures at work it was always nice to experience them for myself – even if just for a drink. The travel agency sometimes sent me to visit various hotels and Pete was more than happy to come along.

After spending five days in Singapore, Pete and I travelled overland through Malaysia to Thailand. We spent Christmas at Ao Nang Beach in Krabi. This is where *The Beach,* the movie based on Alex Garland's novel, was filmed. The beaches are beautiful, set against a backdrop of dramatic cliffs and limestone rocks. The water is a deep turquoise. From the beach you can see tiny islands scattered out to sea, which can be reached by longboats.

Pete and I were at a bar one night when I recognised a man sitting alone a few tables away. It was Dan, one half of the English couple who had been on our flight from Vienna to Kathmandu. We walked over and introduced ourselves again, reminding him that our luggage had been lost with his in Kathmandu. He remembered us and we talked together for a long time. Dan explained that his girlfriend, Lisa, had returned to their room because she wasn't feeling well. Before he left to check up on her, we exchanged email addresses and arranged to meet up again.

A few days later we met up with Dan and Lisa on the island of Phuket, and on New Year's Eve the four of us went into Patong to join the celebrations. Hundreds of people lined the main street to view the fireworks which were being let off in the street just metres in front of us. It was dangerously close but nobody complained because it was so spectacular. It didn't seem too organised and there wasn't a countdown to the New Year. Fireworks and firecrackers were being let off from as early as 9.00 pm and from then on were going pretty much non-stop all night. Some of the firecrackers were lit and then rolled along the ground. It was an accident waiting to happen – but it was fun. We just happened to be standing outside an Irish bar and from time to time one of us would step inside to buy a round of drinks. At around 11.00 pm it was my turn to go to the bar. It turned out the Irish had drunk the bar dry before midnight. The barman told me he'd sold out of most drinks and handed me the last bottle of champagne. I paid and when the barman handed me my change, I held it out to check it as there seemed to be too many notes. An Irishman standing at the bar leaned over to me and said, 'You'll not get ripped off in here, love.' He was right, the barman had given me back more than I had paid him. I tried to give it back to him but he wouldn't accept the money. I love the Irish.

On New Year's Day we said goodbye to Dan and Lisa, arranging to meet them again in Sydney in a few months' time. Pete and I continued to travel north through Thailand and explored the island of Koh Samui by motorbike. One day we came across a wildlife park. The park was new and not quite finished so supposedly hadn't opened to the public. Pete and I wandered in with a few other tourists. There weren't many animals, but I did see a tiger and its baby cub. We'd been in Thailand long enough to know that the Thai people were happy to give you what you wanted . . . for a price. I wanted to cuddle and feed the tiger cub so Pete paid a few hundred baht and the keeper handed the cub to me. It was cute and playful and I didn't want to hand it back. Pete paid the keeper another few hundred baht and I got to cuddle the cub for longer. The keeper eventually prised the cub from me and suggested we get in the cage with its mother for a photo. I felt apprehensive and, although I'm smiling and looking relaxed in the photo, I can assure you I was ready to leap out of the cage door. I was very aware I was sitting next to a wild animal.

As we were about to leave we walked by a crocodile enclosure and a man with an American accent asked if we could take a photo of him sitting on the back of one of the crocodiles. I was incredulous, but agreed. When he returned to collect his camera from me he suggested that Pete and I should have a go. Pete was keen and he climbed over the fence to join the American. I often found myself shaking my head at him and saying 'I can't believe you just did that!' Personally, I declined the offer, jokingly saying, 'I don't think my travel insurance will cover this.'

Once Pete and I reached Bangkok we decided on the spur of the moment to go to Cambodia, to visit Angkor Wat. We went to the Cambodian embassy to collect the necessary visas before catching a train to the Cambodian border, where we had to queue outside in the heat to pass through immigration.

Pete and I had bought a money belt for our trip but we never used it around our waists, we used it like a wallet. While we were in the queue Pete told me to put the belt on. I fully intended to but never actually did. Instead I put the money belt containing a few hundred US dollars, credit cards and flight tickets in my backpack. I didn't realise it then but while we were in the immigration queue someone must have stolen the money belt out of my pack.

We spent two days blissfully unaware. I assumed Pete had the money belt and he assumed I had it. We used the cash from our pockets and had an awesome time visiting the ancient temples. When we had both run out of money we asked each other for the money belt. It didn't take long to realise we had been robbed. Anyone else may have lost their temper but Pete was always so chilled. That was what made him such a great travelling companion . . . and boyfriend. If he wasn't habitually late for everything, he'd be perfect.

We were stranded in Cambodia with no money or onward tickets. It was only through the kind generosity we received from other travellers and my helpful colleagues from Thomas Cook that our small crisis was overcome.

3

Beaches and skyscrapers

Pete and I arrived in Sydney on the 16th of January 2001. We had been backpacking in South-East Asia for about two months before we boarded the flight to Australia and were looking forward to settling in one place for a while. It was after midnight when we touched down. As we walked through the airport, the surf shops and advertisements made me feel like I was on a beach in the sunshine. Even though we were walking under fluorescent strip lighting, my mind was imagining the sun and surf.

As we stepped out of the sliding doors, the night air was warm and Pete and I were wide awake. We were in a new place and we felt incredibly alive. We hadn't pre-booked any accommodation in Sydney. We'd slipped into a very relaxed routine in Asia and had drifted from one guesthouse to another, not panicking about the finer details. We'd always landed on our feet and we both had the attitude that we could overcome any obstacle together.

We had come to rely on our Lonely Planet guidebooks and after reading through the Sydney section we decided that Kings

Cross was our best bet to find a place to stay that night. It was closer to the airport than the beach and was described as being open twenty-four hours and full of travellers. We caught a cab and took off.

Our first glimpse of Kings Cross was the huge Coca-Cola sign that hangs over the district, and we were soon surrounded by the neon lights of the strip bars, the pavements full of revellers, internet cafes, women hanging around looking everyone else up and down...it was seedy but exciting. The Cross had an energy that buzzed. By the time the taxi pulled up outside a rundown backpackers' hostel I didn't know where to look, there was so much happening.

We went inside and spoke with the man working at reception. We wanted to stay in Kings Cross for about a week while we looked for jobs and found shared accommodation, near a beach. Though the man at reception was friendly, the hostel itself seemed too rowdy. He offered to mind our bags, so we could walk around the area and see if there was anywhere else to stay. Not far away we discovered a rundown hotel called Springfield Lodge we liked the look of. It was very basic, but cheap, clean and very quiet. It was perfect and we went back, collected our bags and booked in. In the whole duration of our stay we never saw another guest.

* * *

After that initial feeling of sun and surf as we walked through the airport, I woke up to a disappointing grey and cloudy sky. The weather stayed that way for our first few days in Sydney so I told Pete we would have to wait to go sightseeing. I was just as eager as him to explore the city, to see the Harbour Bridge and the Opera House, but I had always imagined seeing the Opera House gleaming white in the dazzling sun, against a backdrop of rich blue sky. So we waited for the perfect day.

We spent two days lazing around in Kings Cross. Pete and I were both hit with jetlag and would spend all morning sleeping and the afternoons watching the Australian Tennis Open. It wasn't the best way to adjust to a new time zone and we struggled to sleep during the night. We let ourselves be entertained by the many bars, cafes and internet cafes that Kings Cross had to offer. My first impressions of the place began to change and in a short time I grew to like it. I was starting to see beyond its seediness to find its charm.

Despite growing to like the Cross, Pete and I were still keen to find somewhere to live closer to the beach. We answered an ad for a flat in Bondi and arranged to meet the owner, Jesse, for coffee at the Aubergine Cafe in North Bondi. It turned out Jesse was from Amsterdam. He was very tall with a golden tan and blond wavy hair that reached down to his chin. He had bright blue eyes and a wide grin. Many people wrongly assumed that he was a surfer and I ended up teasing him about this unfounded reputation. He was a beautiful man with, as we were to find out, an equally beautiful soul.

Jesse had his five-year-old daughter, Tess, with him and he explained that her mother was doing a course in Canada for a while. Tess is incredibly similar to her father in appearance. She is a little ray of sunshine. We hit it off with them both straightaway. Among the usual questions, Jesse asked if either of us played chess. Sadly we didn't, not to a reasonable standard anyway. I was convinced if we had done, he would have rented us the room there and then. Instead, we went back to our hotel room and waited for him to call when he had made a decision.

We didn't have to wait long. Jesse called to say Pete and I were his and Tess's new flatmates. We arranged to meet him that night at the Bondi RSL to collect our keys and have a celebratory drink. The Bondi RSL (or Returned Servicemen's League) is quite an institution, as Pete and I were to discover. Pete and I ended up joining the club. It had regular live music, movie screenings, and served cheap food and drinks.

The next morning we checked out of the hotel. We had enjoyed the experience of living in Kings Cross but we were looking forward to staying in a more homely environment. Pete and I caught a taxi from outside the hotel to the flat in Bondi. Jesse had told us he would be at work but he still made us feel immediately welcome. He and Tess had left a note on the coffee table that said: 'To Jo and Pete, welcome home.' Tess had signed her own name, writing the letter 'e' in her name backwards. I thought that was adorable.

The flat was perfect. I instantly felt at home. It was open-plan and spacious. The walls were painted a pale blue and the floors were timber throughout the hallway and living room. As you entered the flat, a long hallway stretched before you with bedrooms leading from it on one side. The bathroom and separate toilet were on the other side from these, and at the end of the hallway was a huge living room. The kitchen was also off the hallway, and could be accessed from either the hall or the living room. I felt this room epitomised Jesse. It was bright, casual and on the walls hung photographs of Tess that Jesse had taken. Paintings that Tess had brought home from school were taped to the walls. My favourite was a colourful picture of a butterfly that Tess had painted. A tall bookcase stood against a wall, crammed full of books and old, worn copies of *National Geographic*. My favourite thing in the room was a black polished wooden screen with a traditional Japanese design across it. There were wide glass sliding patio doors leading on to a very big balcony. Every room had a balcony off it, including our bedroom, and the view was spectacular; being on the top floor of a three-storey apartment block we could see the crescent of Bondi Beach, hear and see the waves. We slept with the doors open as often as the weather would allow.

* * *

Once Pete and I had sorted out a place to stay it was time to begin searching for work. I had no idea what job I would be able to get in Sydney. Before I left the UK I made sure that I had an up-to-date CV and copies of this and my references ready to hand out. The day after we moved into the flat, Pete and I caught a bus from North Bondi to Bondi Junction. My plan was to walk around and ask for work anywhere that I thought I'd enjoy working. Pete came along to keep me company. He was looking for specific work in construction planning, so he was going to register with a number of employment agencies in the city.

We walked around Bondi Junction for a while and though there weren't many places that I felt I would like to work, I did narrow down the places I was going to approach. I love listening to music and reading books so I decided that I would like to work in either a music store or a bookshop. There weren't many of those in Bondi Junction so Pete and I caught a train to the city to widen our search. It was a hot, sunny Sydney day but the tall high-rise buildings blocked out the sun and I felt cool in their shadows. Pete and I walked together until we reached a bookshop on George Street called Dymocks. Pete kissed me for good luck and waited outside, out of sight, while I took a deep breath and stepped into the shop. A friendly young man approached and asked if I needed any help. I asked him if there were any job vacancies; he told me that there were and suggested that I leave my CV. I thanked him as I handed over my paperwork. As I left the store I noticed other staff members of a similar age to me throughout the shop. I could see myself working there and was determined to make it happen.

I walked outside and told Pete I wanted to work there. We kept walking and weaved our way through bustling streets full of office workers rushing along the pavement. Every now and again I would look up to admire the strip of dazzling blue sky that appeared between the tall skyscrapers. I'd never worked in a major city before and was excited by the thought of it. The hustle and bustle in the city centre was a stark contrast to the laid-back atmosphere of Bondi Beach and I was looking forward to having the best of both worlds.

With Pete's encouragement, I continued to hand out my CV at book and music stores throughout the city. As soon as we arrived in Australia, Pete and I had bought a mobile phone to share. I had put this phone number down as my contact whenever I left my CV. As we walked our phone began to ring. Pete answered it and then passed the phone to me. On the other end was a man called Gary Sullivan, the owner of the Dymocks bookshop I had been into earlier. He invited me to come in for an interview the next day. I was both surprised and delighted at the speed at which he'd got back to me.

I was on a complete high after Gary's call, but unfortunately Pete didn't get the same positive response. The employment agencies that we visited that afternoon told us that construction employers weren't willing to employ travellers on working holiday visas. I could understand why they wouldn't want to employ somebody for only a few months but it wasn't good news for Pete. I tried to encourage him and suggested that he look at alternative types of work but he felt disillusioned. He had been looking forward to learning about the Australian construction industry and working in it. On the way home Pete joked that I could go out to work and support him, while he surfed all day.

* * *

The next day Pete and I headed back to the city. While I went to the interview Pete was going to try his luck with a few more employment agencies. At the doors of Dymocks I arranged to call Pete on the mobile when I'd finished and then we'd organise a place to meet up. As I said goodbye to him I began to feel nervous. Pete could instinctively tell. He gave me one of his reassuring, winning smiles and winked at me before turning around and walking down the street.

I took a deep breath and let it out slowly. I felt my inherent optimism return. I walked down the stairs that led into the cool basement of the bookshop and walked over to the sales counter. I told the girl serving that I had an appointment with Gary Sullivan. A man with a kind face, who looked to be in his late forties, appeared, introduced himself and ushered me into his office.

Our conversation flowed freely and it wasn't an intense job interview. We chatted about books. While I'd been travelling I'd been reading a lot and talked about the different titles I'd read. Gary explained that Dymocks was a chain of franchises and that he owned two of them. They were family-run stores; his wife, son and brother all worked in the shops.

Working for a small family-run business appealed to me. I'd only ever worked for multinational companies before, reaching sales targets and generating profits for shareholders that I never knew. I thought the interview went well and Gary told me that he would let me know as soon as he'd made a decision, as he had other people to see. I thanked him for his time and left.

When I got outside I went to find a pay phone to call Pete and I suddenly realised that in my excitement getting to the interview I'd forgotten to bring any money. I thought about walking back to the bookshop to ask if I could use their phone, but instantly dismissed the idea. I didn't want to look like an idiot and risk putting them off employing me.

All I needed was forty cents to make the call. I decided to ask a passer-by. I was embarrassed at having to do this, but thought that they would be willing to help if I explained the circumstances. I must have chosen the most unsympathetic person to approach because the lady I asked looked at me as if I were distasteful and bluntly refused. After that I didn't have the heart to approach anyone else.

I didn't know anyone in the city, it was too far to walk home (and I didn't have a key to get in even if I did). I decided to call Pete anyway. I should have made a reverse-charge call but back then I didn't know this was possible. I dialled our number and heard Pete's voice for a second before the line went dead. I looked around for a shop name or a landmark that had a short title. I could see a shop in front of me called Lush. I dialled the number again and as soon as I heard Pete answer I yelled the word 'Lush'. I called a couple of times and did the same thing, then went and waited under the Lush sign.

To my absolute relief, Pete worked it out and found me outside the shop. He felt so guilty about having left me with no money that he took me inside the shop and insisted on buying me lots of beautifully aromatic soaps and body lotions. I told him that it wasn't his fault, but he felt better once he had spoiled me. He was like that.

* * *

A few days passed by and I heard nothing from Gary. Pete persuaded me to call him. I'm not usually that assertive and I didn't want to appear too pushy but I was so keen to work at the bookshop I decided that I would. Gary had given me his mobile number, explaining he often travelled between his two bookshops and it was the easiest way to catch him. I didn't know it at the time but have since learnt that Gary is a keen golfer and plays religiously on Wednesdays.

It was Wednesday. I called Gary and, not surprisingly, he was on a golf course. He didn't make small talk and told me that I could have the job. Later my Dymocks colleagues would tease me, saying that Gary gave me the job so he could get off the phone quickly and get back to his golf game.

My first day at work was the 14th of February, Valentine's Day. Gary introduced me to everyone. My colleagues were mostly Australians and New Zealanders around my age. Gary told me that an English backpacker called Tim had started work the day before and suggested that I should go with Tim to a particular shop in the city to try on uniforms and place an order for one. I was pleased to hear I was going to be working with another English backpacker and had a picture in my mind about what he would be like.

When I saw Tim for the first time, he was nothing like I had imagined. He was tall, skinny, wore glasses and had ginger hair. I am ashamed to say that I thought he looked like he would be a computer nerd. I was worried we wouldn't have a lot in common besides being English.

As Tim and I walked to the uniform shop together that morning, we chatted and I soon realised how wrong I was about him. Tim was softly spoken and had a relaxed manner, which I liked. I soon found out that he was intelligent, well-read, witty and very, very funny. He wasn't a nerd at all, far from it. He was into skateboarding, playing pool and having a beer. Trying on a navy-blue skirt inside the uniform shop, I remarked to Tim that I thought it was too short. Tim shook his head, took one look and said, mock seriously, 'It should be shorter.'

Tim became one of my closest friends and we looked out for each other. I enjoyed his company and he was always there when I went out.

Later that day another colleague by the name of Marelle insisted on taking me to a coffee shop called Earls to meet Simon, a fellow Northerner, from Leeds. Earls was at the back of our building and to get there we went through the bookshop's delivery door. Marelle was in her forties, enthusiastic and motherly. She had picked up on the fact that Simon and I had similar accents. I felt a little awkward but we exchanged travel stories and I soon relaxed. I told Simon that I was travelling with my boyfriend, Pete. Simon asked where he was working and when I explained that he was having trouble finding something Simon told me that there were jobs available where his mate Craig worked. It was an office furniture installation company called January Design. It sounded promising and Simon gave me a number to pass on to Pete.

I couldn't wait to get home and tell Pete about my day. As soon as I got back to the flat I kicked off my shoes, settled into a seat with a beer and told Pete and Jesse all about my first day at work. Every so often Pete would interrupt me to suggest that I go and get changed but I kept talking about the books I could borrow, trying on my uniform, meeting Tim and the rest of my colleagues, how Simon had a mate that might help Pete get a job. After talking for over an hour without taking a breath, I started to see their eyes glaze over. I walked to our bedroom to get changed. I opened the door to find Pete had bought me a huge bouquet of colourful flowers. It made me feel very special and happy and I loved Pete for being so thoughtful.

* * *

It was easy to settle into a routine. Pete had called Craig and had started work at January Designs. Most nights I'd go for drinks with my friends from work. Gary, my boss at Dymocks, was really pleased that his employees had bonded so well. He'd sometimes shout us drinks or tag along on a night out. There was always something to celebrate – a birthday, a new arrival, or someone would be having a drama that needed sorting out over a beer.

Pete would often join us and my friends became his. He also made friends with some of the people he worked with and they would occasionally join us as well. The weekends were our time together and we spent those days around Bondi or exploring Sydney. One weekend we travelled up to the Blue Mountains to go bush walking, and stayed in a hotel overnight. We would often go out for meals together or as a group with some of our friends.

Monday nights were what Pete and I referred to as our 'TV night in with the family'. Wherever I was and whoever I was with, I would make my excuses and leave so I had enough time to get home by 7.00 pm. Pete would do the same. On those nights we would all pitch in to prepare dinner and then settle in around the television to eat. We watched Tess's favourite program about wildlife and by the time 'Ally McBeal' started she would be falling asleep. Jesse would put her to bed and then we would watch 'The Practice'. What I enjoyed the most was relaxing in the company of my new Bondi family. When 'The Practice' finished I would go to bed and read while Pete and Jesse shared a joint and talked into the early hours of the morning about world politics, globalisation and conspiracy theories.

I made the most of having access to so many books. I read constantly and as well as borrowing books from the shop I was encouraged to read any of the advance copies of new releases the publishing companies sent in. I read while sitting on the bus and train to work, in the park or staff room on my lunch break and every night before I went to sleep. Everyone who worked in the shop was a keen reader and we were constantly recommending books to each other.

Marelle told me about a book she had just finished which she wanted me to read so we could compare interpretations. The book was called *After You'd Gone* by the Scottish writer Maggie O'Farrell. It was about a woman dealing with the loss of her partner. It was a multi-layered story that explored mother/daughter relationships and jumped forwards and backwards in time. I read and enjoyed the story but never could I have imagined that one day I would be questioned about it in a court of law.

Pete and I were happy and loving our time in Sydney. We both became very quickly attached to Jesse and Tess and planned Jesse's thirty-fifth birthday celebrations together. I had to work so Pete took Tess shopping in the city to buy presents. When I got home that afternoon to set up for the party, Tess couldn't wait to show me the beauty set Pete had bought for her. It included glitter powder and nail varnish. We decided to make Tess's gift a feature of the party. We hung fairy lights across the glass patio doors in the living room and set up a table in the hallway near the door. Tess and I made a sign that read 'TESS'S BEAUTY PARLOUR'. As guests arrived Tess painted their nails and put glitter on their face. She took special care making up Pete and Jesse. It was a great night and a memory I will cherish.

4

I hate goodbyes

Lisa and Dan arrived in Sydney two months after us. While Pete and I had spent time settling into our Sydney life, finding a home and jobs, they had continued their round-the-world trip, including travelling around Australia. They had kept in touch and sent us postcards from various places.

Once they arrived in Sydney, Lisa and Dan rented a flat in Potts Point, near Kings Cross. Pete and I would often call round for a drink and to watch football with them as they had subscribed to the Pay-TV sports channel (FOXTEL). Having them close by was great. The hardest part of travelling is missing the people you love, but Pete and I had made such good friends it made it easier to be so far away from home.

Lisa's mother, Bren, came out to visit Lisa. She'd missed her daughter and while she was in Sydney she mothered us all and cooked us roast dinners. On the day of Lisa's birthday we all went to Star City to celebrate. Casinos are not my scene but I had a great time. Dan and Pete wandered off gambling and Lisa and I sat in a lounge bar chatting with her mum. There was a singer performing on stage and from time to time Lisa and her mum would comment that he wasn't very good. At one point Lisa got up, saying that she would be back in a minute. I assumed she'd gone to the bathroom.

All of a sudden we heard a woman's voice begin to sing. Bren exclaimed, 'It's my Lisa!' I turned round to see Lisa standing on the stage. She had told me that she wanted to be in a band some day but I'd never heard her sing before. She was good. I listened in surprise, finding it hard to believe that she'd got up on stage without warning us. I was impressed and blown away by her confidence.

My time in Sydney was full of wonderful moments like that. One Sunday afternoon I decided to spend time with Tess. It was a glorious sunny afternoon with clear blue skies. I asked Tess what she would like to do and she brought out a packet of coloured chalk. I decided that our whitewashed balcony walls would be the perfect surface to chalk on. I set up a chair for each of us out there and Tess and I spent all afternoon sitting in the sun and drawing on the wall. From time to time I would look across to see what Tess had drawn. It was always the same as mine. She was copying me. I'll remember that afternoon always.

* * *

Not all my memories are as heart-warming. Anyone who has paid attention to our story in the papers and on the news will know some of the particulars of our lives. But to give you my account I have to reveal things I would prefer not to talk about. I am about to tell you about a choice I made. A choice I wish I had been strong enough to resist. In the telling I am betraying a friend. I am also betraying my wish to leave this far behind me. Because what happened impacted so much on what was to come later I know I must explain how I felt at the time and why I made the choices I did.

In the previous chapter I have tried to give you an idea of what our life was like while we were living in Sydney. Our relationship was good and we were happy.

Living and working in Sydney was a thousand miles away from the realities of my life back in the UK. Even though Pete and I hadn't been in Australia long, it was an intense time for me and I had forged strong friendships quickly. Most of the girlfriends I'd made were single. It was a live-for-the-moment time and I was caught up in the reckless immediacy of the backpacker's life. Though this was kept balanced by living with Jesse and Tess, I was in holiday mode and it was very easy to get caught up in the Sydney nightlife. Most nights of the week I would go for drinks after work with my friends from Dymocks and sometimes a group of Tim's friends would join us.

One night, quite early on, a group of us were out and Tim brought along a mate of his called Nick Reilly. Nick was from Brighton and on a working holiday in Australia. He was a guy who was always the life and soul of a party. We developed a playful friendship and I enjoyed being around him. He paid me lots of attention and when he flirted I responded. I didn't think anything of it in the early stages, I thought it was harmless. I just liked the way I felt when he was around.

Nick and I were never alone at first. We would see each other in pubs among our large group of friends. I enjoyed the energy and the new friendships, but Pete was happier at home in Bondi, discussing global politics with Jesse.

After two months of Nick and I flirting and teasing each other things went too far ... and I let it happen. Over a short period of time Nick and I slept together twice. I was caught up in the moment and I didn't think about Pete or my real life until afterwards. If you have travelled for any length of time you will know what I mean when I say it was something that happened outside my normal realm. I would never have done something like this at home in Huddersfield or Brighton but in Sydney it didn't have the emotional weight it would have had in my 'real' world. I am not trying to make excuses for what happened and I hope that it doesn't sound like I am. I was a grown woman capable of making decisions and making her own choices.

As soon as we had stepped over that line everything changed between Nick and me. The flirtatious, charming, exciting exchanges evaporated. Something had been taken further that never should have been. We both knew this was something that couldn't go on, that we didn't want to continue. The attraction was gone but there was still a friendship and we were both able to accept this and see what had happened for what it was. Not long after, Nick left Sydney to continue travelling and though we stayed in touch by email, if things had been left to a natural course the email contact would have eventually faded out.

I never told Pete about Nick. It had been a momentary madness and I didn't want to hurt Pete and make him doubt us when what I had done had only made me realise how much I wanted him in my life. What had happened was separate from my life with Pete and was no reflection on our relationship. It was a holiday fling that would have been quickly forgotten. The thing I struggled with most was not what I had done but that I now had a secret that I could not tell Pete. Until this point we had shared all our feelings and our worries.

I was twenty-seven years old then, and looking back I can see it was all part of growing up and working out what I wanted from my life. I obviously had no idea this would have such momentous ramifications and possibly jeopardise the hunt for Pete's murderer.

The only person I owe an explanation to is Pete and I would give anything to be able to do that. But Pete isn't here and I can't continually beat myself up about Nick. What happened wasn't important and it shouldn't define me. The defence counsel would use it as an attempt to discredit me during the committal hearing. The media picked up on this and turned it into a sensational story, which it did not deserve to become. I cringed at the time but I refuse to be ashamed or embarrassed about anything that I have done. It has helped make me who I am.

I should make two things clear. I did not hide this information from the police; in fact I gave them the password to my email account knowing full well that all Nick's emails were on there. I knew Nick was completely irrelevant to what happened to me and Pete on the Stuart Highway.

Later, knowing that the details of my fling with Nick had been given more weight than they should have by the police during the investigation and that copies of all my statements and interviews were available to the defence many months before the committal hearing, I knew I would have to tell the Falconio family about it. I was determined that they would hear the details from me rather than in court or through any other source. The fact that I had to expose Pete's family to unnecessary hurt caused me a great deal of stress and anxiety and I wouldn't be truthful if I didn't admit I was worried about what they would think of me.

I couldn't bring myself to tell Luciano and Joan directly. I called Paul and was completely honest with him. I told him that the only reason I was telling him about Nick was because it would no doubt be brought up by the defence during the committal hearing. I didn't want him or his family to first hear about it in court. I told Paul that I had never wanted him or his family to find out. I hadn't wanted them to think any less of me. I asked Paul if he could tell the rest of the family on my behalf.

Paul was quiet. I think he appreciated my candour. It has never been referred to since by him, his brothers or his parents and I've never been treated any differently by any member of the Falconio family since they found out. If anything I feel closer to them.

I don't know if I would ever have told Pete about Nick. It is impossible to say. What I do know is that any chance to make choices together, any highs and lows that we would have had to face, were violently taken away from us on the 14th of July 2001.

* * *

At the beginning of May, Pete and I began looking for a campervan to travel around Australia in. One Sunday we went to a well-known place where travellers sell their campervans after they have finished their trips around Australia. It was in an underground car park in Kings Cross.

Stepping from the pavement we walked down a ramp and into what felt like a hidden world. Inside the car park there were campervans of all different shapes and sizes. Their doors were wide open, inviting anyone to come and look inside. The owners of the vans sat lazily beside them in deck chairs, listening to music blaring out from various car stereos. There was a cacophony of noise and the atmosphere was more like a carnival than a car yard.

I liked looking inside the many different campervans and meeting their owners. It was great to talk to people who had just returned from similar journeys to the one Pete and I planned to do. They had fascinating stories to tell and recommended various places to visit.

Despite looking at lots of campervans that day we didn't find the one for us. Even though we had weeks to keep looking, Pete was keen to buy something as soon as possible. I understood his eagerness. Once we had bought the van, our trip would be one step closer. It would be 'real'. Having our own vehicle would also make it easier to explore more distant parts of Sydney.

On other occasions, I was quite content to let Pete look for a van without me. He knew much more about cars and engines than I did and enjoyed checking out prospective vehicles. He used to go with a few mates. I thought of it as a boy thing.

One day Pete called me at work. He was excited because he said he'd found the perfect VW Kombi for us. I arranged to meet him in the city after work to inspect it with him.

Later that day, Pete and I walked towards a burnt-orange VW Kombi which was parked at the side of the road beside Hyde Park. Sitting inside were a young couple. As we approached their side window they opened their doors and climbed out to greet us.

As soon as they spoke I recognised their accents and asked them where they came from. 'Huddersfield,' they both said. I couldn't help thinking, it really is a small world. I teasingly chastised Pete for not telling me earlier that they were from our hometown. After chatting some more I discovered that the man, Anthony, came from the same village as Pete. His girlfriend was from Barnsley. In Pete's enthusiasm for the Kombi and his fixation with engine and mileage details it had slipped his mind to tell me what I considered to be important information. Another boy thing, I thought.

Before I had even had a good look around inside the Kombi, I had decided that we were buying it. After all, these people were from Huddersfield. My attitude is that if you can help each other out, you should.

We organised details, agreed on a price and the van was ours. Pete and I drove the couple to where they were going and then drove home to Bondi. A few days after buying the Kombi, Pete received a phone call from his mum, Joan. We both kept in touch with our families regularly so there was nothing unusual about this. Joan told Pete that she'd heard that we'd bought a Kombi. Pete's mum and dad owned the local post office and Anthony's aunt had been in and told Joan that we had bought a Kombi van from her nephew. I thought this was hilarious: you can be 12,000 miles away and your mum still finds out what you've been doing without you telling her!

* * *

Over the weeks leading up to our departure from Sydney, Pete would often work on the Kombi. He made improvements and alterations and would even stay behind after work to modify the Kombi with his workmates. He fixed a safety deposit box underneath the backseats for us to be able to store our passports and important documents safely. He also installed a pair of spotlights in the back above the bed. It was a very thoughtful gesture, because he knew I'd have a pile of books to read on our journey. He also installed a new table, a shelf underneath the dashboard and re-panelled the interior doors.

At weekends Pete and I would pick up our friends and we would all go on day trips. I would insist on making cups of tea and lunch on the little stove inside the Kombi for our friends, even if we were parked just metres away from a string of cafes. It was a novelty and I enjoyed playing hostess.

I'm not sure exactly when it happened but I gave the Kombi a name. I called it Taz because of the Tasmanian registration plates. Taz was parked on the street outside the flat and from time to time Tess and I would take our dinners down there and sit at the table inside the Kombi to eat. Tess loved it and it was fun for me as well.

* * *

We were both excited at the thought of the next stage of our journey but I was dreading saying goodbye to all the good friends I had made. Not just Jesse and Tess but also my friends from Dymocks, people like Amanda, who was my closest friend in Sydney. It was strange to feel happy and sad at the same time.

Towards the end of June my work friends organised a leaving party for me at a restaurant at Cockle Bay Wharf. Pete's mates organised his farewell for the same night in Kings Cross. Pete and I planned to merge the two groups after my party had finished at the restaurant and continue our night all together. My time in Sydney had been a bit of a party and this was my last night out with my friends.

Because there were so many people involved, it was hard to coordinate everything. Eventually we all ended up at the Kings Cross Hotel, which has a bar and a dance floor. It was relaxed, everyone knew everyone and it was fun dancing and chatting. It was one of those nights you don't want to end.

After a while it was decided we'd move on to a seventies-themed club called the Carwash. I'd heard about it and had told everyone I thought it would be a great place to finish off the night. Half the group were ready to go, while the other half wanted to finish their drinks. I suggested that those who were ready should go on ahead and the rest of us would catch them up. I stayed back with Pete. It wasn't long before they were back. Apparently they'd been queuing to pay the entrance price when the police stormed past them and raided the club for drugs. Consequently, the club was closed that night. I didn't really care where we were as long as there was music to dance to. I was in a dancing mood. For me this was the end of a wonderful stage of my life and I was making sure I celebrated the time I had with the friends I'd made.

In the early hours of the morning, when the bar shut, we went to a friend's house nearby. Everyone had that end-of-the-night languor and sat around the kitchen table, chatting and passing around joints. I knew most people but there were a few strangers there too, friends of friends. As it was quite crowded and there weren't enough chairs I sat on Pete's knee. I listened to snippets of conversation and then fell asleep in Pete's lap, with my head against his chest. He woke me softly to tell me our taxi had arrived. I said a sleepy goodbye and we headed home.

The sun was already up when we climbed into bed. Pete and I snuggled up together and I was just drifting off to sleep when I remembered that Jesse had told me he had someone coming at 10.00 am to view the flat. He had obviously been interviewing prospective housemates to fill our spot. I set the alarm for 9.00 am so that we could be out of the flat when they arrived. There was no way I'd let Jesse down.

It seemed like I'd just closed my eyes when the radio alarm woke us. We got up, dressed and headed down to the beach for breakfast. Eating breakfast out is a rare treat; normally I'm rushing around getting ready for work. That morning we didn't eat at the cafe, but took our breakfast down to the beach and sat and watched the waves lap against the shoreline. We stayed there for a while, mesmerised by the waves, until we thought enough time had passed and then headed back to the flat.

When we got back Jesse was still there. He told us how much he enjoyed living with us, which made Pete and me feel great. Jesse explained he'd been worried about having a couple move in but he had been so pleased with how it had worked out he thought he would probably try to get another couple to take our room.

I took a shower and got dressed. I had left some things at work so Pete and I decided to drive into the city to get them. To most this would have been no big deal, but I hate goodbyes and popping into Dymocks meant I would have to say goodbye to people all over again. I used to get very emotional but, sadly, since then I've been getting better at goodbyes. I've had a lot of practice in the last few years.

The bookshop was much quieter on the weekends and so there were fewer staff rostered on. That day it was Tracy and Corinne. I walked down the stairs and into the shop basement. Tracy and Corinne were standing by the counter; walking over to them I explained that I needed to pick up a few things. As I approached them, they stared at me. I felt self-conscious and puzzled; I asked them what was wrong. They both said, 'It's because you're leaving', and ran over to give me a hug.

As I walked out of the shop I was holding back tears. Pete didn't say anything; he just put his arm around me. That was just what I needed.

* * *

A few days later, Pete and I were finally ready to leave Sydney. We set off a couple of days later than we'd initially planned, but that's the great thing about travelling – we didn't have a rigid schedule to keep to. We said our final goodbyes to our housemates and Jesse gave us a book, which he had inscribed with a message, and some photos of Tess. I also had pictures that Tess had drawn of us at the beach. After getting to know Tess it was very difficult to say goodbye. But I was the adult so I held it together and promised I would keep in touch. I meant it. I watched Jesse and Tess walk back into the flat and felt so sad that we were moving on.

Just before we drove off Pete told me that he had bought me a present, to cheer me up. He climbed out of the driver's seat and walked through to the back of the Kombi. He turned around to face me holding a small portable television. My face dropped; my first thoughts were that I don't want or need a TV and that Pete had actually bought it for himself. Pete could see the unimpressed look on my face, and still beaming with enthusiasm he nodded his head and said, 'Wimbledon, babe.' Then I knew that he *had* bought the television for me. It was a wonderful gesture and it did cheer me up. I love watching the Wimbledon tennis tournament.

5

3391 miles

After weeks of working on Taz and modifying the vehicle for our trip, Pete was thrilled to be on the road. I was too but it took a little while for me to shake off the sadness of so many farewells, especially saying goodbye to Tess. We left Sydney and headed to Canberra and from there made our way to Thredbo. It was cold and wet and I was looking forward to warm days and sunshine so I can't say this was the highlight of my journey so far. The drive down the Great Ocean Road was amazing and we loved looking down on the wild ocean and feeling so insignificant against the aged cliffs.

We were the typical tourists and visited Phillip Island to see the penguins and, of course, made sure we went to Brighton Beach. It was nothing like home but we thought the brightly coloured bathing sheds were better than ours. While we were there we watched a wedding on the sand. We felt good being on a beach again.

From Victoria we headed across to Adelaide and then to all the Port towns – Port Pirie, Port Augusta. I was pleased when we left Adelaide and escaped the city. We had settled into Taz well, but for me cities are not really the place to be when you're living in a Kombi. I was looking forward to heading up north, into the outback country and wide-open spaces.

The scenery kept changing dramatically as we drove up through the centre of Australia. We drove past salt mines, which just seemed to appear from nowhere and glisten like snow. I'd never seen a salt mine before.

We arrived in the opal-mining town of Coober Pedy and I couldn't help thinking it was a slightly bizarre place. The desert landscape was strange, dramatic and almost alien. As we drove in there weren't many people or houses that you could see and it felt and looked like a ghost town. On the horizon I could see rows of mounds of dug-out sand that from a distance looked like pyramids.

Every day Pete and I would see places and landscapes that until that moment we'd only seen in tourist brochures and in movies or on television. It was wonderful. When we got close enough to see Uluru (Ayers Rock) we pulled onto the side of the road to stop and admire it peacefully from a distance. It felt strange to be finally seeing for ourselves an image we had seen so many times. I had seen Uluru's picture on thousands of holiday brochures and learnt of it at school. From time to time Pete and I would pull over at a tranquil spot to take in a view only to have a coach full of tourists pull up beside us with the same idea. It never failed to spoil the moment but we'd always laugh as it was kind of funny that even in the most remote area busloads of tourists were never far away.

Thankfully, we weren't disturbed that day and after a time we started Taz back up and drove to the Uluru car park. I wanted to climb the rock straightaway but we were told in the visitor centre that it was closed due to windy weather conditions. Instead, Pete and I walked all around the base of the rock. It was a cool, fresh day and it was invigorating to be out of the confined space of the Kombi and to be walking in such a breathtaking place. I felt a sense of freedom and energy being out in all that space. Vast open land lay in every direction, for as far as I could see. After so long in cities, we were beginning to feel as though we were now on the once-in-a-lifetime adventure we had planned.

Pete and I didn't see many people as we walked around the rock. It probably took us about two hours to walk all the way around, but I wasn't really conscious of the time. I didn't need to be. Pete and I had slipped easily into the travelling lifestyle and we had started to lose track of what time it was or even what day of the week it was. We didn't have to answer to deadlines or have a work schedule, so time wasn't important. We got up when we felt like it, ate when we were hungry and moved from place to place when we were ready to go.

I thought that Uluru was magnificent. The rich colours were amazing and changed with the movement of the sun. It is the whole setting and endless open landscape that adds to the striking presence of the place. I can't explain it but I felt some eerie moments as I walked the ten kilometres around the pitted rock. Perhaps it is because of the sheer size of the rock itself, combined with the isolation, but there is an otherworldly feel out there. I tried to imagine its history and the different generations of people who had also visited. It was such a familiar landmark and I felt privileged to be able to see it for myself.

The sun was beginning to slide down across the sky as Pete and I drove away from the Uluru car park so we stopped on a stretch of road to watch it set over Uluru. Many other people had the same idea. Cars lined the road; people stood beside their vehicles or sat on their car roofs to admire the magnificent red rock changing colour as the sun began to sink slowly behind it.

Strangely, watching the sunset surrounded by strangers didn't spoil the moment as we thought it would. It actually made it feel more special to be sharing the experience. Everyone looked at each other, smiling in satisfaction and appreciation, and for a short moment complete strangers were united. We knew what everyone was feeling because we were feeling it too.

Once the sun disappeared, Pete and I drove over to a nearby campsite and stayed there for the night. It was cold and dark outside and there wasn't anything to do there but Pete and I weren't worried. I filled my hot-water bottle, closed all the curtains in the Kombi and tuned the TV to the men's Wimbledon final. Sitting curled up next to Pete we cuddled under the blankets and watched one of the most dramatic games of tennis. Goran Ivanisevic was playing against Pat Rafter. I was cheering for Goran. He had entered Wimbledon on a wild card and was the underdog. I always support the underdog if my favourite players aren't competing. I was almost in tears when Goran won in a five-set victory. I was completely caught up in the excitement and tension of the game and was exhausted when it was all over.

In the morning Pete and I woke up early and drove back to Uluru to watch the sunrise. Afterwards, we noticed people climbing up the rock, looking from a distance like small ants crawling across the red surface. We parked Taz and got ready to climb.

It didn't take very long to reach the top and the view of the endless flat land around us was awe-inspiring. I was surprised to hear other climbers making calls on their mobile phones. I could overhear them saying, 'Guess where I am?' It didn't sit well with me. It seemed completely wrong and disrespectful to use modern technology at the top of such a sacred site. Though I know some would say the same about Pete and me for climbing the rock in the first place.

After climbing back down we had breakfast inside the Kombi and then decided to head off. I was in the passenger seat and Pete was driving. Up ahead I could see two hitchhikers standing on the side of the road, a male and a female. I felt concerned for them because they were in the middle of nowhere. Pete turned to look at me questioningly and I nodded. We had never picked up any hitchhikers before but something made me want to stop and help this couple. I thought it would be good karma, especially after people were so kind to us in Cambodia after our money belt was stolen. It just felt like the decent thing for us to do, to help out other travellers.

Pete pulled over and the hitchhikers ran up to my window. I opened my door to greet them and, to be honest, to check them out. I climbed out of the Kombi and Pete climbed over the passenger seat to join me. Pete asked them where they were going, and they told us they were headed up to Alice Springs. I explained that we were travelling to Kings Canyon and planned to stay overnight there before travelling on to Alice Springs. I invited them to join us and they happily agreed.

Their names were Isobel and Mark and they were Canadian. Mark wore his hair long in two very distinctive plaits. They were both friendly and had a good energy about them. They settled into the backseats and we set off.

It was fun having new people to chat to as we drove and I could tell Pete was enjoying being 'host'. When we arrived at Kings Canyon we headed straight to the campsite. We parked and Mark and Isobel pitched their tent next to Taz. Sitting outside in the late afternoon sun we took turns playing backgammon and shared stories about our travelling experiences. As darkness fell we lay back to look up at the stars. The night was clear and we could see thousands of bright shining lights. Mark was quite knowledgeable about astronomy and pointed out various constellations to us. We talked for hours and eventually it was time for sleep. We agreed to set off early in the morning to walk around Kings Canyon.

When we woke it was a warm, bright morning. After breakfast we all set off to trek around the canyon. We stopped occasionally to take photographs, admire the views and look down over the dangerous cliff overhangs. We jumped into the natural water springs, shrieking out to each other as we entered the cold water. Our shouts echoed loudly around the canyon.

When we got back to the Kombi, Pete checked out the map and worked out two possible routes to Alice Springs. He explained both options. One route, which was the shorter of the two, meant driving across an unsealed road. The other option was longer but was on sealed roads. Pete was confident in the Kombi's ability to drive across an unsealed road without any problems so we all agreed to take the shorter route.

We headed off and soon enough we were driving along on an uneven red dirt road. As the Kombi bumped up and down I looked at Pete's face and knew we'd made a mistake. There was nothing we could do, we were committed to this track and just had to see it through. The road was empty and there was nothing in sight except for the dusty road. The only way the Kombi was going to cope was to go slowly, and I mean *really* slowly. I think we could have walked faster.

It was tedious driving so the four of us decided to take it in turns to drive to break up the monotony. What I thought was going to be a very boring trip turned into a fun adventure. We all wanted to get to the end of the unsealed road but we laughed and joked and talked together so it was far from an interminable journey. Every so often I would ask Mark and Isobel if they were regretting accepting a lift from us. They both said they were happy to share the ride.

From time to time a four-wheel drive would speed by without pausing, leaving behind a cloud of red dust. One driver did stop to check that we were alright but we assured him we were and off he went.

Finally, just as it was getting dark, we reached the end of the rough road and saw a sign pointing to Alice Springs. It had taken over six hours to get to this point. Once we were on a sealed surface we sped up and in no time we arrived in Alice Springs. We dropped Mark and Isobel outside a backpackers hostel on the main street, but not before Mark and Pete exchanged email addresses, and then Pete and I drove off to find somewhere to camp for the night.

The next morning Pete and I left the Kombi at the Stuart Park caravan site and explored the town of Alice Springs. It didn't take us long. We needed to spend some time in Alice doing chores. First we booked the Kombi in for repairs. The steering rod had suffered on the way there on the unsealed road. Pete made an appointment with an accountant to discuss his tax return and we also dropped into a travel agent on the main high street. Pete made enquiries about adventure trips to Papua New Guinea. It was something that he and Dan (the Englishman we had befriended) had talked about doing while they were in the Southern Hemisphere. Pete didn't confirm a booking because he needed to check dates with Dan but he was pretty confident it was something he could make happen. I was happy for Pete to have a boy's own adventure and I would spend the short time he'd be away with my friends in Sydney.

Because we were in Alice Springs we did what most tourists do...we went to the Camel Cup. The Camel Cup is an annual fundraising event held in a park on the outskirts of the town. As the name suggests, the main event is camel racing. Pete and I stood near the start line and watched most of the races. It was quirky and hilarious. Half the camels ran in the right direction while the other half headed off in the totally wrong direction. We couldn't stop laughing as we watched their jockeys struggle to control them.

On the way to watch the races Pete and I had stopped off at the airport. I purchased a return flight ticket from Brisbane to Sydney at the Ansett desk. I'd been encouraged to do this by the travel agent in Alice Springs, who advised me to book as soon as possible in order to obtain a low fare, something I knew all about from my own work experience. Pete held off booking his ticket as he was keen to do his adventure holiday with Dan and was still waiting to hear if Dan could fit it in. If Dan couldn't make it, Pete planned to buy a ticket and return to Sydney with me.

That day at the Camel Cup we wandered around the park to look at the other attractions; there were food and souvenir stalls, belly dancers and a Miss Camel Cup contest. It reminded me of our local village galas back home. There was a lot to see and so we stayed there until late afternoon and then we decided to hit the road again.

We weren't worried about travelling at night. We had fuel, food and the Kombi was our mobile home. Pete and I were both used to driving between Brighton and Huddersfield, which we usually did late at night to avoid traffic. Just before we left Alice, Pete pulled into the car park of the Red Rooster fast food restaurant. The restaurant was all but empty, and it was chilly inside from the airconditioning. In Australia, I'd got used to the need to wear a jacket or a jumper inside a building because of fierce air-conditioning, and having to take it off again as soon as you stepped outside. It was kind of like England in reverse. I was wearing a denim jacket that day, wrapped around my waist most of the time. I was glad to have it to put on inside the restaurant.

We only hung around long enough for Pete to order and eat his food. I wasn't feeling hungry and Red Rooster wouldn't have been my first choice if I had been. We had healthier food inside the Kombi and our cupboards were stocked with pasta, herbs and spices for whenever I wanted to put a meal together.

As we drove out of Alice Springs, Pete was sitting in the passenger seat beside me. I'd selected a CD by a band called Texas and it was playing as I drove on to the Stuart Highway. I relaxed back into my seat, singing along to the music, and Pete picked up his book from the shelf below the dashboard and began to read.

After a few kilometres he decided to move to the back to read more comfortably. I was content in the front by myself. The road was long, wide and open and driving was a pleasure. There weren't very many cars on the road and some of the drivers I passed waved at me and I waved back. The road was continuous and the scenery never changed. From time to time I would glance back through the rear-view mirror then look straight ahead through the windscreen. The image was exactly the same. White line, red road. Pete calls this white-line syndrome. At one point I saw a dead cow lying at the side of the road. It caught my attention, that's how boring the stretch of road had become. I called out to Pete to take a look. He didn't answer me. I turned around to look at him. He was lying down on the back seat fast asleep. I didn't disturb him and kept driving.

6

Never give in
Never give up

I was driving and Pete was asleep in the back when I saw a petrol station up ahead on the right. Pete had done far more of the driving than me on the trip but I liked being behind the wheel. Rather than wake Pete right next to a petrol pump I saw a lay-by on the left just before the petrol station. It was the perfect place to stop and wake Pete. I had to brake heavily to swing in and the sudden movement roused Pete without me even trying. As I stopped I looked to my left and saw a wide area of flat scrub land with a few trees scattered here and there. There was a gathering of Aboriginal people sitting in groups in this clearing. The sun was beginning to set and the scene was golden and languid. I felt incredibly happy as I sat there and watched. I was beginning to understand the vastness of Australia's heart and to appreciate the diversity of its land and people.

Pete leaned up to the passenger seat and I told him I'd pulled up to watch the sunset before I got petrol across the road. I pointed out the service station. Pete nodded his approval and got out of the Kombi by sliding open the side door which leads through to the back of the Kombi. The outdoor air raced into the vehicle as I moved across the seats and got out through the passenger door, leaving it wide open. Pete stood and stretched for a moment and then reached out and pulled me close. He leaned back against the Kombi and I leaned back against him. We stood in silence like that, absorbing our surroundings and breathing in the late afternoon air.

Pete decided he'd roll a joint to smoke as we watched the sun set and he unwrapped his arms from around me and went to the passenger door. He leaned in and picked up his cannabis, Rizla papers and cigarettes, which were lying on the shelf below the dashboard. He came back and sat in the side doorway while he put together a joint. When he finished he lit it, smoked some, and then passed it to me. I smoked a little but soon passed it back. I'm not really a smoker. The only effect the cannabis had on us was to relax us more.

The temperature had been getting warmer the further north we drove. Shortly after we left Alice Springs we saw a big sign that told us we had just passed the Tropic of Capricorn line of latitude. The setting sun softly illuminated the land. There were a few thin, scattered clouds and the light gave them an appearance of having a white-gold lining. The sunset was beautiful but it was the whole landscape that was so unique and memorable. I felt empowered as I stood there, almost overwhelmed by a feeling of freedom and adventure.

Once the sun had set, Pete took over the driving and drove us across to the service station. I noticed there was a police station next to it. The service station was small but it had a shop, a bar and restrooms which you accessed through the shop. From the petrol pump I looked into the bar through a window. I could see two men staring at me and they looked like rough and tough bush men. I had to pass by them on the way to use the bathroom and I felt uneasy going alone. I don't know if I imagined it but I sensed their eyes following me. When I walked back, Pete had finished refuelling. I sat in the Kombi and waited for him to come back from paying for fuel. We had a system and when he got back to the Kombi he handed me the receipt and I wrote the mileage on it and then added it to the rest of the receipts, which were clasped with a bulldog clip to the shelf. We were collecting all of our petrol receipts from around Australia and recording our mileage so we could calculate at the end of our trip exactly how many miles we had travelled. Pete had bought sweets, chocolate and Coke. The sweets were called Lifesavers and as Pete drove I fed them to him.

We were headed north, that was our only plan. We were just going to drive until we got tired and then we'd stop somewhere for the night. Now I can see it wasn't the most sensible thing to do, but at the time I was unaware of the dangers. We were young and carefree; I was with my boyfriend and felt completely safe and untouchable.

As Pete drove I sat in the passenger's seat with my feet either resting up on the dashboard or up against the shelf that Pete had built. It was warm in the Kombi with the heater on and the denim jacket that I'd worn throughout the day lay at the back of my seat.

Not long after leaving the service station we came across a fire at the side of the road. It was on the left-hand side of the road, and though it was only small, it had extended into the road and was enough to cause Pete to swerve to get past it. Pete asked me if I thought we should go back and put the fire out. I can't explain why but I felt uneasy about stopping and told Pete not to. For the first time, as the darkness began to draw in, I became acutely conscious of the remoteness of the outback and the lonely highway we were on. Looking out through the windscreen, all I could see was a dark ribbon of road ahead. I started to think about the fire and thought maybe it was some kind of trap or ambush, an attempt to get a car to stop and then hijack it. I didn't tell Pete what I was thinking and he drove on, seemingly unperturbed.

Pete and I love music and had lots of CDs with us. It had become our practice to allow the driver to choose the music that played while they were at the wheel. When we started out the passenger had to dig around through our extensive collection and find the requested CD. After one exasperating search for a CD I wanted to hear, Pete had modified the ritual so that the passenger could name three CDs for the driver to choose from. That night I suggested three CDs and Pete chose The Stone Roses.

I put it on and sat back, only moving to unwrap a Lifesaver to give to Pete. The sweets were quite sticky and sometimes the silver foil would attach to them, so I would put on the interior light for a minute while I unpeeled the foil from the sweet and then placed it in Pete's mouth. Pete called me a Lifesaver. It was pitch-black outside. Pete drove with the full-beam lights on, which attracted moths, flies and other insects. The effect reminded me of some of the scenes in *Star Wars* movies in which the stars, planets and galaxies zoom towards the screen.

Every so often I would spot a kangaroo darting out across our path. I'd point it out to Pete to make sure he'd seen it as well. He'd slow down a little to make sure it passed safely.

We started to plan our birthdays, which were in September, two months away. Our birthdays were five days apart. This was always how we were. When Pete and I weren't travelling we were planning trips, and when we were travelling we were planning our next trip or side trip. For us the planning was part of the fun. There was so much we wanted to see and do, and the more places we visited the more we realised there were so many places we hadn't been.

We planned to go to Fiji in September and we knew Lisa and Dan were going to be there around that time. I thought it would be nice if we were all in Fiji for my birthday so we could celebrate it together. Pete was happy enough with this but he wanted to go skiing in New Zealand for his birthday. Pete loved skiing; he went skiing every January in Europe with his brothers. We talked about how we would arrange this and were discussing these birthday plans when the inside of our Kombi was lit up by headlights behind us. That was the first time I became aware of another vehicle on the road with us.

Pete said, 'I just wish they'd overtake us.' The vehicle began to drive up alongside, and both Pete and I looked across to check it out as it overtook us, but it didn't.

The vehicle was white, which appeared ultra-bright against the black night. I could see the driver clearly in the cabin, as he had his interior light on. He appeared to be in his forties, had a moustache and was wearing a black baseball cap. He looked to me like a local not a traveller. There was a dog sitting next to him in the passenger seat. As Pete and I looked across at him, the man stared intensely back at me. I felt afraid. The driver was gesturing, pointing across to the back of our vehicle. Pete said that we'd better pull over and check out the problem. I felt uneasy and didn't want to stop. I said as much, but Pete smiled and told me it was okay, there was only one man. Pete's calm and casual manner always put me at ease; I felt safe when I was with him.

Pete stopped Taz on the left-hand side of the road, partly on the gravel and partly on the tar. The four-wheel drive pulled up and parked behind us. Pete got out and I moved across into his seat and began to climb out too. Pete stopped me and told me to wait inside, where it was warm. I positioned myself in the driver's seat and left the door slightly ajar so I could try and see and hear what was happening. I began to think there must be something wrong with our vehicle. Pete walked towards the back of the Kombi and the other driver met him there. I heard Pete say, 'Cheers, mate. Thanks for stopping.' From what I could make out, there seemed to be a problem with the Kombi's exhaust. I heard Pete ask the man if it had been doing that all the time he'd been following us. The words 'following us' stood out and gave me a chill. I turned my body and looked out to the back of the Kombi. I couldn't see Pete and I thought he must have been crouching down, looking at the exhaust. The man stood on the right of Pete and I could see him fully. He looked directly at me. He was tall, taller than Pete, and his posture was stooped. He seemed to have his hands in his shirt or pockets.

Pete came back to the driver's side and told me everything was okay, that the man had seen sparks flying from our exhaust. He picked up his cigarettes from the shelf below the dash and asked me to rev the engine. I started to relax a little. Pete disappeared again and I started to rev the engine. I'd never been asked to do this before and I wasn't really sure how much pressure to put on the accelerator. I revved the engine and listened out, with the door slightly open, for further instructions from Pete. I did this a few times, each time taking my foot off the accelerator pedal.

There was a bang and my first thought was that it was the exhaust backfiring. It had done this before. I sat there with my head in my hands, elbows resting against the steering wheel, hoping that we hadn't broken down in the middle of nowhere. I sat up straight and looked out of the driver's side window to my right. The man filled the window and stared back at me.

Time stood still for that moment. In that instant all the fears I'd ever had hit me all at once. I stared back into his cold eyes, paralysed. My focus was drawn to the silver revolver he held in his right hand. I could not believe this was happening but I knew without a doubt my life was in danger. He opened the door, which was already ajar, and his upper body entered the vehicle.

'Turn the engine off.'

My whole body was shaking with fear. I slowly stretched my hand out towards the ignition key. It was as though I was in slow motion. The man's hand was there before mine and he turned the engine off. He moved towards me and I instinctively backed away, moving across into the passenger seat. All the time he was getting closer and closer to me. My eyes jumped from the silver revolver to his eyes.

I searched deep into his eyes hoping to get a flicker of some emotion but they were empty.

I managed to stutter, 'Why? Why are you doing this?'

The man was huge and I felt his deadly presence all around me. He didn't reply to my questions. He just stared into my eyes.

The man had a long oval face with deep-set eyes surrounded by wrinkles and dark circles. He had wrinkles across his face and lines around his mouth. His handlebar moustache came past the corners of his mouth and had flecks of grey in it, as did his eyebrows and the hair poking out from underneath his black baseball cap, which had a yellow motif on the front. He was expressionless, cold and seemed to radiate evil.

I kept repeating, 'Why are you doing this?'

He didn't answer but said, 'Put your head down and your hands behind your back.'

I started to do this but something happened. I got angry. I wasn't going to allow this man to do as he pleased with me. Nobody can say how they will react in such a situation. I'd never given it a thought before; why would I have?

I put my feet up against the dash to get some leverage to swing my body around. I screamed for Pete. I began turning my body around and reached out for the door handle. The man's hand came down on my shoulder and he put the gun to my head.

'Put your head down and your hands behind your back,' he repeated. I thought I had no choice. I had to do what he told me. I slowly put my hands behind my back and lowered my head to my knees, with my head turned to the driver's side. As I lowered my head my glasses began to slide off, and the man ripped them from my head.

He moved from my right side and disappeared out of view, but I could feel him still behind me, over me, all around me. He positioned my hands, then I felt something fasten tightly around my wrists. They were bound but not touching each other. It happened so quickly and I was helpless to stop it. I'm not sure exactly what happened next but all of a sudden I dropped knees-first to the ground outside the Kombi. The ground was rough and the gravel cut into my knees. I was then pushed forwards and fell on my stomach. I instinctively raised my head to protect my face from hitting the ground. I screamed 'Pete!' over and over and over again. I needed Pete to help me, to get the man off me.

I screamed his name but Pete didn't come. For the very first time in my life I felt completely alone. It was just me and this man. No one could hear my screams. No one was going to come and save me.

I was lying on the ground with my feet towards the passenger side of Kombi and my head towards the bush, slightly raised and turned to the right. The man was straddling me, his legs at either side of me. He was bending over and attempting to tie my ankles together. Again I got angry. I wasn't going to let him. I frantically kicked my legs apart, up and down. The man bent lower to get a better grip on my ankles. I was able to reach between his legs by lifting my arms up above my back. I tried to punch him in the crotch. I felt a blow to my right temple. Everything seemed to stop for a second.

I felt some kind of tape around one of my legs. Then the man roughly pulled me to my feet. I could hear a ripping noise and before I knew it he was trying to wrap tape across my mouth. I swung my head backwards and forwards and from side to side, screaming for Pete. There was tape wrapped around my throat and attached to my hair but it didn't even get close to my mouth. The man gave up. He walked behind me with one hand gripping the base of my neck and his other hand on my left shoulder. His body obscured my view of the back of the Kombi and his grip on my neck made it impossible for me to look around to search for Pete.

I was marched to the passenger door of his vehicle. The tape that he had tried to bind my legs with didn't stop me from walking. His interior light was on. I was positioned so I was facing the passenger door. He lifted up a loose corner at the bottom of the canvas canopy directly behind the passenger door. He pulled out a sack. All of a sudden it was over my head. I couldn't breathe. I was suffocating and began to panic. I used all the energy I had in me to wriggle my head and body. I screamed out, 'I can't breathe.' The sack came off. I'm unsure how. He'd opened the passenger door and began forcing me in, grabbing me and shoving me in backwards. He lunged forwards towards me and I edged backwards further into the vehicle trying to distance myself from him. Looking out of the windows all I could see was darkness, pitch-black darkness. I had reached the driver's seat, his dog was blocking me. I hadn't noticed it as I had been edging backwards. The dog did not react to me at all. As I glimpsed it I noticed that it was a short-haired dog with a broad head. It wasn't a breed I recognised. My body was twisted and I was sitting with my back to the dog facing the man. Screaming, I looked helplessly out of the windows into the darkness. The man's face leaned down towards mine and I tilted my head as far back as I could. There was nowhere for me to escape. He looked down at me, grabbed me and the next thing I knew I was in the back of his ute. This was to become a major issue in the police investigation – but I have said from the beginning I am unsure how this happened. All I know is he put me there.

I found myself in the back of the ute, lying on my right side, my head pointing to the front cabin and my feet towards the rear. I felt completely drained of energy. I was alone. It was dark under the canvas and I couldn't see anything. I still couldn't believe this was happening to me.

I turned my body round and sat in a half-upright position, my legs stretched out in front of me and my arms behind my back. I was lying on something soft and flat, it felt like a firm mattress. I stared straight ahead and I could see that there was an opening at the rear of the ute. I couldn't see the man, we were separated by the canopy of the ute, but I could hear him on my right-hand side. His footsteps crunched the gravel underneath, scraping; it sounded like the man was scraping something on the ground. He sounded close to me, just the other side of the canopy.

I sat there for a moment in disbelief. My life wasn't supposed to end this way. I shouted out to the man. 'What do you want? Is it money? Is it the Kombi? Just take it!' The man came to the rear opening. He poked his head through. I couldn't see him clearly but I could make out his silhouette.

'SHUT UP or I'll shoot you.' His shadow disappeared, he returned to the scraping on the ground.

The word 'shoot' echoed through my mind and I thought of Pete. Had he shot Pete?

I needed to know. I became hysterical and began calling out to the man again.

'Where's Pete? What have you done to Pete? What have you done to my boyfriend? What have you done to him? Have you killed my boyfriend? Have you? Have you? Have you shot Pete?'

It was probably only seconds or a few minutes but it felt like an eternity before the man returned and his silhouette appeared at the rear opening. I held my breath. The man simply replied, 'No.' I didn't believe him. The realisation was starting to sink in. He'd shot Pete and he was going to shoot me too. He was going to kill me. I was going to die. I was going to die. A strange calmness came over me. I accepted that I was going to die. I was all alone. I had no fight left in me.

Then, like a bolt of lightning, I had an image of this man raping me. I felt as if I'd just woken up. I regained some strength, adrenaline rushed through my body. I could hear the man outside, the sound of him scraping gravel on the ground. I was aware that he was preoccupied and I knew what I had to do. I summoned all the strength and courage I had.

Staying in the same position I silently, slowly, began to edge feet-first towards the opening. When I reached the end I sat and hung my feet over the tray of the ute, not touching the ground. I glanced once to my right. I couldn't see the man. I dropped to my feet a short distance from the ute, the sound of crunching gravel echoing as I hit the ground. I shot into the darkness. I ran down a gently sloped embankment towards the trees. My sprint was impeded as my hands were tied behind my back. I was conscious of the man following me but I never turned back to look. The land was uneven. I stumbled over small shrubs but remained on my feet. I ran further through the trees and bushes and the vegetation became thicker. I could hear the man behind me. I knew I could not outrun him. I changed direction and darted off to my left. I ran down a line of trees. I came to a tree that appeared blanketed in complete darkness, more so than the others. The tree's branches were low and I had to crawl inside backwards. I crouched down and crawled under the tree, my hands and arms going through first. The branches were low and scratched my skin as I passed through them, but that was the least of my concerns. I brought my knees up to my chest and buried my head into them. I covered my knees with my hair, which had fallen loose at some point throughout the struggle. I tucked my feet as close as I could to my body. I held my breath. The night was still and I had to remain silent, or I would die.

I was facing the bush with my back to the road. I was in an uncomfortable position. I could feel a branch against my back and I tried not to lean my weight against it for fear it might snap. My body weight was suspended dangerously against it. I remained frozen.

I could hear the man nearby, the crunch of dry scrub with every careful footstep he took. That was the only sound that echoed throughout the lonely outback. The sound of crunching came closer. My heart was pounding and I felt sure he could hear it. I kept frozen still. I didn't dare move, or look up to see how near he was.

The crunching began to fade away. The sound of his footsteps headed off in another direction. I lifted my head slowly and glanced up for the first time. I could see a light, a torchlight, through the trees deeper down into the bush from where I was hiding. I was wearing a pair of green boardshorts that had reflective white stripes down each side. My immediate thought was why hadn't I worn my jeans today. I buried my head again. I was petrified. What would he do to me if he found me? I could feel his controlled fury with every slow, steady step that he took. The sound cut through the air.

I kept visualising the silver revolver striking towards me. I had to look up several times to ensure it wasn't there. Sheer terror was making me hallucinate. My head was raised just enough to enable my eyes to see above my knees. All around was darkness. I could just make out the dark silhouettes of the trees and bushes in front of me. I could see the man's single spot of torchlight moving through the trees. I noticed a few stars in the sky and wondered if I would ever see daylight again, would I live to see the sunrise? Would I live to see tomorrow? Would I ever see my friends and family again? I thought of my friend Carol, who'd been winning her fight against cancer, she was strong, a survivor. Maybe I could be too. I began to gain faith. He hadn't found me yet. My hopes began to rise that I might stay alive.

The sound of crunching drew nearer again, and then passed by. I heard vehicle doors open and slam. I remained as still as I had been but felt it was safe to breathe out more heavily. I listened intently to what he was doing. All I could make out was the sound of doors opening and shutting. I envisaged him ransacking our Kombi. I could hear him dragging something, it sounded heavy. I thought it could be a body, it could be Pete. The sound appeared to be coming towards me and then it stopped. I thought the man had left Pete in the bush somewhere close to me. Vehicle headlights came on. I hadn't moved, my back was still to the road. Looking straight ahead I could now see the faint outlines of trees and bushes illuminated in the headlights. Oh my God. I fought back the urge to run, fought back panic and prayed that he couldn't see me. I heard the engine turn on and then the sound of the vehicle drive away. It sounded as if it was headed north.

I was too frightened to move. I believed he was trying to trick me and that he was just pretending to leave but would really come back into the bushes to look for me. I remained still and listened.

It only felt like a short amount of time had passed when I heard his footsteps crunching through the scrub again. I heard him to the right of me. I wanted to cry. He'd come back to search for me.

I didn't allow myself to cry. I buried my head to my knees again and tried to take controlled silent breaths. I don't know how long he was out there in the bush with me but it felt like an eternity.

The man finally returned to the road and I heard him open and close a vehicle door. I could hear some activity but I couldn't make out what he was doing. Headlights came on again. The engine started up and then I heard him drive away. It sounded as if the vehicle was heading south; in my peripheral vision I could see headlights driving south.

It felt safe to move now. I wasn't going to chance moving out from underneath my hiding place but I repositioned myself more comfortably. I brought my hands from behind my body to the front by placing my hands and arms underneath my buttocks, then slipping my thighs first, then legs and feet through my arms in one single movement.

It was too dark to see the handcuffs but I was able to feel them. They were made up of thick plastic cable ties, one on each wrist, with three looped cable ties joining them together. My wrists were tied about four inches apart, which gave me some limited movement. The loops in the centre of the handcuffs were covered with tape. I realised that there were in fact two cable ties around each wrist taped together. They gripped my wrists tightly. The ends of the cable ties were long and I had to be careful they didn't poke me in the eye as I tried to examine them.

I believed that Pete lay nearby and I wanted to be with him. I believed that he'd been shot. Maybe I already knew that the man had murdered Pete but I didn't want to believe it. I hoped that Pete was injured but alive somewhere close to where I was. I desperately wanted to leave my hiding place and find him but I was too afraid. I felt guilty for choosing to remain where I was. I decided I wouldn't leave unless I was able to remove the handcuffs from my wrists. For the moment I was free from the man and I wasn't prepared to venture out of hiding, for my escape efforts to have been in vain, for him to find me, rape me, murder me.

I began trying to pull the cable ties from my wrists, intending to slide one down over my hand. The cable ties had been fastened tightly to each wrist and I could only move them a centimetre or two. I got frustrated and began frantically trying to tug them off but it was futile. I only succeeded in stripping skin from my wrists and making them sting with pain. If I couldn't get them off what would I do? I was too afraid to go out into the darkness. I decided that I'd wait until daybreak.

It was then that I remembered I had a tube of lip balm in my pocket. I got it out and bit the lid off, spitting it out onto the ground. I softened the lip balm in my right hand and, dropping the now empty tube, I rubbed the balm around the cable ties on my left wrist. I hoped that the balm would act as grease and I would be able to slide the handcuff off. It didn't work. I was determined to free my hands. I felt the centre cable-tie loops that were covered with tape. I tried feeling for the stuck-down end of tape. When I found it I put it to my mouth and gripped with my teeth. I tried to pull it slowly and unravel the tape in one piece. I only had a tiny corner of tape in my mouth and it broke off in a small piece from the loop. I spat it out and tried again. The same thing happened. I tried again. The same thing happened. I gave up.

I sat there in the darkness. I heard a vehicle drive up the Stuart Highway, saw headlights speed past. I thought about the driver of that vehicle, they would have been oblivious to the violence that had taken place and my continuing terrifying ordeal. Help felt so near yet so far away.

I was beginning to feel very cold, my body felt stiff. I thought of all the warm clothes that I had in the Kombi. I began to wonder where the Kombi was. My thoughts returned to Pete. Pete had been really keen to go skiing in New Zealand. No way was that going to happen. I was going to take him home to England and never let him out of my sight again, once I'd found him. Once we were safe.

I remembered the date. It was Saturday the 14th of July 2001. We'd received an invitation to our friends Kate and Simone's housewarming party. They had known we wouldn't be able to make it but had given us an invite anyway. I could visualise the invitation. All our friends would be there, having fun right this very moment. I couldn't believe I was here, shivering, not knowing where Pete was, fearing for my life, a man with a gun determined to find me.

I had no idea what the time was or how long I'd been hiding for. Hours passed. I felt cold and I thought Pete must be feeling cold too. I had to get help. I didn't feel that it was safe to move but knew I had to do something. I slowly crept forwards. I couldn't see a thing. The branches creaked and ripped across my body as I passed through them. I stood outside my hiding place and looked around. It was so dark. I couldn't even see the hiding place I'd just crawled out of. My body was very stiff and I took one careful step at a time, looking all around before taking another. The sound under my feet echoed and I lost my courage. I retreated back under the tree.

7

A long way from home

All around was darkness, the night was silent and still. The only sound was the loud crunch of dry spinifex beneath my footsteps. I edged carefully, slowly, towards the road, looking in every direction before taking each small step. I didn't know where the man was or if he would appear. I was terrified.

Reaching the road, I could see the white line that marked the edge of the bitumen. I looked both ways and then started to cross. As I walked, I kept imagining that headlights would suddenly switch on and the man would appear. I listened hard for any sound but all I could hear was the noise of my own steps. I made it to the other side of the road and collapsed in what seemed to be long grass. I wanted to stay hidden so tried to keep low. I felt stabs of pain when anything touched my knees so positioned myself carefully so that nothing touched my cuts.

I was confused and scared and I wanted Pete, wanted to be safe. I wanted to cry but wouldn't let myself. I had to be silent in case the man was waiting, watching. I felt like my life depended on it.

Headlights came towards me from the south. A car was fast approaching. I let it pass without moving. As soon as it went by I was angry with myself for not being brave enough to flag it down. I didn't know when I'd get another chance, but I was too afraid of what might happen if I left the safety of the darkness. I fought my tears and desperately wished I could see my Mum.

I knew I was alone. There was no one to help me, no one who could lift me up and save me. I had to save myself. I knew I had to pull myself together and do something. Time passed. Thoughts came and went. My Mum's voice, the fear of the man, the need to find Pete. To help him. What if he was seriously injured? I wouldn't let myself think that he could be dead.

Alone in the dark, pressed against the earth, I started to think about road trains. I had seen these huge transportation vehicles while travelling on the road with Pete. To stop a car seemed too risky. What if it was him? I wouldn't be able to see inside a vehicle as I flagged it down. The dazzle of headlights meant I would have to have blind faith about the person driving and any passengers. I couldn't do it. It was too unsafe. I decided that if a road train were to come past, I'd run out in front of it and make it stop. My logic was that the driver of a road train would be on a job and therefore have a reason to be on the highway late at night. I thought it unlikely that the man could be in a road train.

I'm not sure how much time passed but I suddenly realised I could hear a road train approaching in the distance. From far away I watched as it lit up the curve of the road ahead of it and then straightened to accelerate along the long, straight section of road that I lay beside.

I got to my feet and started to slowly move to the road. The road train was coming towards me, fast. I felt like this was my only chance of getting to safety and reaching help. I had to make the driver see me. I started to hurry. I had to show the driver that my hands were tied, so they would realise I needed help. That was the only thought I had. I was completely focused on stopping this vehicle.

I started running on the bitumen, caught in the beam of the road train's headlights. I held up my hands in front of me. It was getting closer. I started to run forwards in the same direction it was travelling, my head and body twisting around to see where it was. I could feel its weight and power bearing down on me and leapt out of its path, back under the cover of darkness at the side of the road. I heard the road train's brakes slam on. I stopped still, trying to catch my breath, and watched as its clearing lights came on. It was slowing down.

It took maybe 1000 metres to come to a complete stop. I found out later the driver had swerved to avoid hitting me, though I didn't realise this at the time.

I was still breathless but started to run along the road, and down the length of the road train, calling out, 'Help me! I need help.' There were three long carriages between me and the driver. He had got out of the cab thinking that he'd hit someone, so had started checking underneath the trailers. He was looking for body parts.

As I reached the middle carriage I heard a voice call out, 'Over here, love'. We were separated by the load; he was on the driver's side and I was on the passenger side. He started shouting out instructions. The road train was huge and sat very high up. There was a gap between each load where the separate trailers were attached by a bar. The driver told me to bend down and pass underneath the bar sideways, like a crab. I did what I was told and when I emerged at the driver's side I came face to face with the driver.

I felt immediately vulnerable and uncertain. I was terrified that the driver might hurt me too. I knew I couldn't defend myself as my hands were tied. I had to fight the urge to run back into the dark. At that moment all I could do was surrender myself to the mercy of a complete stranger on this isolated outback road.

I held my wrists out in front of me to show the bindings and pleaded with the driver to untie me. He looked down at my wrists but couldn't see them in the dark. He led me towards the beam of the headlights. Looking down at my wrists and then back up at me he shook his head and said, 'Jesus... Jesus... Struth he meant business.'

My fear heightened as the driver walked over to the driver's door and called into the cabin, 'Can you get out here, mate? We've got a bit of a scene. We've got a sheila out here and she's all tied up...'

I suddenly realised that there was someone else inside the cabin. I watched anxiously as a man appeared at the door and began to climb down. Looking shocked and completely bewildered he stepped towards me. I held my wrists out to him and he began to examine the plastic cable-tie restraints.

I asked again to be untied and told them both that a man had attacked us. My words came tumbling out in a jumbled rush. The driver looked apprehensive. I hadn't thought about how he must be feeling, that he could be frightened too.

I was grateful and relieved by the driver's calm actions that followed. He got a toolbox from the truck and, together with his co-driver, cut the cable-tie handcuffs away from my wrists. They were very tight so they had to be careful. One man held the wire cutters while the other tried to pull the wrapped plastic away from my skin so the cutters could get underneath. Once they had them off I knew that these men weren't going to hurt me. I knew they would help me. It is impossible to describe the relief that I felt.

The driver removed tape from around my ankle and began to remove tape from around my neck. The tape had matted into my hair and after a second he stopped, not wanting to hurt me. Then both men held tight to my hair at the scalp as I tugged and ripped the tape off. The driver took the handcuffs and tape and placed them together in the toolbox. He said he should keep them as evidence. Looking back now, I can't believe how sensibly they went about dealing with the situation they had found themselves in. They carefully noted the position we were on the road.

I kept saying over and over that I needed to find my boyfriend, I needed to find Pete. I pleaded with them to help me search with their vehicle. They were willing, though I don't think I would have picked up on any reluctance. I was in shock and fuelled by adrenaline and fear.

It took a while for them to unhitch their load from the prime mover. Once that was done, they helped me inside the cabin. I sat in between them on the engine cowling. They each told me their names. The driver was Vince Millar and his co-driver, Rodney Adams. I told them that my name was Jo. I had no idea that they were shocked by my sudden appearance and apprehensive about what had happened. My only thoughts were of being reunited with Pete.

Vince turned the vehicle around and we drove north in the direction I'd come from. Despite the road train's headlights we could see very little along the roadside. Vince did notice two piles of dirt at the side of the road. They were shaped like pyramids. He stopped and got out to take a closer look. I would later learn that Pete's blood lay underneath the dirt. Rodney and I stayed inside the cabin. When Vince climbed back inside he said that he could see two sets of tyre marks, where two vehicles had been parked close together.

We continued driving and looking out from the cabin. There was nothing out there. No lights. All we could see was darkness. Vince saw a track that led off the road to the left. He stopped and said that he could make out fresh tyre marks. We followed the track.

As soon as we left the road I started to feel panicky. We headed into the bush and I warned Rodney and Vince to be extremely cautious, as the man had a gun. This must have been the first time that I'd mentioned a gun because Vince and Rodney looked at each other in shock.

One of them said, 'Well, what are we doing here? Let's get the police.' We turned, made our way back onto the road and started heading back south to pick up the load. Vince reattached the trailers and then we drove to a nearby roadhouse.

When we stopped we were in a car park. I was told we were at Barrow Creek. I didn't want to be there. I wanted to be at a police station, to let the police know what had happened. I wanted them to start looking for Pete. I remembered the police station I'd seen when Pete and I stopped at Ti Tree and told them about it. Vince got out of the cabin and went to talk to the people inside the roadhouse. I stayed inside the cabin. I didn't want to leave the safety I had found. While we sat there, Rodney offered to clean my wounds. My knees, elbows and forearms were badly cut and there was visible dirt and stone fragments in the cuts.

Rodney brought out a first-aid kit and started to clean my wounds. It stung a little. Vince came back and told us to come and wait inside. I didn't want to. I wanted to stay in the cabin with Rodney. I had no idea who'd be inside the roadhouse. What if the man was there? I just wanted to see the police. Another man appeared at the open passenger door of the cabin. As I looked down from my elevated position he looked small. I had curled up and he asked me to come inside with him. Rodney had started to get out and the panic came back. I didn't want to go inside a roadhouse. I wanted to drive back to Ti Tree. Rodney stood beside this new man and they both kept coaxing me to come inside. I refused, curling my body up further and wrapping my arms tightly around my shins. After ten minutes the stranger said, 'It's okay, you're among friends now.' These words broke through and though I was still reluctant I climbed down from the cabin. I stayed close to Rodney as we walked into the roadhouse.

As I stepped in through the door I stopped to survey the room. The room was wide, with a timber floor and beams. There was a bar on one side opposite the door. There were about twenty people in the room. It was well after 1.30 am and most of those inside appeared drunk to me. Paul Young's song 'Love of the Common People' was playing on the jukebox.

> 'Cause she's living in the love of the common people
> Smiles from the heart of a family man
> Daddy's gonna buy you a dream to cling to,
> Mama's gonna love you just as much as she can and she can...

It was like I had dropped into a strange new world. I scanned the room frantically with my eyes to make sure the man wasn't there before I stepped in any further. I didn't see him. I stayed with Rodney as he walked towards the bar.

The man who had coaxed me out of the cabin turned out to be the publican of the Barrow Creek Roadhouse. He told me that his name was Les Pilton. Les and Vince rang Ti Tree Police Station but all they got was a recorded message telling them that it was closed. They then called Alice Springs Police Station, 280 kilometres away from where we were. They were on the phone for a while and it was my understanding that the police thought Les was making a hoax call. He passed the phone to me and asked if I could speak to the policeman on the other end. He wanted me to convince the officer that he was for real. I put the phone to my ear and was surprised at what the policeman asked me to do. He asked me to describe the gun.

After I'd spoken, Les finished the call and then led me to a bar stool beside the bar. He settled me down and went back behind the bar, serving drinks and cleaning up. He offered me a drink, telling me that I could have anything that I wanted, on the house. I didn't want anything. Later, I was offered a cup of tea.

I sat at the bar with my back turned to the rest of the room. It was the only way I could deal with the situation. I didn't want twenty pairs of eyes watching me and tried to become invisible. A man came up and stood beside me. He was obviously drunk and he tried to strike up a conversation. He was slurring and started to tell me a joke. He was completely oblivious to my state of shock and my appearance. The blood from my cut knees had smeared onto my T-shirt while I was curled up hiding in the bush.

Les looked at me apologetically and explained that it was New Year's Eve there tonight. I felt like I was underwater and couldn't understand the words that were spoken. I thought to myself: Where the hell am I?

I was later told that building work had recently been completed on the roadhouse and they'd had a party that night for the builders and their families as well as the usual clientele to celebrate. They'd given the party the theme New Year's Eve. I had walked in at the tail end of the night.

I sat on the stool and stared straight ahead. From time to time I'd sense movement and look down to see a mouse dart across the floor. I noticed that the wall behind the bar was covered with various bank notes, each with the name of the person it belonged to penned across the front. Some had messages written on them. Les proudly informed me that customers left them there, so that they would always have money for a drink when they next returned.

Everything was bizarre and I started shivering so Les decided to light the fire. He moved me and my stool so I was closer to the warmth and told me to sit there. He'd noticed my red, raw wrists and gave me ice wrapped in a towel to soothe them. Vince went out to the truck to get his jumper for me to wear.

I didn't want to be there. I wanted to find Pete. I wanted my Mum. I wanted this night never to have happened. All I could do was sit and wait for the police to arrive.

I didn't see Rodney again. I didn't know at the time, but he'd gone back to the cabin of the road train to sleep. Someone asked me if I wanted to call anyone. I didn't want to phone anyone until Pete was with me. I told myself the police were on their way. Pete would be okay and we'd be able to let both our families know what had happened and that we were safe.

I waited and waited. So it would be fresh in my memory to be able to tell the police I went through every detail I could remember in my mind. The hours passed by and I got frustrated and impatient. A few phone calls went back and forth between the police and the people at Barrow Creek. At one point Les's girlfriend, Helen Jones (though I didn't know her name then), appeared in her dressing-gown to complain about the noise of the telephone ringing.

Two dogs roamed past while I was waiting in the bar. One dog caught my attention. It was a medium-sized short-haired dog, with a broad head and body, speckled black and white in colour. It looked very similar to the dog the man had. I asked who owned the dog. Apparently it belonged to a young girl who worked at the roadhouse. I asked her what breed it was. She told me her dog was a blue heeler cross. I stored the information to tell the police when they arrived.

Someone suggested that I go and have a lie down. The roadhouse had rooms off the bar where people stayed. I didn't want to have a lie down but did so under pressure. I am sure they had no idea what to do for me as I sat there like a zombie in the centre of the room, staring at the door.

I was shown to a small bare room; it looked like a prison cell. It was painted white with a single bed in it. I lay on my side on top of the covers, facing the door. I kept the light on and the door open. I kept going through the events of the crime over and over again. I hadn't really discussed what had happened to me with anyone at Barrow Creek or with Vince and Rodney. I didn't know where to start or whether I trusted any of them completely. I wanted to tell the police everything so they could find Pete and arrest the man who had attacked us.

Lying on the bed I wondered if the police had arrived and were in the bar. I couldn't stay there not knowing so rolled off the bed and walked back into the bar area. The police hadn't arrived. I sat back down on the bar stool in the centre of the room and continued to wait, in silence. I had never felt more out of place than I did there. My eyes were fixed on the door and after a time I noticed daylight creeping underneath it. It was a reminder of the many hours that had gone by. It had been pitch-black when I had arrived. It was now Sunday morning. It had been the longest night of my life.

I was aware of people in the bar and activity taking place around me but I felt distanced from it. I sat separate from everyone else. They were just a blur in the background. As I write this now I am slightly bewildered that no one tried to comfort me or talk to me. I wonder what I looked like through their eyes. I was a traumatised English backpacker wearing bloodstained clothes. When I picture myself from their perspective, it is not surprising that they left me to myself. I am glad that they did. I didn't want to talk to anyone. Only my Mum or Pete could have comforted me.

Even though I had been watching it for hours, I was startled when the door opened. Daylight and fresh air raced in as a man and a woman, both dressed in beige uniforms, entered the bar. I let out an audible sigh of relief. Finally something was going to be done. The policewoman walked towards me and introduced herself as Erica Simms. She explained that she had travelled down from Tennant Creek. I was confused and asked where the police from Alice Springs were. Erica told me they were still on their way.

I didn't understand. We had driven from Alice Springs to Ti Tree, which is just before Barrow Creek, in two hours and we had been driving slowly in an old Kombi. Five hours had passed since Les had first contacted the Alice Springs Police Station. I couldn't work out why they were taking so long. Surely they could travel quickly?

It was after 6.00 am. Erica arranged with Les for us to use his back office so she could take my statement. While Erica was listening and entering my words onto the computer belonging to the Barrow Creek Roadhouse the police arrived from Alice Springs. They didn't have much contact with me, but occasionally would enter the room and interrupt to ask me questions. I didn't mind. I was just glad the investigation had finally begun. Surely soon they would start searching for Peter.

Giving my statement took a long time and I wanted to make sure I told the police every detail I could remember from the moment I knew there were headlights behind us. I was asked our parents' addresses, our dates of birth, and our occupations. I gave a description of Pete and then of the Kombi. I detailed our travel itinerary. I tried to give as much detail as I could and I answered lots of questions. I was asked if I wanted to inform our families what had happened or if I would prefer the Foreign Office to do it. I didn't know how to find the words to tell them what had happened. I didn't want it to be real.

After Erica and I had finished, Erica realised the statement hadn't saved on the computer. She told me we would have to start again and this time she would handwrite it. I tried to repeat what I had said in my first statement but I felt rushed and I didn't go into as much detail. I was interrupted on a number of occasions. At one point I overheard that the Kombi had been found. My heart leapt but there was no mention of Pete. I learnt later that Taz had been found not far from the crime scene. It had been driven off the road and into the bush in an attempt to conceal it. Nobody told me anything officially. I felt distant from everyone and like it was all not quite real. I wanted to wake up from my nightmare and find myself next to Pete in Taz.

While giving my statement for the second time I was asked to take a look at a vehicle. I followed a policeman outside to see a white four-wheel drive utility. There were a few policemen gathered around it. My heart started racing as I jumped to the conclusion that the police had caught the man. A policeman asked me if this was like the vehicle the man had. I said that it looked similar. I walked around it and I noticed a man standing beside the ute. It belonged to him. He looked shocked and was protesting his innocence. My heart sank. They hadn't caught the man who had attacked me. This was not the vehicle. I didn't speak to the owner and simply turned and walked back inside the roadhouse to finish my statement.

My completed statement was eighteen pages long. It was broken down into numbered paragraphs and there were forty-four in total. This is what was recorded by Erica for number nineteen: 'Somehow, the man manages to push me into the back of his ute. I landed on something that was flat but quite soft. The man stood outside of the vehicle on the bush side. I could hear him doing

something – no voices, just the crunching of gravel, so I knew he was nearby.'

I couldn't explain to Erica how the man put me into the back of his utility and I never have been able to vividly recall. I wish I could. All I can say is he put me there quite easily. On reflection I believe he pushed me through the passenger-side canopy. However, at the time of giving my statement I didn't know how he put me in the back. I didn't know then what an issue it would become.

The final sentence of my statement read: 'I have never seen this person before but I would definitely recognise him if I saw him again.' I hoped that the police would find him and Pete soon and this would all be over.

While Erica was taking this statement a police forensic officer photographed my injuries. No one had called a doctor, or even a nurse, so I had no medical assessment. I was then asked to undress down to my underwear and to place my clothes and sandals into paper bags. These would be forensically examined for evidence. Because I had no other clothes to put on, someone spoke to Les's girlfriend, Helen Jones, and she gave me a white T-shirt, jade-green tracksuit pants and a pair of size seven trainers without laces. I am a size five.

Once the police had finished recording the second statement, it was decided by the police that I should wait with Les and Helen until they were ready to take me to Alice Springs. Les and Helen had a unit at the back of the roadhouse and I was taken to sit on their verandah. I didn't query what was happening; I was dazed and numbed by having to relive, twice, what had happened to me and Pete. Shutting down was the only way I could get through it. I know Les and Helen were trying to be comforting and kind but instead they freaked me out by telling me that I must prepare myself to identify Pete's body. At that point the numbness gave way and I started to cry. Helen Jones put her arms around me but I didn't react. I was in shock. This wasn't a nightmare, it was my reality. I was alone in a strange place and the police were leaving me with people I didn't know. The man was still out there somewhere. And so was Pete.

8

c/- Alice Springs
Police Station

I sat on that verandah staring off into the distance but seeing nothing. I desperately wanted someone to come and tell me they had found Pete and that he was okay. No one came. By late afternoon the police told me I was to be driven from Barrow Creek to Alice Springs for further interviews. I know there were many conversations about me that day, though I wasn't present for any of them, and in one of them it was decided by the police that Helen Jones should act as my guardian and that I would stay with her. Helen had told the police she had a house in Alice Springs. It would be revealed later that this house was actually owned by her boyfriend Les Pilton's elderly parents.

The decision to allow this woman to look after me was a strange one but at the time I was still in shock, traumatised, dazed and confused. Everything was so surreal I had no grasp of what should be happening to me. I didn't think about the right way or the wrong way to handle the situation, I just went along with it. Surely the police knew what they were doing?

I was driven straight to the Alice Springs Police Station with Helen Jones but she didn't come into the station with me. I hadn't eaten for over twenty-four hours but I had no appetite. I hadn't slept in over thirty-six hours but I doubt that I would have been able to, if I had been given the chance. The police weren't going to give me time to do either; they wanted me to give further statements. I was ready to do whatever they wanted, whatever would help them find Pete.

I was taken to a room within the police station and left there, alone. I curled up on a sofa and waited for someone to come back and interview me. This was to become a regular occurrence, waiting for detectives and being questioned by the Northern Territory Police. It never occurred to me that my every action was being scrutinised.

Eventually Senior Sergeant Helen Turnbull came to interview me. She was a tall, heavily built woman who wore her blonde hair short and spoke in a broad Australian accent. Senior Sergeant Turnbull asked me to repeat what had happened to me from the beginning to the end. She did not seem at all concerned for my welfare or emotional state or concerned about how reliving this over and over might affect me. The truth is I didn't care about myself; I would keep talking for as long as they wanted.

When I got to the point where I arrived at Barrow Creek with Vince and Rodney, I was asked to repeat what had happened from the finish to the start. Once I had done this, I was asked to recount different moments and then she would switch to ask about other details. I did not know this at the time, but this is called cognitive interviewing technique. Cognitive interviewing technique attempts to guide a witness through 'four memory-jogging techniques: thinking about physical surroundings and personal emotional reactions that existed at the time of critical past events; reporting everything that comes to mind about those events, no matter how fragmentary or seemingly inconsequential; recounting events in a variety of chronological sequences (beginning to end, reverse order, forward or backward) from highly memorable points.'

When I told Senior Sergeant Turnbull that the man had punched me on my right temple, she remarked that she could see a bruise there. I hadn't looked at myself in a mirror, so I didn't know this until she pointed it out.

I demonstrated to Senior Sergeant Turnbull how I had brought my hands from behind my back to the front of my body. It was never a disputed point and she never went back to it once I'd showed her how I did it. It was very easy for me to do and I didn't have to exert myself at all. I found it easier to demonstrate how I had done it rather than to describe my actions.

While I was being interviewed by Senior Sergeant Turnbull I was interrupted at various times by Constable Isabelle Cummins to assist in compiling a COMFIT (Computer Facial Identification Technique) image of the man who attacked Pete and me.

The first step in putting this image together involved me giving a physical description of the man to Constable Cummins and then choosing individual features from a small selection shown to me from a folder. I had to concentrate on each of the man's individual facial features and decide the one that most closely resembled his. There were only a limited number of options of male hairstyles to choose from and because the man had been wearing a cap I couldn't be sure about his hair. Once I'd made the choices Constable Cummins would leave the room and Senior Sergeant Turnbull would ask another question. We wouldn't get far before Constable Cummins returned with a computer-generated image. I would then suggest improvements to make the picture a more accurate representation of the man.

'He looked older ... His moustache came down past his mouth.'

This continued off and on for hours. It was after eleven at night but I wasn't conscious of the time. I had to keep going so they could find Pete. There was a sense of urgency, which was not manufactured by me. I believed that the police were pushing this hard because they thought it would help the investigation. I wanted an image to be ready as quickly as possible so the police could release it to identify and locate the man. I just wanted Pete back safe and the man arrested.

Constable Cummins took a DNA sample from me, which meant swabbing the inside of my cheek with a cottonwool bud, and she also cut my fingernails. I was told it was a long shot but that there may have been some of the man's DNA underneath them. I didn't think that there would be, as I'd showered and washed my hands since the attack. Nobody told me not to.

* * *

It was almost 11.30 pm when Senior Sergeant Turnbull told me that we were finished and that she would drive me to the place where I would be staying with Helen Jones. On the way she took me past some car yards and pointed out a few white four-wheel drive utilities, asking me if they were similar to the one that had stopped us on the Stuart Highway. In the dark they all looked very similar to me.

Shortly after midnight we pulled up outside what I thought was Helen Jones and Les Pilton's home. Senior Sergeant Turnbull told me that she would collect me at 8.00 am the next day and didn't hang around.

I was surprised to find an elderly couple waiting up to see me. They were Les Pilton's parents and they told me that I was very welcome in their home. I was confused but too tired to question anyone. Helen Jones was there and was concerned that I hadn't

While we were exploring the island of Koh Samui, Thailand, we discovered
a wildlife park. I took this photo of Pete in the crocodile enclosure.
This was typical of Pete. I was often shaking my head and saying,
'I can't believe you did that!'

Pete and me in Thailand.

Pete and I travelled through a jungle in Nepal on top of the ultimate 4x4.

Pete and me with fellow travellers Dan and Lisa.

Once we bought our Kombi, Taz, Pete and I made a number of day and weekend trips out of Sydney. I took this photo of Pete in the Blue Mountains.

I made many good friends while I was working in Sydney — people like Tim.

When we got to Uluru I felt a sense of freedom and energy being out in all that space.
This is Taz parked at the side of the road as Pete and I got ready to watch the sunset.

Above: The crime scene in daylight.

Left: The bush that I hid under for hours.

Below: These are the homemade restraints used by Murdoch to bind my wrists.

Right: Vince Millar was driving a road train when I ran out to stop his vehicle. He was shocked to find some 'sheila' all tied up.

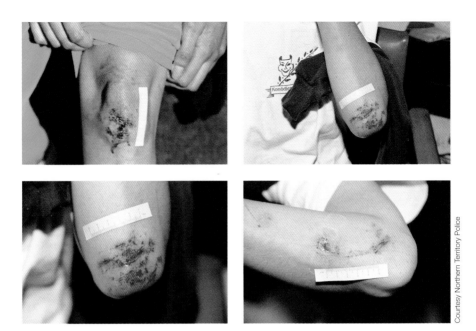

The police photos documenting my injuries. But they could only photograph the physical … the emotional scars run deeper.

On the 18th July 2001 the media waited at a roadblock while the police filmed a re-enactment of that night. At one point the policeman representing Murdoch pointed a gun to my head. I couldn't stop the flashbacks or stop the terror from overwhelming me.

BARROW CREEK ABDUCTION

MISSING PERSON

PETER MARCO FALCONIO

$250,000 REWARD

We were all hopeful that a $250,000 reward posted by the Northern Territory government would provide information that would help us find Pete.

Pete's brother, Paul and father, Luciano, flew to Australia to help find Pete.
Their anguish is obvious.

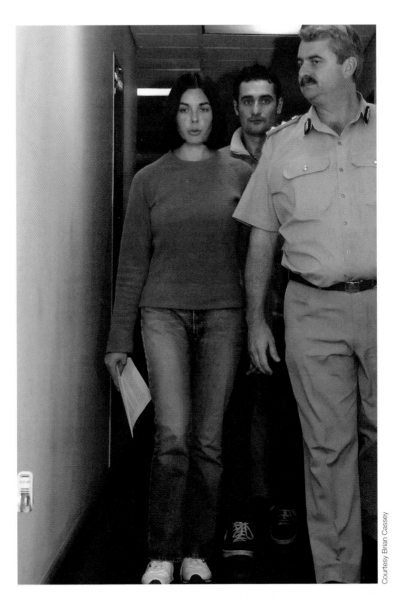

Courtesy Brian Cassey

Here I am walking to the media conference with Paul Falconio (*centre*). If I look shocked or uncomfortable, that is because I was. Apparently I didn't behave like a 'true victim' and from that moment the whispers about me became louder. How do true victims behave?

received any of the messages she told me she had left when she called the Alice Springs Police Station.

I desperately needed to have some time to myself. I was exhausted and I wanted to have a bath. I was directed to the bathroom. When I pressed the light switch to the bathroom, the light didn't come on. I asked Les's parents if they had a spare bulb and they got one for me. I wasn't too steady on my feet but I managed to change the light bulb while balancing on the bath edge to reach the ceiling. I ran a bath and lay in it for a long time. I replayed the day's events over in my mind. I thought to myself that this really could not be happening to me, but I knew that it must be, because Pete wasn't with me. I was alone.

I had none of my possessions, no clothes, no phone or money. I didn't have a toothbrush or any night clothes. I got back into the clothes I had been wearing before I came out of the bathroom, Helen Jones showed me to the room I would be sleeping in and left me to settle in. I kept the bedside lamp on and crawled into bed to try to get some sleep. I spent most of the night watching the door. I was too scared to close my eyes. As tiredness overcame me, my eyes would flutter shut and instantly the image of the man standing outside the Kombi's window would appear. I would snap my eyes open and push sleep away. Even now, I feel a chill writing this and I vividly remember the terror I felt as the man appeared.

After a sleepless night I was collected by Senior Sergeant Turnbull and taken back to the Alice Springs Police Station. At the station I was informed that the police were receiving lots of enquiries from the public who had heard about our attack through the media and were concerned to know the names of the backpackers who had been ambushed. The police asked if I would give my permission to allow them to release our names to the press. I had no idea what to do. All I knew was that I had to break the news to my friends personally before they heard about it through the media. I rang Pete's brother Paul and asked him what he thought I should do. I don't remember the entire conversation, we were both upset, but he realised I was all alone and told me he was going to get there as soon as he could. I needed someone with me, someone to help me find Pete, and I was so grateful. I asked him to promise that he'd come and he did.

After I hung up the phone I felt even more alone. Talking to Paul had made me crave the comfort of my family or my friends. My Mum was so far away and it was so late at night in England that I didn't want to wake her, so I called my friend Lisa in Sydney. Her phone went straight to voicemail. I didn't know at the time that she was on the phone frantically ringing around trying to get information about me and Pete. I left her a message and gave her Helen Jones's telephone number as I had no other contact number.

Next I rang the bookshop in Sydney. One of my colleagues, Michael, answered. I was glad it wasn't one of my close friends as I might have completely fallen apart hearing them. I could hear the concern in Michael's voice. I didn't know how to say it so I just said, 'It *was* me and Pete.' He needed no further explanation. Everyone in the bookshop had already heard the news that two English tourists aged twenty-seven and twenty-eight had been ambushed on the Stuart Highway, while driving an orange Kombi. Despite my friends hoping and praying that it wasn't Pete and me, deep down they had already known. I told him that I would call again soon and put the phone down.

That day I went through what had happened again and tried to help the police in whatever way I could. Later that day, when I returned to the Piltons' home, Helen Jones gave me some good news. My friends Amanda and Lisa were flying in from Sydney the next day, the seventeenth. They were both on working holidays and neither of them had much money. I found out later that Gary, my boss from the bookshop, offered to pay for Amanda's ticket. Lisa's mum paid for her to get to Alice Springs to be with me. I was so pleased that people who cared about me were arriving. I would gladly have paid for their airfares myself but I had no access to my money and bank cards. They were being withheld by the police.

Helen Jones then told me she thought I looked drained and that the police were wearing me out. I didn't argue. I had a permanent headache from concentrating and trying to answer all their questions. Helen declared that I should not see the police the next day and that, instead, I was to go with her to meet my friends at the airport.

The police had refused to give me any of my possessions from the Kombi but Helen Jones had bought me some pyjamas and a toothbrush so I went to bed to try and get some sleep. I couldn't sleep. I lay in bed and Helen Jones sat on the edge of the bed talking to me. She said she was concerned that in the morning the police would arrive to take me back to the police station for more questioning. She was worried I would be trapped there and not able to get away to meet Amanda and Lisa when they arrived.

I thought this over and began to panic. I was longing to see familiar friendly faces. I just wanted to be able to collapse into the safety of their arms. I didn't want to feel so alone. Helen seemed to have it all worked out and told me the plan. I was to get up right then and get dressed. She would contact a friend of hers, who would come over and drive us to her son's home, which was also in Alice Springs. We could sleep there overnight and no one would be able to find us, so in the morning I could get to the airport without any problems.

I didn't feel at ease about going out in the middle of the night, but the desire to be reunited with my friends was stronger than my fears and I agreed to the plan.

I jumped out of bed, got dressed and Helen Jones and I crept out of the house. We waited at the end of the driveway for her friend to arrive. It was a chilly night and there wasn't much street lighting. A car pulled up. I could see a man behind the wheel of the car. He was wearing a black baseball cap. My fear escalated. I knew he was not the man who had attacked me, but that did not stop me from physically shaking. I stood and stared at him for a moment, assessing the danger. Helen Jones ushered me into the car. I got in cautiously. I did not feel comfortable with this. I felt vulnerable. I didn't know these two people. My heart raced, my head spun and I felt nauseous. What was I doing? Why was I putting myself in jeopardy again?

I sat in the car and didn't say a word on the short journey. I was relieved when the car stopped and I was able to get out. The driver, who Helen had introduced as Mark, drove away. I followed Helen Jones into her son's house. Her son and his girlfriend were expecting us. They had a baby son named Paddy. Despite feelings of great despair I thanked them for allowing me to stay the night with them and their beautiful baby boy. I excused myself as soon as was possible and went to bed in their spare room. I couldn't sleep. I was in yet another stranger's home. I didn't want to sleep. I just wanted the night to be over. I couldn't wait to see Amanda and Lisa.

Morning eventually did arrive. A friend of Helen Jones's son drove Helen and me to the airport. We stood waiting next to a glass door that led onto the tarmac. I watched as other passengers disembarked from the plane. I was so relieved when I saw Amanda and Lisa walking towards me. I walked through the glass door towards them and watched their expressions changing from apprehension to concern, through to shock and then horror as we drew closer. God knows what I looked like to them.

When we reached each other we all stopped for a moment and searched for the right words to say. There weren't any. Lisa broke the silence in her unique forthright manner and in her Essex accent said, 'Aww, honey. Come here.' She gave me a huge hug and I allowed myself to relax into her arms. I had no idea until then how tense I had been and how tightly controlled my emotions were. As she held me for a split-second I felt a tiny part of myself return, then it disappeared. I was left feeling shell-shocked at the contrast to my old self and what I'd become. I didn't recognise who I was anymore. I broke free, turned and hugged Amanda.

Neither of my friends could hide their concern at my appearance. Amanda was especially shocked at how pale I was and at how much weight I had lost and didn't hesitate to say so. Lisa, God love her, simply stated that it was obvious I was a mess, but that they were here now to help me get through this.

Helen Jones gathered us up and took us to a bar called Bojangles, in the centre of Alice Springs. I had no idea where we were going. Pete and I hadn't gone to any bars while we were there. Lisa had though; she'd visited Alice Springs when she had toured around Australia. As we walked in she told me that it was a popular bar. Amanda, Lisa and I all thought it was an inappropriate place to visit and whispered this to each other. We didn't say anything to Helen and we went along with her plans. I don't know why we didn't speak up but I do know that none of us were thinking straight.

The bar was decorated as a traditional outback drinking hole. It reminded me of the saloons in American Western films, where a fight always breaks out and someone is thrown across a table. Helen told us to sit at a table in the corner towards the back of the bar. Amanda, Lisa and I found a quiet table and huddled together. We felt able to talk freely for the first time while Helen went to the bar.

'Who is she?' Lisa asked.

I didn't know what to say. I didn't really know who Helen was or why the police had asked her to look after me.

Helen brought over champagne, which, when you think about it, is pretty strange. I was in no mood for a celebration. She had also ordered food for us. Although it was lunchtime I had no appetite and did not want to drink any alcohol. Lisa tried to persuade me to drink a glass of brandy; she thought it might calm me down and stop me from shaking. I hadn't realised I was but I looked down and saw that my hands were trembling. I declined the brandy.

Helen Jones had told us she would give us some privacy and she sat at the bar talking to some people that I assumed she knew. I quietly told Amanda and Lisa what had happened to Pete and me. My voice broke at times but I managed to get it all out. I wanted them to know what had happened and how much I needed them. I felt that they needed to know everything in order to support me. This was the only time that I have ever told any of my friends what happened that night, and my friends have respectfully never asked.

Recently I asked Lisa her recollections of this moment and this is what she told me. 'You were extremely shaken. You didn't get upset; you appeared to be in shock and in a daze. You said that it had taken the police an age to get to you in Barrow Creek and you were shocked that they had thought it was a hoax call. You went through your ordeal from beginning to end and your story has never changed in any way.'

I'm not sure how long we stayed at Bojangles but not long after arriving back at the Piltons' house, Helen let in a visitor. That visitor was Mark, her friend who had driven us both to her son's house the previous night. He was introduced to me as Mark Wilton, a journalist for *The Advocate*, the Alice Springs local paper.

Helen led me into the sitting room with Mark. It was just the three of us. I found out later that Helen had stopped Amanda and Lisa from entering the room. I didn't feel comfortable, I wanted to leave but where could I go? Mark spoke at high speed and told me that the police had arrested a man on the Tanami Track. I fully believed him. Why wouldn't I? Why would anyone lie about something as serious as this? I was disturbed that I was being informed of this by a journalist, even though the news was positive.

Mark Wilton began asking me some questions. I paced around the room. My thoughts were elsewhere. I answered some of his questions honestly without really considering them. I confirmed to him that yes, it was correct that a man had ambushed us, deceiving Pete and me into believing there had been a fault with our Kombi's exhaust. He then asked what happened next. I told him that I had heard a bang and at first I thought it was the sound of the exhaust backfiring. I then told him how the man had appeared at my driver side window holding a gun. My words began to trail off.

He kept prompting me to continue. I didn't want to talk about this with him. My heart was racing and I was scared so I refused. He wasn't concerned about Pete and me, he was just interested in a story. He was after the chilling details. I wasn't able to repeat what had happened to a stranger, especially one whose only interest was to sell newspapers. I told him that he could use his imagination. I left the room and went and found Amanda and Lisa, who were sitting in the kitchen looking extremely concerned.

That was my first introduction to the media.

Mark Wilton left the Piltons' home without saying goodbye. Shortly afterwards, Senior Sergeant Helen Turnbull arrived. She entered the kitchen where we were all standing. I introduced her to my friends. Senior Sergeant Turnbull asked Helen Jones directly if any journalists had been to the house. Helen Jones replied, 'No.'

My friends and I gave each other puzzled glances. A journalist *had* been here. Helen Jones had arranged the meeting with Mark Wilton, inviting him into the house. Why was she lying? I couldn't stand the thought of this woman looking after me anymore when she seemed to have her own agenda. I told Senior Sergeant Turnbull that a journalist had in fact been here and had left not long ago. I told her that the journalist had said that the police had made an arrest on the Tanami Track. Senior Sergeant Turnbull told me she had no knowledge of this. She was alarmed that a journalist had been given access to me so easily and excused herself to make a phone call. After finishing her call she announced that we were leaving. Amanda, Lisa and I got up from our kitchen chairs and walked out the door. It was as quick as that. I had no possessions to pack and didn't stop to get the toothbrush that Helen Jones had bought for me.

It was early evening and Senior Sergeant Turnbull drove the three of us to a motel. Everything happened so quickly. Senior Sergeant Turnbull and I were out of the room for a moment when Lisa answered a phone call from Helen Jones on her mobile. Helen Jones had taken Lisa's number earlier. Lisa, unaware that the police wanted our location kept secret, had told Helen Jones the name of the motel we were staying in.

When Senior Sergeant Turnbull and I returned to the room, Lisa informed us that she had just spoken with Helen Jones. Sergeant Turnbull immediately barked, 'You didn't tell her where we were staying, did you?'

Lisa looked upset as she nodded her head. She could tell by Senior Sergeant Turnbull's face that she had done the wrong thing. Lisa was apologetic but it was completely unnecessary; she hadn't been told not to tell anyone and Helen Jones had been given, up until thirty minutes before, the role of my guardian by the police. Senior Sergeant Turnbull left the room, shouting back to us, 'Don't talk to anyone.' Lisa continued to apologise to me and Amanda but I told her she had nothing to be sorry for. I was starting to recognise the police's dramatic change in attitude towards my protection and who I spoke to. Sergeant Turnbull returned and declared we were leaving because Lisa had disclosed our location to Helen Jones. This made Lisa feel even worse. We were driven to the Plaza Hotel.

I have never seen or spoken to Helen Jones since that day and I have no desire to. How can I not suspect that she set up the interview with her friend Mark Wilton? In my opinion she did not fulfil her caretaking role.

* * *

After three days of wearing the clothes that Helen Jones had given to me at Barrow Creek I was given a few items of my clothing from the Kombi by the police. It was late evening and I was very pleased when these were handed over. I went straight into the bathroom to have a bath. All I wanted to do was get changed. Amanda, Lisa and Senior Sergeant Turnbull waited in the bedroom. When I walked out of the bathroom wearing my own clothes Amanda stared at me, looking horrified. Because I was wearing a vest, it was the first time that my bruises were visible to her. I hadn't really taken much notice of them but my body was black and blue.

It felt good to be able to finally wear my own things, to wear clothes and shoes that actually fitted. I felt clean for the first time since I was attacked. Dressed in my favourite old blue denim jeans I felt a little bit more like myself.

I lay on the hotel bed with Lisa and Amanda and we talked. I was trying to make sense of all that was happening and we were reassuring each other that Pete would be okay. From time to time Amanda and Lisa would go out on to the balcony for a cigarette and even though I don't smoke I would join them.

At one point Senior Sergeant Turnbull marched out onto the balcony and accused us all of smoking what she called 'wacky baccy'. Lisa pointedly told Senior Sergeant Turnbull that we had more common sense than to do a thing like that in the company of a police officer. Lisa has since read me a line from the diary she kept at the time which says: '... It was always hard to feel comfortable around the police and they seemed to make sure of that.' Looking back, I would have to agree.

The police had booked Amanda and Lisa into a different hotel room and even though I would have preferred we all stayed in the same room, they wouldn't allow it. I use the word 'allowed' because that was how it felt. The police were keeping me as isolated as possible and that meant discouraging me from spending time with my friends. I still had no money or phone so I couldn't contact anyone unless I asked to use a phone at the police station. A police officer was with me at all times, but I still had not been offered any counselling or victim support. I never asked about this at the time because I didn't know such things existed.

I was in shock. I had no idea what had happened to Pete and if he was okay. I had lost everything. You'd think someone in authority would have realised I needed help, but in those first days no one did. I wish that I had spoken up, had told them I was struggling to cope, but all I was focused on was finding Pete. I didn't register my own needs. And it wasn't in my nature to expose myself to people I didn't know. I closed in on myself and held my emotions in tight. I wouldn't let myself break down. As far as I was concerned, all I could do was put my trust in the police and fully cooperate with them.

* * *

On the morning of the 18th of July 2001 I was permitted to see Amanda and Lisa for less than an hour before being driven to the Alice Springs Police Station by Senior Sergeant Turnbull. I was questioned and interviewed and made every effort to recall everything that had happened. I was asked to take part in a re-enactment of the crime. The police told me it would greatly help them with the investigation. Though the very thought of going back to that spot on the Stuart Highway made me physically ill, I agreed to do it. I'd do anything if I thought it would help find Pete.

As Senior Sergeant Turnbull drove out of Alice Springs, I sat low in the front passenger seat. I stared blankly out of the window for most of the two and a half hour journey as we headed up the Stuart Highway. I replayed in my mind the last time I had driven this stretch of road. It was only four days earlier but it felt like it was much, much longer. I thought about how happy I'd been as I sang and drove while Pete slept peacefully in the back of Taz. Abruptly and violently everything had changed in an instant. I wanted to scream, to cry, to go back in time.

I looked across at Senior Sergeant Turnbull's expressionless face and determinedly fought back the tears. I sunk lower into the car seat and snuggled deeper into the fleece jacket I was wearing. My fleece had been a present from Pete and hugging it close gave me comfort.

The sky was grey and the light was fading as we approached a police roadblock. Cars were lined up waiting to pass through on both sides of the highway. Journalists and photographers were also there, hoping to get a glimpse of me. I didn't fully take in the scene; I was more concerned with the fading light and hoped that the sky would not become any darker.

Senior Sergeant Turnbull was waved through the roadblock. She drove a short distance into what I can only describe as no-man's-land. The small stretch of road was empty, it felt cold and eerie. Senior Sergeant Turnbull parked on the right-hand side of the road. Opposite, I could see an orange Kombi, but it was not Taz. I could also see a white four-wheel drive utility. As soon as I saw it a shiver went through my entire body.

I reluctantly climbed out of the car and followed Senior Sergeant Turnbull over to where the two vehicles were parked. A group of six police officers were standing next to them. A member of the forensic team held a video camera in their hand and for the first time I realised that this was going to be filmed. It felt more like a performance than a crucial piece of police investigation.

Senior Sergeant John Nixon was there and he was in charge. He acted like the director of a film. He spoke straight to the camera and declared that a toy gun and a black baseball cap would be used as props. I felt numb and disconnected from what was happening. I wasn't sure how this was going to help find Pete, and I was scared. I didn't want to fall apart here in front of these strangers, even if they were police. Senior Sergeant Nixon instructed me to sit in the passenger seat of the Kombi as I had on the night of the 14th of July.

Two police officers were playing the roles of Pete and the man. My role, besides obviously playing the part of myself, was to direct the acting police officers and tell them how to position themselves and what to do. The officer playing Pete got out and went to the back of the Kombi. It was getting darker as I moved over to the driver's seat as I had on that night. The policeman representing the man came to the driver's side window holding a toy gun in his hand. He entered the vehicle and pointed the gun at me. On the night we had been stopped this was the moment that I first knew my life was in danger. Face to face with the gunman I had become paralysed with fear. I looked at the policeman. I knew that this was a re-enactment but I couldn't stop the flashback or stop the flood of terror from overwhelming me. I burst into tears and buried my face in my hands. The policeman moved out of the vehicle and Senior Sergeant Nixon shouted, 'Turn off the camera.' I was left alone to compose myself until Senior Sergeant Turnbull came over and patted me on the back.

While writing this book I watched this re-enactment. It seemed badly organised and the equipment didn't seem to work properly. When I saw myself burst into tears I wanted to shout out, 'It will be okay, you can get through this.' I could see the look of impatience creep over the policeman's face as he got out of the Kombi. It was cold and the wind was howling so the audio is distorted and hard to hear clearly. Perhaps I am imposing my knowledge of what happened later, but there is no sense of compassion towards me from the police present at that re-enactment. If anything they are cool and seem awkward with this pale, dark-haired victim of a violent crime. I had no idea they doubted my every word.

Once I had pulled myself back together, the policeman who was acting out the part of the man returned and the filming began again. Sensibly, someone had decided that it wasn't necessary for him to hold a replica gun. Instead he formed a gun with his hand.

I continued to re-enact the sequence of events. This meant having to lie down on the ground outside the Kombi. It felt degrading but I kept reminding myself that this was to help the police with the investigation. On several occasions I was asked to speak up or go back and replay an action because the camera didn't pick it up. I was asked how the man had hit me and how I had fallen. I explained how the sack had been placed over my head; about how the man barely spoke and how I was screaming constantly. I didn't do this for the camera.

At one point I was asked to get inside the back of the four-wheel drive. I felt enclosed, trapped and vulnerable. I showed how I had escaped from the back tray. Hanging my legs down over the tray I dropped slowly to my feet, as I had done on that night. In the dim light I was able to see just how close the man had been to me, before I had run into the bush and into the cover of darkness. I could not control my emotions; it was the first time that I had allowed myself to acknowledge how lucky I had been and how narrowly I had escaped being raped and murdered. The feelings of terror came back and again I felt nauseous. Not one of the police acknowledged that what I had just done must have been difficult, nor was I asked if I was okay.

When it was over, Senior Sergeant Turnbull and I went back to her car and began the drive back to Alice Springs. As we passed through the roadblock a photographer jumped out in front of our car, risking his life to take a photograph of me. Senior Sergeant Turnbull only narrowly missed him. It shook us both.

The next day that photograph appeared on the front page of a newspaper with a headline that basically said 'Joanne Lees looks desperate and lonely as she revisits crime scene'. Senior Sergeant Turnbull was with me when I saw it and she joked that they had confused me with her, saying that she was the one who was desperate and lonely.

* * *

I had been told that Paul and Luciano Falconio were arriving in Alice Springs that evening and I was desperate to see them. One of the things that had helped me through the re-enactment was the thought that they would soon be here. I had convinced myself that once I saw them they could somehow make everything better. But as the moment of seeing them drew nearer, I began to feel anxious. I was not sure how I would cope when I came face to face with their pain and anguish. I knew the distress they were feeling because I was experiencing it too.

Senior Sergeant Turnbull accompanied me to Paul and Luciano's hotel room. We hugged each other and soothed one another by saying that Pete would soon be found. All the while, we were watched over by the police. I remember trying to lighten Luciano's pain by saying that this was typical of Pete, that Pete was always late for everything but that he would come back to us. I was clinging on to that hope. I didn't stay long and was back in my hotel room by 10.30 pm. As it was every night, my sleep was constantly interrupted by a man with cold, hard eyes.

* * *

The following morning I saw Amanda and Lisa in my hotel room. Senior Sergeant Turnbull was with us as well. While we were there, Constable Libby Andrew was introduced to me for the first time. She was to act as my chaperone during the day and Senior Sergeant Turnbull would do the night shift. I didn't question why I had to have a constant police presence. In the end it wasn't that constant, because a couple of times during the next week or so I would wake in the night to find I was alone.

Amanda and Lisa weren't with me long and then they were taken to the police station. They each had to provide a statement. We were all puzzled as to why. They had been in Sydney when it happened. They had only come to Alice Springs to support me.

Lisa was interviewed at length by Detective Senior Sergeant Jeanette Kerr. Amanda was in another room with someone else. Lisa recorded everything in her diary later that day. Despite her protestations of my innocence she realised Detective Kerr was suggesting that I had something to do with Pete's disappearance. Lisa stated that I would never do anything to harm Pete and never wavered from that belief. At the end of the interview Lisa was asked to type up her own statement. She did but thought it very strange and unprofessional that she should be required to do this.

After they were interviewed, Lisa and Amanda were told that the police were not prepared to take them back to the hotel where I was staying. Detective Kerr told Lisa that they would not be seeing much of me as I would be too busy assisting the police with their enquiries. Detective Kerr went on to say that the police would prefer it if they left Alice Springs and let the police get on with their job. They were told by Detective Kerr that she would be more than happy to escort them both to the airport to catch a flight back to Sydney.

It was 9.00 pm when Amanda and Lisa left the police station. The police had agreed to pay for them to spend the night in a backpackers hostel called Malanka's. Lisa refused as she and her boyfriend, Dan, had stayed there on their previous visit to Alice Springs and had thought it a horrible place. Instead Amanda and Lisa caught a taxi to Elsie's backpackers. Detective Kerr told them that if anyone asked what they were doing in Alice Springs, they should say they had been on a tour to Ayers Rock.

That evening I called Amanda and Lisa to make plans to see them the next day. I was completely unaware of their experience and the treatment they had received from the police. I was desperate to see them. Lisa broke the news to me that they were leaving the next day.

I was devastated and very confused when I got off the phone. I spoke to Detective Kerr and told her I needed my friends to stay. She said that I was being selfish, that Amanda and Lisa were travellers and they didn't have any money to pay for accommodation. I offered to share with them. I said that if the police returned my bank cards I would pay for them. Detective Kerr told me that Amanda and Lisa had jobs and family to return to in Sydney and I should consider that. She had no idea how badly the attack had affected me and I didn't understand her coolness. Now, knowing I was a suspect, it all makes sense.

The next day, the 20th of July 2001, the police picked Amanda and Lisa up from the backpackers and brought them to my hotel. We had fifteen minutes to say goodbye. It was heart-wrenching. I didn't want to be left alone and Amanda and Lisa didn't want to leave, but the police had made them feel unwelcome and they didn't think they could go against the authorities. The police were there the whole time we were talking, and when Amanda and Lisa left me they were taken to the police station to wait for Detective Kerr, who was going to personally drive them to the airport. The only reason I didn't completely fall apart when Lisa and Amanda left was because I knew Paul and Luciano were still in Alice Springs.

* * *

I was alone and isolated and the police were pushing away anyone I was close to who could have supported me (I have discovered since that this was happening to other friends and relations). I was desperate for news of Pete and was sure that any day there would be answers to what had happened to us. Having Constable Andrew there was the only good thing in my day.

Constable Libby Andrew, who had been appointed the day before as my daytime chaperone, was incredibly professional in her dealings with me. She treated me with the respect and compassion that I needed – that anyone who had gone through a violent and traumatic event would need.

The next few days were strange and confronting and I was focused on trying to help the police, even though I was puzzled by some of their methods. I had never experienced anything like this before. I had no comparison, no context, so I went along with what was asked of me. What I know now is that it wasn't only a unique experience for me but also for the investigating police. This was quite possibly the biggest case they would ever have. They had no idea how to deal with me, the evidence, or how to control the interest and media frenzy that was building.

Senior Sergeant John Nixon sent a request to me via Constable Andrew that I work in collaboration with an artist to create an impression of the man's gun and utility vehicle.

I was, of course, willing to assist so Constable Andrew escorted me to the Alice Springs Police Station; we arrived there at approximately 9.30 am. Senior Sergeant Nixon directed me into a room, telling me an artist was waiting for me. Inside I was greeted by a bespectacled older man with white-grey hair who introduced himself as David Stagg. He told me he was an art teacher. He seemed kind and sensitive and extremely nervous. His hands were shaking, and this made me feel nervous and uncomfortable.

After he had introduced himself he produced two examples of his work. He obviously wanted to show me he was up to the task. One of his pictures was of a horse, and the other a drawing of the solar system. Constable Andrew and I exchanged puzzled glances. I praised Mr Stagg honestly, telling him that I thought his drawings were very good.

He explained that he'd never done anything like this before and I told him with a wry smile that neither had I. He made it clear he had not been given any instructions but told me he was eager to help in any way that he could.

Constable Andrew left the room to speak with Detective Senior Sergeant Nixon, and a short time later she re-entered the room with a detective called Mick Lauser. It was my understanding that he was there to oversee the process. Detective Lauser sat in the corner of the room with his back turned to us for half an hour, then left the room and never returned. David Stagg and I worked together all day until 6.00 pm.

When I got back to the hotel my head was full of guns and utes. It had only been six days since the attack and I felt I had aged a lifetime. I wasn't sleeping or eating properly. Constable Andrew recognised the pain I was in and was the only person who tried to give me the skills or the outlet to get my body and my mind back to some sense of normality, if that was possible. She set up an exercise circuit in the hotel room so I could burn some energy and brought punching pads and boxing gloves so I could get some emotion out. She recognised the different emotional stages I was going through – from shock, to anger, to tears, to frustration and to disbelief – and she didn't condemn me for any of them.

I am lucky that Libby was with me when I was asked to go to the forensic building to identify the Kombi. It had been found abandoned in the bush the day after the attack, and the police now wanted me to tell them if anything was missing.

I didn't realise how confronting I was going to find this. The Kombi, Taz, had been our home and now it was a visual reminder of what had happened and that Pete was missing. Everything inside was a shambles; it had been trashed. I assumed the man had wrecked it, but I found out later it was the police.

When I was looking through Taz, among the tangled mess on the floor of the vehicle I saw my bracelet. I picked it up and put it on my wrist. Detective Senior Constable Paula Dooley was there and she snapped at me to take it off. She told me I couldn't touch anything or remove anything. Her tone and attitude were extremely rude and dismissive. I felt like a naughty child and I reacted angrily, telling her to 'Fuck off!' I hadn't lashed out at anyone up to this point and never did again. She was just so cold. I am sure she had her opinions about me, but I'll never forgive her or forget how she made me feel. She had no understanding of how emotionally draining it was to enter that vehicle, to see Pete's and my life on the floor. To realise this was my reality. It wasn't a bad horror movie or something to gossip about at the pub, it was my life. After my outburst I went and sat on the kerb and cried, for me, for Pete, for everything.

* * *

At this time my stepfather Vincent arrived in Alice Springs to support me and to help look for Pete. It wasn't easy to see him, or Paul and Luciano. It was so hard to watch their suffering. I was barely holding it together myself and had no reserves to help them. My stepfather made sure I was physically okay and then went back to the UK to look after my Mum. She had not been well for a long time and the best thing he could do for me was look after her, so I didn't have to worry how she was. Paul and Luciano stayed. They wanted to be there when Pete was found.

I felt like I was caught between two worlds. I was with the police all the time and had two chaperones, one at night and one by day. I was never alone. I never had the time to cry or scream or just be myself. I was constantly scrutinised and watched.

I had no idea at the time that Pete and I had become a huge news story in Australia and the UK. I knew journalists, like Mark Wilton, were hanging around but I had no clue how newsworthy they thought I was. I was completely isolated and all my time was spent with the police. Shortly after the crime I was asked to attend a press conference. Paul, Luciano and Vincent had already done one, days earlier. They were happy to be able to do something that might help find Pete or our assailant. I didn't appear with them; I wasn't ready to face the world just yet. Maybe I was wrong, but I couldn't see how me talking to the media was going to make a difference. I thought that it was enough that Paul, Luciano and Vincent were making public appeals for information. I didn't think I would be able to hold myself together and I didn't want to cry in front of a room full of journalists. I didn't want my Mum to see me crying on the news.

A few days after Paul, Luciano and Vincent's press conference the police asked me to address the media. They told me it might make a difference. I agreed, but in retrospect I wish that I had stood up for myself and refused. Maybe if I'd been given the necessary victim support the outcome would have been very different. We will never know. But I was given no guidance or advice before either of my two press conferences. Apparently I didn't behave like a true victim and from that moment the whispers about me became louder. How do true victims behave?

I was criticised for not breaking down in front of the cameras and for only answering three out of the thirteen questions that were asked. I doubt if anyone stopped to wonder what the other ten questions were. If I looked shocked and uncomfortable, that is because I was. I was positioned in front of a room full of media. One face stood out from the rest. Mark Wilton. His presence made me feel even more uncomfortable. I felt like an exhibit.

Before I entered the room where the conference was taking place I had stopped to drink a glass of water. A cameraman filmed me doing this. I didn't understand why. My only comfort throughout was that Paul Falconio was sitting beside me, and that Libby was standing at the back of the room behind all the journalists and cameras.

As I began to speak I watched all the media in the room lean forwards. They had never heard me speak before and they seemed to struggle to understand my Yorkshire accent. Maybe that was part of their problem?

I received even more criticism after the second press conference I attended. This time I was criticised for wearing a pink top with the words 'cheeky monkey' written across it. I learnt later this is something a 'true victim' would not wear. I didn't know there was a dress code for people who had survived a traumatic event. I have to admit I gave no thought to what I was wearing. My mind was focused on more important things. I was a backpacker with a limited wardrobe consisting of T-shirts, sarongs and shorts. I didn't have a white pressed shirt to hand or a navy-blue suit. Would I have been taken more seriously if I had? Would people have judged me less harshly? I am able to think these things through now, but at the time I was an emotional wreck. I had no idea that everything I did, said or wore was going to be examined, analysed and debated. I still was not completely aware that more and more people were questioning my recollection of events.

* * *

As a reaction to this media interest, Northern Territory Police Commissioner Brian Bates and Superintendent Kate Vanderlaan organised to meet me in a cafe in the local mall for morning tea, to perhaps reassure the media and themselves that they had acknowledged the victim. I didn't realise how unusual it was for the Commissioner to visit the victim in an active investigation. Though the police have a hierarchy, it meant nothing to me. For an officer like Libby it was eye-opening to see people she would never normally have dealings with. I wasn't focused on a person's rank, but a number of times I was surprised that some of those I dealt with of higher rank could be inept, unsure and even rude.

After a strained time making small talk with them both, I was relieved to get away. I was tense and not sure what was going on. I couldn't see how morning tea with me would help find Pete. To make me feel better, Libby teased me about having access to someone so high up.

* * *

Every morning I would get up early and head off with Libby for a long walk. It was cold on those mornings and Libby gave me an Australian Rugby jumper and beanie to wear – it was comforting in a strange way. At other times, Libby would take me for a drive to Simpsons Gap or Stanley Chasm, to take my mind off everything. These drives and our morning walks were times that I valued. That night, while I was hiding from the man searching for me, wondering where Pete was, I wasn't sure if I was going to get away alive. There were moments when I thought I would die, that I would never again be able to see a sunset or sunrise. I can't describe everything I felt as I tried to be invisible and tried not to breathe while crouched under a bush in the outback in the dark, but there were moments of utter despair, terror and dread. To see the beauty of the Northern Territory, away from hotel rooms and police stations, helped me feel better. I drew power from knowing I was seeing things that one man had almost stopped me from ever knowing existed.

I was torn between being happy to be alive and despairing that Pete wasn't with me. I was lucky, but he wasn't. I didn't know where he was, what had happened to him, and I was struggling to deal with this and my escape. Trying to get a grip on how I felt and what had happened wasn't helped by how I was living. I was in an unreal bubble and so any hint of normality was something I seized. When Luciano and Paul told me they'd had a haircut one day I thought it sounded like a good idea. My hair was damaged from the tape that had been wrapped around my head and having it cut was, I thought, a positive thing to do. Libby arranged an appointment for me. I was surprised my haircut made the paper but apparently it was something a 'true victim' was not supposed to do. I didn't know that.

Time was passing and there was no news of Pete. Libby was trying to keep me moving, and when I wasn't needed she took me to places to keep my spirits up. I am not a complicated person and I like down-to-earth places and genuine people. I don't like pretence or being treated differently because of what happened. Libby picked up on that. We did things like visiting a desert park and taking long walks. One day in late July, Libby and I went to the local YMCA to climb a rock wall. I know it will sound strange but I was proud of myself (and so was Libby) when I reached the top. My feelings all went back to that awful night. It was a weird roller-coaster of emotion that I was riding. One moment I was fearful and having trouble sleeping, but then at other times I felt invincible. Climbing that wall was caught up in that. I was alive. I was strong. I could stand up for myself.

But no matter how empowered I occasionally felt, the fact was nothing was ever going to be the same again. I could try and act normally, have my hair cut, climb rock walls, but the events of the crime were always in my thoughts. Around this time it was announced that the Northern Territory government was posting a reward for information about our attack and Pete's disappearance. Everywhere I went I'd see his picture. It must have been devastating for Luciano and Paul. However, we all knew that to find Pete we needed the public's help and needed to keep people focused on Pete.

It was hard to spend a great deal of time with Luciano and Paul. Partly this was the police keeping me from anyone I knew and partly because it was emotionally difficult for all of us. We were just waiting for news. One afternoon I sat with Luciano around his hotel pool while Paul went to the dentist. We didn't talk a lot but it was comforting for me to be with him.

That day I found out the police had developed the photos Pete and I had taken since we'd left home. They'd given some to the media and some to Luciano but hadn't bothered to give them to me or tell me that was what they were doing. I didn't know until

Luciano told me he had them. We sat there and looked through a stack of photos. It was an incredibly bittersweet moment. There were lots of photos of Pete that I had taken. It reminded me of all our good times and I couldn't help but think I should be with him.

When I got back to my hotel room, Libby took one look at me and instinctively got out the punching pads.

Luciano had decided to go back to the UK. It was very hard for him because he'd vowed not to go home without Pete. He'd been in Australia for two weeks and he must have felt so helpless not being able to do anything. He and Paul had visited the crime scene and made themselves available but there wasn't a lot they could do. Joan was back at home, trying to cope with her fears and grief, and Luciano felt he should be with her. I asked him to take a letter back with him for my Mum. I wanted to reassure her I was okay. Taking the time to write to her made the distance between us feel a little less.

The day before Luciano went home I was asked to go to the police station to look through their offender books. I so wanted to be able to point to a picture and say, 'That's him'. The man wasn't in there – and much later I would wonder why, because I would eventually learn our attacker had a criminal history. While I was looking through the books, Libby arranged for me to get copies of my photos.

Once Luciano left for the airport, Paul, Libby and I cycled to Centralian College. At that point, Paul and I couldn't see ourselves leaving Alice Springs until Pete was found but we didn't know what to do with our time. We didn't think there was any other option but to wait around, so we talked about renting an apartment and studying... something.

With Libby's help we tried to fill our days with exercise, bike rides and touring around to places like Flynn's Grave. One evening I went to the movies. I hadn't been out since Sydney and I have to say it was very strange. What was even stranger was watching *Bridget Jones's Diary* with Senior Sergeant Helen Turnbull. Nowadays I can't see that movie without flashing back to 2001. My friends see it as a feel-good chick flick but for me it is an unpleasant reminder.

On Thursday the 2nd of August I was struggling. It was my Mum's birthday and I was missing her. As much as I was still trying to believe that the police would find Pete, in my heart I knew that hope was fading with every day that passed. I had thought the reward money would generate information and lead to the man but I hadn't heard anything. Again Libby knew what I needed and drove me to an isolated property on Undoolya Road, outside town. We got out of the car and walked a little way. There was nothing around. Libby encouraged me to scream at the top of my voice and release my anger, frustration and despair. I did. Probably more than she thought I would. It all exploded out of me in a cathartic primal rage. When I finished I collapsed and started to cry. I didn't recognise the woman I was or understand what had happened to me and Pete. Why us?

* * *

On Friday the 3rd of August the police arranged for me to be hypnotised. I had been told that they thought it might help me to remember something important. I felt apprehensive but was desperate to help and agreed to give it a try.

Libby escorted me to a room, Senior Sergeant Nixon was standing outside. He didn't speak to me directly, he never did. He was nervous around me and never made eye contact. He was usually looking down at his shoes whenever I passed him. In years to come I would notice a lot of detectives do this.

I began to enter the room and turned back to see if Libby was following. She wasn't. I asked Detective Senior Sergeant Nixon if

Libby could come inside the room with me and he gave an abrupt 'No'. I felt tense and very nervous as the door closed. I was alone in the room with the hypnotist. She was an older woman who had been flown in from Sydney. I was conscious that this was also being filmed.

The hypnotist asked me to sit down in a chair that had been set up for the purpose and to close my eyes. I did as she asked but from time to time I lifted up an eyelid to take a peep at what was happening.

She began the process and spoke in a deep throaty voice. I was startled at first because she suddenly sounded like a man. I was told to imagine myself walking along a beach. I was then asked to visualise my footprints in the sand, to follow them getting further and further away, becoming fainter and fainter. I was not hypnotised. She tried other methods to hypnotise me but they did not work either. I told the woman that I was fully conscious but she told me that I was in fact hypnotised. I disagreed but went through the motions anyway. The woman asked me to describe the events of the crime. I told her. She asked me to scream out like I had done that night. I opened my eyes and explained that I couldn't do that. On the Stuart Highway I was screaming out for my life, I could not re-create this at will for her or anyone. I wasn't prepared to put myself back into that terrifying time. The whole experience was a waste of time and didn't reveal anything. I was disappointed but not surprised.

I left the room and was told Libby had gone. I wouldn't see her again until the trial. I can't begin to explain how I felt when she didn't come back and didn't say goodbye. Nobody told me that she was being removed from the case. The one person who had treated me with respect and had been concerned with my welfare was gone. Paul was around, and he was helping as much as he could, but he had enough to deal with. I was thrown back to not knowing what was happening and I was confused and thought I had done something wrong. I found out years later that Constable Andrew had been told she was getting too close and that she was forbidden to have any contact with me. The reality is that she behaved as a compassionate professional and only did what she had been trained to do.

After Libby's removal I had another chaperone called Karen. In the days that followed I warmed to her. But it was hard to trust another person after Libby was removed. Karen was my chaperone during the day and the night chaperone was cut. I was still having trouble sleeping and sometimes Paul would stay in my room. He managed to talk me into sleeping with the light off – but I still made sure the television was on in the background. I had the sound turned down but needed some light. Since that night I have been scared of the dark.

* * *

One night in early August, Superintendent Kate Vandalaan came to my hotel room. She asked for Paul to be present before she gave me some news. Paul was staying in the room next door and was there in a flash. A body had been found. I don't know whether I took in all the details right away. All I remember is her leaving and Paul and I hugging each other and convincing ourselves it wasn't Pete. I don't think either of us slept that night. We waited for more details to come, for someone to contact us, but no one ever came back to my room to tell us anything. I kept phoning the detectives to see if they had more information but they wouldn't tell me anything. Finally, twenty-four hours later, I got through to Senior Sergeant John Nixon and he told me it wasn't Pete. I couldn't believe I'd had to pester them to get an answer and that no one had told Paul and me earlier.

I think that was the moment when I started to realise that being in Alice Springs wasn't helping get me closer to Pete. It wasn't healthy being there, and the police were not handling things well as far as I was concerned. Looking back, I should have realised they were doubting my story. It was time to leave the Northern Territory.

9

Oh my God!
You think it's me

After twenty-four days in Alice Springs there had been no word
about Pete. The police had no news, or at least no news they were
telling me. Every minute of those days I thought about that man
and hoped that somewhere Pete was okay. The sound of the
gunshot would fire through my mind day and night. Where was
Pete? What had he done with Pete?

I had spent a great deal of my time trying to help the police:
giving statements, looking at similar vehicles, looking through
photographs of known criminals to see if I recognised the man,
taking them through our movements in the lead up to July the
14th. I relived the crime, over and over again. It was draining,
suffocating and taking its toll on my health. I didn't care about
my own wellbeing if what I was doing helped, but I was starting
to wonder if it would make any difference.

I couldn't remember what it was like to feel like me anymore.
I needed Pete. I wanted my Mum and I craved some normality.
I never went anywhere without a police officer accompanying me.

I knew I couldn't take much more. I talked it over with Paul and I decided to leave Alice Springs. It was one of the most difficult decisions I have ever had to make. I felt torn. I didn't want to leave Pete or the investigation behind but I couldn't stay there. I had no freedom from the media, I had no friends, and though Paul was there it was too hard to talk with him about my fears. He was hurting as well. And somewhere, that man was out there and I couldn't feel completely safe.

I made plans to return to Sydney. I would be far enough away to give myself some space to heal but still only a short flight away if Pete was found and the man caught. I was still in the same country so the police could contact me whenever necessary and could keep me updated. I planned to go back to work, keep busy and try and think of something other than the crime. I wasn't ready to leave Australia – I still hadn't given up hope.

When I told the police of my plans, they didn't seem at all surprised or disappointed. If anything, I sensed relief. I'd been told a couple of times in subtle and not-so-subtle ways that it was costing a lot to pay for my accommodation and to use police officers as chaperones.

My flight was booked for the 8th of August 2001. Mick and Karen, two police officers who had acted as chaperones for Paul and me while we were in Alice Springs, organised a farewell dinner for us both the night before my departure. Mick's wife worked at the local RSL club and so we went there. Mick thought the RSL would be a safe, private place to have dinner and a few drinks together. The RSL was a members only club and Mick knew most of the locals and knew they would respect our space.

After such an emotionally fraught time it was good for us to get out, have a meal and a few drinks. I hadn't really been drinking while in Alice Springs. I was holding myself in emotionally the whole time and not drinking was part of keeping in control. We were halfway through our meal and I was on my second glass of wine when Mick's mobile phone rang. It was about eight o'clock at night. He answered it, and after ending his call he turned to me and said that I was wanted at the police station. Mick looked as confused as I felt. We left and headed to the Alice Springs Police Station. My heart was racing. Did they have news of Pete?

When we got there, I was told that the detectives wanted to interview me. Pete hadn't been found. After waiting an hour, I was told the detectives were ready. At 9.30 pm I was led into an interview room. There were lots of detectives and police officers milling around the room, looking at me. I felt selfconscious and very much alone but I pushed those feelings aside and tried to focus on what the police wanted.

Once inside the small interview room I was shown to a seat. I could see a video camera positioned on a tripod pointing towards where I would be sitting. I sat down at a small rectangular table that jutted out from the wall. Detective Senior Sergeant Jeanette Kerr and Detective Tony Henrys sat opposite me. Detective Senior Sergeant John Nixon entered the room to adjust the video camera and then left.

I waited and Detective Kerr explained that because I was leaving the next day they needed to go over my statement to clarify some inconsistencies. She spoke to me as if my plans to leave had created difficulties for the police. I was confused; I had let it be known for a while that I was leaving on the 8th of August. If I had been told it was a problem, and that I was needed, I would have stayed longer.

After the attack I had put all my trust in the police. I had no reason not to; as far as I was concerned they were trained professionals who knew what they were doing. I believed that they would find Pete and arrest the man. I believed what they told me. For example, I asked them a day or two after the crime had been committed if they had obtained any footage from security cameras at any service stations in the area. I was told they hadn't, but this was not true. I don't know why they didn't tell me they had.

Since the crime I'd had very little contact with Detective Henrys but I had met Detective Senior Sergeant Kerr on a few occasions. She seemed quite cold and I felt she was insensitive towards me. I got the impression that she didn't like me. I never wanted or expected sympathy or pity from her, or from any of the police who came into contact with me; I just wanted to be treated thoughtfully and with the respect any victim of a violent crime deserves.

Detective Kerr had photographed me in Alice Springs to record my injuries. I had to stand in front of her in my underwear to display my cuts, bruises and scrapes. While she was doing this she casually asked me if I had been raped but had been too embarrassed to say so earlier. Thinking back now, I can't believe a police officer who suspected something like this would be so careless in their probing. I told her I hadn't been raped but as soon as the words were out of my mouth the realisation that this would have been my fate hit hard. I hadn't shown Detective Kerr how freaked out I was but I had been very relieved when she finished and I could put some clothes back on.

Now that same woman was sitting across from me asking about inconsistencies in my statement. I took a deep breath and shook my head to try and shake off the effects of the wine I'd had.

I was told the interview was to be recorded onto three audio cassettes in addition to being filmed. This, I was told, was correct procedure. As we were ready to start, the tape recorder wouldn't work. Detective Kerr apologised as she tried to rectify the problem. I sat patiently in my seat. I was used to waiting for the police to sort out technical hitches. After a few attempts to get the tape recorder to work, Detective Henrys left the room and then returned with a Dictaphone, which he placed in the middle of the table. After being informed by Detective Kerr that police procedure required the recording of an interview onto three cassettes I was surprised that they were now relying on just one.

Once the Dictaphone was recording, Detective Kerr said that she appreciated that this interview was going to be harrowing and distressing for me; she added that I would need to bear with *them*. Her tone was quite patronising and she went on to say that they needed help to clarify 'aspects of your statement that we can't explain'.

After a few general questions Detective Kerr asked me to describe my relationship with Pete. She asked me to go into detail. I couldn't. I began to cry. I missed Pete. It was too painful to think about him. The only way I had been able to cope with the continuous questioning had been to emotionally detach myself from what was happening and deal with everything in a factual way. I had tried to leave all emotion aside. But that night I'd had some wine and the dam I'd built around my feelings wasn't going to hold.

ME: I really can't talk about Pete right now.

KERR: Okay, there's nothing wrong with that. Would you describe it as a loving relationship?

ME: Mm mm.

Despite being visibly upset and stating that I was too emotional to talk about Pete, Detective Kerr continued to question me about our relationship. I started to worry. I had a strange feeling that I was a suspect but I shook it away.

Detective Kerr moved on. She started questioning me about the Camel Cup, about leaving Alice Springs, about watching the sunset at Ti Tree and what Pete and I had bought at the service station.

KERR: Do you recall what the mileage was?

I had written the mileage down on the petrol receipt over a month earlier, shortly before I had experienced the most traumatic experience of my life. Did they really expect me to remember the mileage?

Detective Kerr, and occasionally Detective Henrys, continued to question me on various aspects of my recollections. At times during the interview they would suggest that some of the statements I had given were untrue. I continued to answer as truthfully and as honestly as I had always done. The whole interview was traumatic and the detectives sitting in front of me were completely unperturbed by the obvious trauma I was experiencing. When I became emotional and could barely speak I was just told:

KERR: Sorry, you are going to have to actually speak.

As time passed, I was getting more and more confused and I didn't understand what was going on. I thought I was becoming paranoid, that they were suspecting me. I put this down to being tired and emotional and carried on.

KERR: You said to one of the, um, I'm not sure who it was that was with you, that you had to get to your email and delete it because there was some sensitive stuff on there.
ME: No. I never said I had to get to my email and delete anything. I said I had to get to my emails and delete some messages off there because otherwise my account would close because there would be too many messages.

I was receiving hundreds of messages from friends and family. Email was the only way they could contact me. My Hotmail account didn't have a huge storage for messages so I had to keep checking it and deleting messages before it got too full and shut down. I had given the police access to my emails. I had nothing to hide from them. I knew they would have read them. I wondered if she was going to mention Nick, but I couldn't see how he could be relevant to a stranger attacking Pete and me on the Stuart Highway. I hadn't seen him for months and as far as I knew he was in the United States.

> KERR: Joanne, we are not trying to upset you, we really just want to clarify some of this information to focus our enquiries.
>
> ME: Jeanette, honestly, you can't upset me, I'm just upset enough, okay.

The interview continued and occasionally Detective Kerr would pick up the Dictaphone to make sure it was working.

> KERR: Okay, also um, we've got a statement from a person who was at Ti Tree at the same time as you and they saw, they overtook you actually on the road.
>
> ME: Right.
>
> KERR: And they saw you pull up at Ti Tree and they said that it was only you in the vehicle.
>
> ME: No, no. That might be because Pete . . . was lying down in the back when we pulled up, that did happen. He was reading his book and I woke him up.
>
> KERR: And that this person said that they arrived at Ti Tree Roadhouse and he had a cigarette and watched the sunset and watched you watch the sunset for about five minutes.
>
> ME: The person did and I was on my own? Is that it?
>
> KERR: Yeah.
>
> ME: Well, no, Pete was there.

* * *

> KERR: Okay. The mileage you wrote on the, um, on the receipt was accurate.

ME: Yes.

KERR: Okay, because it's a hundred point five kilometres from Ti Tree Roadhouse to the site where your van was and the mileage on the receipt indicates that a hundred and seven kilometres may have been travelled.

ME: I wrote it accurately, that's what was on there, maybe our odometer was wrong but I did write it down accurately.

I would find out later that this wasn't the case. Whatever her tactics, I knew I was telling the truth. During the trial I found out that the mileage was all accounted for.

Detective Kerr's questions jumped around and I concentrated hard to make sense of the things she was asking. It was getting harder to do as I was becoming increasingly tired and more and more uncertain about what the police wanted from me. Occasionally I would see the looks Detective Kerr would give Detective Henrys and these made me even more unsettled. It seemed she was almost smirking at times.

KERR: And you describe the revolver?

ME: Uh hum.

KERR: You get a really good look at the gun. It's a silver handgun like a western-style gun. It's about maybe four inches long and we've discussed the engraving on the barrel. Joanne, we've done a complete firearms record check, we've had ballistics experts look at your drawing, and your descriptions, and we have not been able to identify that gun or a revolver of similar in description to what you describe. Like we haven't been able to find a car like you describe. Can you help us with that?

ME: I can't, I can't. I'm just describing what I saw. I'm really, I'm just describing what I saw.

KERR: Can you give me an explanation why we have no gun?

ME: I don't know. I've never seen a gun before in my life. I'm just. I'm getting this feeling that you think that I'm making all this up, but I'm not.

I didn't know what to do. I wanted to find Pete. I wanted to help, but these two police officers were talking as though I was a suspect. I started to feel panicked and wanted to stop and tell them they were wasting their time. I was telling the truth.

KERR: I explained to you that this is really important, and you are a really important witness for us, obviously. Your recollection is what we are working on.

ME: Okay, well, will you make me feel like a witness and not a suspect please? Am I a suspect?

KERR: No, you're not. You're not. I don't believe you murdered Pete.

ME: Good.

KERR: And I'm sure I can speak for Tony as well. And I've said the reason we're going through this is because there are these things that we are having difficulty with. Things that we can't explain.

ME: Hmm. And Pete might still be alive you know.

KERR: Yeah. How long, how long since this day is it?

ME: It's a month today.

KERR: So then you describe the gunman.

I wanted to walk out of that room but I didn't. I stayed and the questioning went on.

KERR: And you've fallen or been pushed from this height face-first onto sharp gravel.

ME: I don't know Jeanette, how I got down there, all I remember is lying down, the next thing I remember is I'm laid down.

KERR: Okay. Can you see the difficulty that I'm having here?

ME: Uh huh.

KERR: You have no injuries to your face.

ME: Uh huh.

KERR: No injuries to the front of your body. And you've come from sitting up in the van, face-first onto sharp gravel.

ME: I don't know how I come up there. I never said I come from sitting up there. All I remember is one minute I'm sitting there in the Kombi in the passenger's side. The next I'm on the ground, face down, yeah, I'm tasting blood in my mouth and, um, my knees are cut.

KERR: Your knees are cut. So, did you pass out?

ME: I don't remember. I don't recall passing out, no.

KERR: Until now you've never claimed that.

ME: No. I'm not claiming it now, I just don't know how I got from there to there. I really don't.

KERR: Did the gunman lift you out?

ME: I don't know.

KERR: Place you there?

ME: I don't know.

I was repeatedly asked where I was when the man bound my hands together. I told them that I'd been inside the Kombi, but they continued to question me and query my injuries.

HENRYS: We're at this point again though, Jo.

ME: Sure.

HENRYS: Where you are our link. You are the one who's gonna help us.

ME: Mm.

HENRYS: Find Pete.

ME: Yeah.

HENRYS: And that's why this is so important.

ME: I know, but is it important how I was tied? Surely there are more important things to know.

HENRYS: Every aspect is important.

ME: (Sigh)

HENRYS: No, it's not a shrug of the shoulders.

ME: I know, I know.

KERR: If you can't remember how you got out of the vehicle.

ME: Maybe I can't remember . . .

KERR: If you can't remember really the way most things happened, how much weight can we place on anything else you've told us?

ME: (Sigh) I can only tell you what I remember.

A thought came to me while I was being questioned and I asked:

ME: Can I ask you, do you know when my Kombi van was found what state was it in?

KERR: Yeah.

ME: What was it like? Was it neat and tidy or was it . . .

KERR: I've already told you that.

ME: I don't remember.

KERR: It was fine, it was clean.

ME: Okay.

KERR: There's no indication.

ME: Okay.

KERR: Okay, I really don't want to labour this point with you.

I don't even know what point either of us was trying to make. I felt completely defeated and they had asked me so many times to clarify myself that I was starting to doubt what I knew was the truth. I was exhausted and my mind was spinning. Things weren't making sense.

KERR: Don't give up on me now.

ME: Oh, I'm not giving up on you at all . . .

Detective Kerr kept going, ignoring my distress. I was asked about how I knew that the man was standing talking to me through the back of his ute while I lay inside.

ME: I know that he is there because I hear him and light is gone.

KERR: Hmm, so for that to be the case the light must have been behind him, which by all accounts is just absolutely impossible because all the lights are forward of this position.

ME: Okay.

KERR: Tell me, how could you see that?

ME: I don't know.

KERR: I don't know. Was there something else, was there another light out there, tell me. I mean.

ME: There wasn't another light that I'm aware of.

KERR: But something's silhouetting him.

ME: I don't know if it's silhouetting him or what but, when he's not there I see more of the bush, and when he comes back I don't, so he's blocking something out and I don't know what light it is.

KERR: But the lights behind you Jo, that's my problem. Out the back is black.

ME: Sure, sure.

KERR: So what light's he blocking out.

ME: I don't know what light he's blocking out but I can see through. If I couldn't see anything I wouldn't even be able to see the gap would I? Wouldn't be able to see the hole and know that there was a way out, that it wasn't totally covered up. Okay, are any of these questions going to help me get to Pete, going to help me find Pete, because I'm . . .

KERR: Yes, I believe they are.

ME: Because, what time is it? Because I'm really tired now.

KERR: I know you're tired. 'Cause we know . . .

ME: What time is it, sorry?

KERR: It's midnight, I know you're tired.

ME: Hmm.

KERR: We don't have much more to go.

ME: I've been here since half past eight.

KERR: I don't know exactly what time, I thought we started at nine.

HENRYS: Yeah.

KERR: I know it's difficult.

ME: Well, I've been downstairs, I've been at the police station since half past eight.

KERR: Okay, I'm sorry for that. You're leaving tomorrow.

ME: Yep.

KERR: I've explained why.

ME: I've been here a month, so you could have got this from me before. I want to go now.

Detective Kerr didn't want me to leave and discouraged me by trying to make me feel guilty and putting words into my mouth.

KERR: You don't want to answer these questions? You don't want to explain the inconsistencies in your statement?

I told them that I was happy to answer them when I wasn't tired. That I had been in Alice Springs a month and they had never queried me like this about any inconsistencies in all that time. Now they were doing it at the last possible moment. I told them I had a flight to catch in the morning. I explained that had I known they had wanted to re-interview me I would have arranged a different flight but that no one had told me this was needed. I had been there three and a half hours and I was tired and not able to focus properly. Detective Kerr continued to try and make me feel guilty.

KERR: To help us with the investigation.

ME: Uh hmm.

KERR: You can't give me half an hour.

ME: Now you're twisting my words. I'm quite happy to help you through this. Another half an hour, is that what you are saying?

KERR: We'll be pretty close to it.

ME: It's just that I'm not thinking straight. So it's not really a good time for me to be doing this.

HENRYS: Why?

ME: Because I'm tired.

HENRYS: Yeah, but.

ME: I've been out, I had a drink, a couple of glasses of wine, I'm not . . .

HENRYS: Why isn't it a good time though. I mean . . .

ME: Because I'm really tired, I can't think straight,

I took a deep breath and pushed my hair away from my face. My body was aching from the tension and from exhaustion but I'd give them another half hour.

KERR: The evidence from the scene says that there's one set of footprints.

ME: Yeah.

KERR: Located at the crime scene, and there [sic] were yours.

ME: Just one or two footprints. The only two of mine.

KERR: Yeah. The only, the only prints there were yours.

ME: And there's only two of them.

KERR: I believe there's more.

ME: Oh, okay.

KERR: And they go in a direct line from the pool of blood to that hiding place, and the length of the stride and the depth of those prints indicate running. Can you account for that?

ME: I was never at the back of the Kombi van. I was never near the pool of blood.

A shudder went through me at this point. They were talking about Pete's blood! That feeling that they suspected me kept hitting me and I tried to ignore it.

KERR: There was no forensic evidence and no evidence of anything being dragged at the scene.

ME: Something was dragged. So maybe your forensics have lost it, there was his footprints, he did go in the bush, so you haven't come up with those either. I was lying in that bush for five hours or more, and you haven't found that, it was a full tube of lip-balm, not just a lid, you haven't found that.

KERR: We haven't found the pieces that you bit off the manacles.

ME: No.

In fact they would do three months later, when they searched the area properly.

Detective Kerr would occasionally glance at Detective Henrys. She spoke slowly and carefully in low tones and I had to strain to hear her.

KERR: We've, um, your statement, we had it, we sent it away to some experts that do linguistic content analysis of statements. They look at the content and they look at the language.

ME: Yeah.

KERR: Practitioners from Victoria, Queensland, Northern Territory and South Australia have had a look at that a number of them [sic].

ME: Yeah.

KERR: And that's done to assist investigators as an investigative tool.

ME: Come on, this is going to be bad news, what do they say?

KERR: The consensus without exception is that there is vital information missing from this statement, from your account. That's the information we need. What? What information's missing?

ME: I don't know, I don't know. How I got from the passenger side to the outside. I don't know.

KERR: What were you and Pete arguing about that day?

ME: We weren't arguing.

KERR: You didn't have an argument at all?

ME: No, not at all.

KERR: Do you. I guess what I want to say about all this at this stage is to get some sort of closure, some sort of closure for Pete's family. I think that you know for them the main priority for them is to be able to take him home, to be able to let go, you know? Can you help us with that?

ME: No. Now you are really scaring me, you think I did this don't you?

KERR: No. But I have to ask you if you've been involved in the disappearance of Peter Falconio.

Interview concluded 12.29 am.

* * *

I understand that what happened to Pete and me wasn't just a unique experience for me. For most of the police handling the investigation it was an exceptional case and like nothing they had been involved in before. I am trying hard not to become bitter about how I was treated, but it is hard. During those twenty-four days that I spent in Alice Springs I was never given any victim care. I was given no media advice, my friends and family were encouraged to leave, and after that interview I realised I was a suspect. I was never offered any legal advice before that interview even though the detectives knew they were treating me as a suspect. I was interviewed under the influence of alcohol. I was isolated, vulnerable and extremely traumatised.

After I left that room I went back to the hotel and the next day Paul and I flew to Sydney. I couldn't tell him what had happened in that room. I couldn't tell anyone. How could I explain that the police thought I had killed Pete, or at the very least was involved in his disappearance?

I don't think I have ever felt so powerless as I did that night. Since then I have seen the tape of this interview and I have watched the person that I was lean forward and place her head on the table in despair. I have watched her break into tears. All I wanted to do was barge into that room and hold her, comfort that girl and tell her, 'I believe you'.

That night Detective Kerr asked me to clear up inconsistencies and yet three years later a member of the prosecution team would tell me that there were no inconsistencies in my statements. It was not until Detectives Kerr and Henrys pushed me so hard when I was exhausted and had drunk two glasses of wine that they made me doubt myself. The only thing that interview would do was to give Murdoch's defence team ammunition.

When Detective Kerr asked me to give some sort of closure to Pete's family, it nearly sent me over the edge. I will never forget those words, or the manner in which she asked them. But what upset me most was the thought that if the police were doubting my story then they wouldn't be looking for that man. They would never find out what had happened to Pete.

I didn't die that night on the Stuart Highway, but in that interview room it seemed that it would have been much easier if I had.

10

Nothing's the same

I was emotionally drained as Paul and I walked across the tarmac and climbed the stairs to board our Qantas flight to Sydney. We were given seats at the very front of the plane and the staff were great and respected our need for privacy.

I was still shell-shocked from the interview the night before, and as much as I wanted to talk about it with Paul, I couldn't find the words. We sat in silence while the plane took off. I sat there and thought about the last weeks. It felt as if I'd been living in another world. A world inhabited entirely by police. I had lost my confidence and independence. I saw my return to Sydney as a return to the real world. Even though it was daunting I knew it was something I had to do, that I needed to do.

To pass the time on the flight, Paul and I started to look through some of the letters that Superintendent Kate Vandalaan had given to me earlier. There were hundreds and most were media requests from journalists. They were all very similar, with most journalists claiming to be of a similar age to me and writing about how they had also travelled around Australia with their partner. When I got to one letter where the journalist had mistakenly referred to my boyfriend as Paul not Peter, I stopped reading. Paul was equally as disgusted that they couldn't get such an important detail right.

Once the flight landed we were the first to disembark. We were met by two members of the British Foreign Office, a lady and gentleman. They were polite, efficient and, for a Yorkshire girl far from home, refreshingly very English. They had organised to have a car waiting. I was enormously relieved to be ushered to it on the tarmac and driven away from the airport without having to enter the terminal. I didn't want to see anyone and I definitely didn't want to have cameras pointed at me.

* * *

When I had told my friends Paul and I were coming back to Sydney, everybody had offered us a place to stay. I had given it some serious thought and had decided the best place to stay was with my friend Corinne. She owned an apartment in Balmain. It was a modern, purpose-built apartment with good security. The good security was an important factor. There was also a communal indoor swimming pool and gym, which I felt would be great for Paul, especially when I was out at work. It was also within walking distance of Dymocks bookshop so I thought I would be able to get myself to work without any problems.

I had no idea how familiar my face had become and how the media storm had intrigued the public. Wherever I went, people would stare at me, whisper to the person they were with and make me feel very uncomfortable. The few times I caught public transport were a nightmare because people would either sit and stare at me the whole journey or keep stealing furtive glances when they thought I wouldn't notice. My hope of sliding back into anonymity was not realistic and there was nothing I could do about it.

Looking back, I can see I was nowhere near coming to terms with what had happened. I was still struggling to sleep, and as much as I wanted to live 'normally', I couldn't. Most of the time I was okay but then I would be overwhelmed by a wave of terror. It would come out of nowhere and I would think that somewhere in Australia that man was going about his life. Occasionally I would see a four-wheel drive vehicle and I would start to panic. I didn't want to be alone. My friends tried to shield me from some of the horrible things that the media were saying about me but I still read or heard stories and found out about some of the conspiracy theories that were floating around. One of my closest friends, Diane, called Paul in Australia in tears to tell him about the nasty stories that were circulating about me in the UK.

The next day Joan Falconio gave an interview in the Huddersfield *Daily Examiner* stating that she had no doubts I was telling the truth. The headline read: 'Joanne's telling the truth, and that's that'. When I heard that Joan had said 'I know the girl so well; she's been going out with Peter for six years. She's like a daughter to me,' my heart felt like breaking for her. For her to stand up for me, to defend me against the media speculation while she was trying to cope with Pete's disappearance, meant a great deal. Joan and Luciano's support has never faltered.

But some of my friends did have difficulties dealing with me. That was hard. They were often uncomfortable, awkward and unnatural, and didn't know what to say to me. After this happened a few times I became anxious about seeing people again for the first time since the crime had happened.

Paul and I settled into Corinne's and Gary was happy to have me back working in the bookstore. I felt like a child on my first day of school as Paul walked me to and from the shop for my shift. The fact that Corinne had made me a packed lunch, with chocolate-coated teddy bear biscuits included, only added to this sensation. I appreciated them both for looking after me.

During the first week back in Sydney the media were quite full-on but that faded away, or maybe I stopped noticing. But the phone calls kept coming and my colleagues gave me a pseudonym to use when I answered the phone at work. They called me Anastasia but I shortened it to Anna. I don't know if changing my name was much help as my accent wasn't so easily disguised.

When I wasn't working, Paul and I would go out with my friends. We'd visit them at home or go for a beer at the local pub. Paul was there, ready to support me whenever I needed him, but I know it was hard for him. He was grieving too, but we couldn't talk about it. It was too raw for both of us. He was in constant contact with Joan and Luciano and he was their link to what was happening in Australia.

To maintain public interest in the investigation Paul and his family decided they would participate in an episode of 'Australian Story', a program made by the Australian Broadcasting Corporation (ABC).

The program went to air on the 18th of October 2001. They filmed in England, Sydney and the Northern Territory. As well as talking to the Falconio family; they interviewed my boss, Gary Sullivan; Vince Millar, the road-train driver; and Helen Jones among others. The program was critical of the police investigation and raised questions about some of the things the police had done, or not done. I only hoped it would lead to someone coming forward with vital information. All we could do was wait.

After weeks in Sydney Paul decided that it was time for him to go home. He wanted to be closer to his parents and it was time he looked after his own life. He knew he couldn't keep a vigil going forever. I was sad that Paul was going to leave but it was healthier for both of us if he did. Before Pete and I were attacked

I had really only ever spent time with Paul when Pete was around. The fact that Pete wasn't there was heightened when Paul and I were together.

Paul had been given a number of cab charges (company dockets that can only be used in taxis) by the producers of 'Australian Story' so he could get around Sydney and to and from their studio without hassle. On the day that he was flying back to the UK he found he still had one and he gave it to me. He hadn't been told to give any unused ones back. Until Paul had been given these I didn't even know of their existence.

After Paul left, I moved in with Amanda and her uncle. I used the cab charge Paul had given me to pay for a taxi to transfer my things to Amanda's. Maybe I shouldn't have, but to be honest I didn't think anything of it. In my mind Paul had been given them and then he had given one to me.

A week after I had moved in with Amanda, a letter arrived at Dymocks addressed to me from someone at 'Australian Story'. It asked why I had used one of their cab charges. It was spelled out very clearly that they thought this was unauthorised use and that they wanted an explanation. I was embarrassed and shocked. They had used my image, my photos and my name in their program but they couldn't absorb one cab fare? Is it wrong to think this way?

I wish I had never used that cab charge and I am sure Paul will be equally as shocked when he reads this and finds out what happened. I've never told anyone in my family or Pete's family about this incident. They didn't need petty things to worry about. I didn't reimburse 'Australian Story' the cost of that cab ride, even though this is probably what they wanted. I didn't want to have any contact with them so I didn't reply. But I kept the letter. It is interesting to compare the tone of this to their first sympathetic letter requesting an interview.

* * *

One day I received some information through the post from the Northern Territory Police. The information included a leaflet detailing the victim support I was entitled to, and it included details about criminal injuries compensation. Apparently I was entitled to claim up to a maximum of $25,000.

I didn't think I would follow it up but I showed Gary Sullivan the leaflets. He suggested that I see a solicitor and told me if I was going to do this I should do it before I left Australia. Gary gave me the telephone number of a solicitor who had been recommended to him.

When I met the solicitor in Sydney, she explained that because she wasn't familiar with Northern Territory law she wouldn't be able to help me. I decided to try and find a solicitor in Alice Springs. I found a directory listing Northern Territory solicitors and chose the name Mark Heitmann from it. Since our first phone conversation I have spoken to Mark Heitmann several times and we have also been in contact by letter, but I have never met him. Mark doesn't have email, which has made contact from the UK difficult. I am not sure how long these things take but at the time of writing this, I have not received any criminal injuries compensation. I have given up hope that I ever will. Since 2001 there have been many times when I have struggled financially while trying to rebuild my life. At times I have worked two jobs to keep myself afloat and that money could have helped. Isn't that what it is for? To help victims of crime move on?

* * *

Every day I would get up and do what I had to do. I went to work, put one foot in front of the other and lived another day. Pete's birthday was the 20th of September. That day I went to work in the bookshop as usual but I spent the entire day thinking of Pete. We were supposed to be skiing in New Zealand together, celebrating his birthday. I felt lost and didn't know how I was going to keep going.

My friend Megan who worked with me in the bookshop knew it was Pete's birthday and she suggested that we go to St Pat's, which had always been our local bar, after work.

Shortly after 6.00 pm Megan and I settled into a quiet corner at the back of the dimly lit basement bar. Megan handed me a wrapped present and told me that I had to open it, but it was for Pete. I felt overcome with emotion. I was touched by Megan's thoughtfulness and her deep understanding of my loss.

I stared down at the gift. I felt guilty, I hadn't even thought about buying Pete a present. I tentatively began to unwrap it. I felt almost afraid at what I might find. I needn't have been. I peeled back the paper to reveal a beautiful candle. It was perfect. I lit it immediately and placed it in the centre of the table. The candle flickered, caught and then burned bright, sending out a warm glow. We sat in silence watching the flame. I wondered what I was supposed to do with all the love I felt for Pete, now that he was no longer here.

* * *

Five days later it was my birthday. I didn't feel like celebrating so I made no plans for that day. I went to work as usual. I felt very confused. I was torn because while I should have been feeling happy and grateful that I had lived to reach twenty-eight, I was devastated that Pete was not with me.

My friends made my birthday as special as it could be. At work I received cards, flowers, phone calls, a birthday cake and presents. In the evening, Amanda and I went home and spent the night with her Uncle Al, Cousin Ben, and her friend Carso. We ordered

Chinese takeaway. I was given more presents; each one was special and thoughtful but one in particular brought tears to my eyes. It was a gold pendant on a chain and engraved on the back of it were the words 'Always in our hearts'.

On the Saturday after my birthday there was a jazz festival in Manly. I went there with my friends and we sat on the beach. Throughout the afternoon more and more friends arrived. We drank beer in the late afternoon sun and listened to the live jazz in the background. As the sun started to set, the beach became deserted but we stayed where we were. Tim was there but he was returning to England the next day. I wished that he wasn't going. He had been a good friend and had helped me a lot since I'd arrived back from Alice Springs. Amanda had told me not to tell him how much his leaving was going to hurt because it would only make him feel bad. She was right. I just had to cherish the time that I had with all my friends.

Whenever I was out with Amanda we would end up talking about what I should do. I agonised over whether I should stay in Sydney, go back to the Northern Territory or go home to the UK. Even though my friends in Sydney were wonderful, nothing was the same as before. No matter what I did or where I went there was always a dark cloud hanging over me.

Amanda and I saw Tim off at the airport the next day. We both put on brave faces. I was genuinely happy that Tim was going to be reunited with his family and girlfriend but I was going to miss him. As I watched Tim walk away after our final goodbye I knew it was time for me to think about leaving Sydney myself. By now I knew that staying in Australia wasn't going to bring Pete back. I knew the police thought I had something to do with his disappearance. And I knew that somewhere in Australia there was a man with cold eyes and a silver gun who knew exactly what he had done.

11

Hard times

It was time to go home. My friends in Australia had been wonderful but I missed my family and friends back in the UK. I wanted to be close to my Mum and this desire had deepened since the September 11 terrorist attacks.

I was feeling frustrated because the police weren't telling me anything. I felt the investigation had stalled. I called often to find out what was happening but I was getting the impression the Northern Territory Police thought I was more a nuisance than the victim of a violent crime who needed to be kept informed. I had wanted to stay in Australia until I knew what had happened to Pete, but as the months went by I realised that I couldn't stay in Australia indefinitely. There didn't seem to be anything more I could do to help.

I'd talked about returning home with my four closest girlfriends in Australia: Amanda, Alison, Danielle and Megan. They knew how much I was missing my family and agreed it was time to leave. In an effort to prevent any unwanted media attention, we decided that I should keep my departure details a secret. However, I did inform Megan Hunt from the British Foreign Office and the Northern Territory Police about my plans.

I spent that last week before I left enjoying the company of my friends, knowing that we didn't have much time to spend together we made the most of every moment. We went to the beach, to concerts, wandered around the city and enjoyed the nightlife, and admired the city skyline lit up at night. We chatted and chilled in cafes, went dancing. I made sure I took lots of photos to capture those good times. After everything that had happened to me I had learnt that special moments should be cherished. Those friendships mean a great deal to me and without them I wouldn't have been able to get through those months after the attack as well as I did.

I have told you before how much I hate goodbyes, and because I was trying to keep my departure a secret I didn't say goodbye to anyone. I felt guilty about that, but thought it was for the best.

For the previous two months I had been living with Amanda and her Uncle Al, Cousin Ben and her friend Carso. We'd been like a family. We'd cooked meals for each other, fought each other for the shower in the mornings, and looked out for one another. In the house, only Amanda knew I was leaving and she and my other girlfriends came with me to the airport. They helped me get my luggage to the check-in counter. I had quite a lot as I had some of Pete's things as well. The police had sent me some of our things from the Kombi. Our plans for a discreet check-in were spoiled when I was randomly chosen for a bag search. Airport security had been tightened since 9/11. Once I'd finished checking in we all went to the outdoor bar for a final farewell beer. I gave them each a present and they gave me a bagful to open on the plane. It had become our tradition, whenever someone was returning home, to give them a bag of presents to pass the time on the flight. Lots of them were handmade, such as photograph collages and mementos.

I waited till the last possible moment before making my way to immigration. Before joining the queue to be processed, I hugged each of my friends goodbye. I fought against crying and to distract myself I dug around in my bag and pulled out my Australian mobile phone and all the Australian dollars I had left. I gave these to Amanda. I knew they would be no use to me in the UK and I thought my friends might as well use them. They all looked so sad as we said our final goodbyes and I told them to go quickly before we all started crying. I promised to call as soon as I got home.

I walked over and joined the queue for immigration and looked back to see my friends disappear round a corner back into the main airport building.

Standing in front of the high immigration counter, I handed my passport over to the immigration officer. I wasn't paying much attention as I waited for my passport to be stamped. My thoughts were with my friends. It would be a long time before I saw them again and I was still trying hard not to cry. After a moment or two of waiting for my passport to be handed back, I suddenly realised there was a problem. I looked up to see the customs officer clutching my passport. The man was frowning and kept looking from his computer screen to me and then back again. I didn't know what was happening. He called for another immigration officer, who was there within seconds. The new officer asked me to follow him. What choice did I have?

I was taken into a small windowless room. The room had a table and a couple of chairs. It reminded me of the interview room at the Alice Springs Police Station, of the hours of interrogation, of Detective Sergeant Jeanette Kerr's voice saying, 'I have to ask you if you have been involved in the disappearance of Peter Falconio.' I started to feel worried. Maybe that was why the police weren't telling me anything. Maybe they weren't searching for the man who had done this. Perhaps they were only concentrating their investigation on me.

The immigration officer explained that the Northern Territory Police had put a freeze on my passport and that I would be unable to travel until this was lifted. I was so astonished I didn't know what to say. I had never been told there was any problem with my leaving Australia. When I'd notified the Northern Territory Police of the date of my departure no one had told me about this freeze. I felt scared and powerless. My plane was due to leave in half an hour.

The officer left the room and a feeling of complete despair overcame me. I was alone, with no phone or money, at the mercy of the authorities. My mind raced with all kinds of thoughts. I began to think that I'd never see my family again. I thought I was going to be arrested. I thought about Pete. He would be furious. I shook my head in disbelief. The man was going to get away with what he had done with us and I was still under suspicion.

After a short while, the immigration officer returned and explained that he recognised me and was aware of my circumstances and what had happened to me in Australia. His voice was kind and I sensed he had not judged me as guilty of something I had not done. He saw me as a victim of a crime, even if some of the police did not. He told me he had tried to contact the Alice Springs Police Station to see if someone could remove the freeze from my passport. I was incredibly grateful for this man's genuine compassion and willingness to help me. He went on to say that the police officer he had spoken to had said they didn't know who I was and that they couldn't help. The freeze remained.

Time was passing and my flight was due to leave any minute. The man left the room again saying he'd make some more enquiries.

I felt a tear roll down my cheek and I wiped it away. I was very glad I hadn't told my Mum I was coming home. She would have been shattered if she'd expected me and then I didn't arrive. I wanted to surprise her.

I sat alone in that room and was overwhelmed by how lonely I felt. I brushed away more tears as the immigration officer re-entered the room. He looked determined and rushed me to my feet. He smiled and said, 'Follow me; you're catching your flight.'

As we hurried to the departure gate he explained that he still had not been able to get through to any senior police officer in Alice Springs. Regardless, he had decided I should be allowed to leave. I know I didn't manage to adequately convey how thankful I was. I'll never forget this man and the compassion he showed me.

I was the last person to take my seat on the plane and I received a lot of disgruntled looks as I walked down the aisle to find my seat. I was relieved when I could finally sit down. I pressed myself back into my seat and tried to disappear. I closed my eyes. I didn't want to look at the stranger sitting next to me. I couldn't help thinking how my carefully planned departure had become a humiliating public spectacle.

* * *

It was a long flight home and I had too much time to think. I landed at Heathrow first, and then caught a connecting flight to Manchester. The flight was fairly empty and I had no one sitting next to me. The closer I got to home, the better I felt. I spent the entire flight gazing down out of the window at the seemingly never-ending patchwork of green fields. As soon as we landed I felt a wave of relief and then incredibly happy. I was home.

My friend Carol and her partner, Keith, met me at the airport. There was a journalist and photographer waiting, but we ignored them and Carol and Keith whisked me to their car. Because of the media presence outside my Mum's home I wasn't able to stay with her. We drove past and saw a pack of journalists hovering outside and waiting in cars. We kept on driving.

I stayed with Carol, Keith and their two children, Junior and Lois. Carol's house was close to my Mum's and I would visit often, cutting across a field and climbing over neighbours' fences to get in through the back garden to avoid the waiting journalists. Our neighbours had watched me grow up and felt protective of me. They wanted to help in any way they could and in many small ways they did.

I just wanted to be me again, to have some privacy and peace in my heart. I couldn't believe I had to sneak into my Mum's house. Staying with Carol was the best thing for me. She treated me like she always had and it felt no different to how it used to be. Carol had been battling breast cancer for the past year and I was very happy to see her looking so well. We had always been close but now we shared a unique bond. We'd both been close to dying: me at the hands of a stranger in the Australian outback and Carol by cancer. There was no one else I could share this experience with and no one I knew at this time who had come as close to death as we had. We both shared the same outlook on life, and had been reminded that it was important to appreciate every moment.

During these first few months I travelled back and forth between Brighton, Huddersfield and Berlin, visiting friends. I was trying to come to terms with what had happened and part of doing that meant spending time with the people who meant so much to me.

I would take long walks along the Hove seafront and breathe in the fresh air, watch the waves crash to shore, all with a big smile on my face. It was November when I returned home and though the weather was cold, the days were crisp with bright blue skies. My friends and I would wrap ourselves up in thick winter coats, hats and scarves to keep warm, and walk on the beach. After our walks we would often sit in a restaurant called Alfresco. The restaurant has panoramic views of Brighton Beach. We would drink hot chocolate and watch the sunset. We'd stay there as the winter pink and lilac skies turned dark. I would often sit there as night fell and look out at Brighton Pier illuminated in the distance. While I'd been in Alice Springs assisting the police with their enquiries I had been sent a postcard of this scene by a friend. Brighton had felt so far away and back then it was difficult to imagine ever seeing it again. Sitting in front of the scene with my friends I felt safe and content.

* * *

I still didn't know what was happening with the investigation back in Australia. The Northern Territory Police were not calling me. Whenever I called to find out if there was any new information I could sense their lack of interest in speaking to me. I was getting incredibly frustrated and I didn't know what I could do. The media were hovering and I would get constant requests for interviews or comments. I turned them all down but I started to think maybe it would help find fresh clues if I did something.

I had no idea at the time that the media were also constantly pestering my Mum. They were always parked on her street and she was often offered a great deal of money to talk to them. They were relentless.

Maybe that is why my Mum was charmed by Martin Bashir. His sympathetic style was such a contrast to all the others. He'd interviewed Princess Diana in 1995 for the BBC's 'Panorama' program and my Mum had watched it. He had started to visit my Mum regularly; he was working in the local area and often turned up unannounced. My Mum was in poor health and unable to get out much; I think she enjoyed his visits. He would talk to my Mum about his mother. My Mum would tell me how lovely he was and that he was so down to earth. I know Martin Bashir was visiting my Mum because he wanted something: an interview with me!

At Mum's request I talked to him and I made the mistake of opening up and telling him I hoped to go to university. He never openly said it but he implied he could help me. Looking back now I can't believe I agreed to an interview and the idea of a program centred on me and what had happened. I thought Martin Bashir was the best of a bad bunch and surely this would help the case, help me financially, and help me get to university.

This was the first media interview I had done and yet nobody from the program prepared me. I had no idea what to expect. I think now this was probably the plan. It was all arranged that Martin would interview me and then they would take me to Australia to retrace my steps.

The interview was to take place in a suite of a Brighton hotel.

I sat in a chair as they fixed the lights and Martin Bashir sat opposite me. He asked me question after question and I concentrated hard so I could answer honestly and concisely.

Then he said dramatically, 'The question the nation all want to know...'

I was so naive I sat there wondering what he could possibly ask. He went on to finish with, 'Did you murder Peter Falconio?' I was shocked. I had been so stupid. I thought this was going to help but it seemed they were interested in sensationalising things and pouring more fuel on some of the ridiculous rumours. I don't know how I got through that interview but as it went on I felt more and more concerned. I was also fighting an internal battle: thinking about Pete, and the way people perceived us and our relationship, stirred up feelings I hadn't ever dealt with. I was so upset. I flew to Australia with Martin Bashir and my friend Mark but I couldn't carry on. Luckily there was a clause in the contract that covered emotional distress, and when it was obvious I wasn't coping, Mark made sure that I was looked after. I couldn't carry on with the program. The thought of re-enacting that night was too much and I fell apart, physically and mentally.

Martin Bashir and his production team continued without me and eventually put a very high-rating program to air. It was a world away from what I had hoped it would be and further cemented my concerns about the media and how it seemed sensationalising a story was far more important than capturing the truth.

* * *

My first months back in England were spent living out of a suitcase and staying with different friends and relatives. I needed to see them but I was starting to crave a space of my own. I needed a home, a place where I could have my possessions together under one roof, rather than stored in various spare rooms. I needed a place where I could close the door and shut out the world. Even though I was determined to live my life and not dwell on the attack, there were times when the loss of Pete would overwhelm me. I needed somewhere I could cry alone; listen to sad songs, somewhere to be miserable without upsetting anyone or giving them cause for concern. I couldn't worry my Mum, and I didn't want my friends to think I wasn't coping when I was overcome with sadness and retreated into myself. It sounds such a cliché but I needed to get to know myself.

I'd thought long and hard about where I should live, Brighton or Huddersfield, and for a brief moment considered flat-sharing with a stranger (something that was not unusual in Hove due to the high rents), but it really wasn't an option. I craved a safe place and wanted to feel relaxed and comfortable in my own home. I wasn't ready to trust strangers.

I had never lived on my own before. I'd lived at home with my family until I was twenty-three years old and from there I'd moved in with Pete. It was an enormous leap for me to take. I needed to be independent and prove to myself that I could stand on my own two feet. I saw it as a step closer to returning to my normal life. I still hadn't realised that nothing was ever going to be the same again.

In April 2002, after viewing eighteen properties, I eventually found one that I thought was suitable. The rent was on the expensive side but I took it anyway. I was desperate to feel settled. My new home was a studio flat in Brighton. It was part of a huge Regency building that had been converted into flats. I loved that flat as soon as I saw it. It had been newly painted in white and it had a massive bedroom/living area with a huge floor-to-ceiling bay window. It had a nice bathroom; the kitchen was fully equipped with a brand new cooker, fridge and washing machine. I thought that I'd be very happy there.

Nicholas and Paul Falconio borrowed a transit van and helped me load up Pete's and my furniture; some had been in storage at Joan and Luciano's place and some had been at my Mum's. After loading up and saying goodbye to everyone, Paul, Nicholas and Percy, Paul's dog, and I all drove down to Brighton. By lunchtime they had everything in my new flat and had assembled my bed for me. They were so efficient that by the time some friends arrived to help, all that was left to do was to go to the pub for a beer.

Nicholas and Paul stayed in my flat with me that first night, just to make sure that I felt safe and secure. They left the next afternoon. I was and will always be grateful to them for the support that they have given me and continue to give me.

I had a limited amount of money to spend on my new studio flat and the only thing I really needed was a light fitting for the main room. One day, shortly after moving in, I took a trip to one of the big home stores nearby. There I found the perfect light fitting to complement my big room. It was a chandelier. I thought it was beautiful. I bought it and my friend Mark had to stand balanced on a chair on top of a chest of drawers to fit it for me. Over the next six months I spent a lot of time staring at that chandelier while lying in bed unable to sleep.

* * *

Once I had found somewhere to live I had to find work as soon as possible to support myself and pay the bills. My job at Thomas Cook travel agency had been kept open for me in case I wanted to return, but even though I really enjoyed the work and liked the people I worked with, I wanted to challenge myself and try something different. I started to apply for other jobs I thought I'd be good at, but at every interview I went to the interviewer was more focused on what had happened to me and Pete in Australia than on my job skills and work experience. The first time it happened I left the interview feeling like an exhibit rather than a person. I knew I was being judged on what had been printed about me in the papers, and so much of what had been written was untrue, sensational and so far from who I really was. I tried to keep going but after one too many questions about Pete and the attack I decided to return to the comfort of my old job at Thomas Cook. My colleagues there knew me well, had known Pete and treated me no differently than before. They were respectful and never questioned me about the crime.

I worked with a good team of women at Thomas Cook whose ages ranged from sixteen to fifty-plus. Most of the women had been there for years and you could say that I had grown up with them. We'd celebrated engagements, experienced heartbreak, discussed wedding arrangements, thrown baby showers and then welcomed people back from maternity leave. It often felt like I was working with sisters, aunts and grandmas.

The first month back at work I received a lot of unwanted, unnecessary and highly inappropriate media attention. One day I was sitting at my desk, which was reasonably close to the front door, discussing holiday choices with a group of young girls. I was completely engrossed and caught up in their excitement. We were interrupted by a man. My first thought was that he was just an impatient customer. He introduced himself as a journalist and asked if I would agree to be interviewed sometime. The young girls who I was serving stopped talking among themselves about pools and beaches and stared at me. I gave the man a polite but firm refusal and told him I was busy working. He didn't leave and started to tell me he had a film crew outside. He wanted me to agree to be filmed while I worked. I told him emphatically that I would not. He offered to pay me. I repeated my refusal and told him I really had to work. He apologised for disturbing me and left.

I focused my attention back on the girls, who were now more intrigued by me than their two weeks in the sun. I started talking them through some destinations and thought we were back on track until one of the girls said, 'Hey, look!' and pointed towards the door.

A man was standing with a huge film camera directed at me. He was blocking the door, obstructing customers from entering or leaving. It probably wasn't the most sensible thing to do but I ducked down below my desk and crawled along the floor using the other desks for cover until I reached the other side of the office. I stood up, entered a security code in the door panel and exited through the staff-only doorway. I made my way up the stairs to the staff room. From there I could watch what was happening downstairs on CCTV. I used an internal phone line to call one of my colleagues and ask if she would apologise to the group of girls for my strange exit and if she would find them a fantastic holiday.

I didn't know where I could go and I had no idea how long the film crew would hang around. I was upset and couldn't believe the rudeness of the journalist and his crew. I had been asked if I would consent to be filmed and I had said no. That should have been the end of it. I sat and tried to calm down and then I remembered the office brandy that was kept for emergencies. Emergencies had come in many forms during my time at Thomas Cook: family crises, boyfriend problems, even rude customers, but we'd never had an intrusive cameraman problem before. I decided that this moment called for a stiff drink.

On another occasion, I was standing by the rack of brochures close to the front door. A young couple bounded in full of enthusiasm and asked me for a selection of holiday brochures. They seemed like a charming couple who were very much in love and excited to be going away on holiday together. While I was gathering up some brochures for them, the girl turned to me and said, 'You look like the girl whose boyfriend was murdered in the outback.' Up until that moment I had ignored many similar statements, denied that I was or removed myself from the situation, but for some reason this time was different.

I replied, 'That's because I *am* the girl whose boyfriend was murdered in the outback.' I didn't want to deny Pete. I was proud that he was my boyfriend. She burst into tears. I couldn't help thinking 'Oh, for God's sake,' before I started to comfort *her*. Her boyfriend looked both embarrassed and apologetic. Once the girl had composed herself I excused myself. I watched as her boyfriend put his arm around her and led her out the door. It felt strange.

I should have been the one to cry but I did not have time. It was a busy Saturday afternoon and I had a shopful of customers waiting to be served.

* * *

Cool night air filled my room. I lay awake in the blue shadows staring up at the high ceiling. The music had just stopped. I stretched out my arm and reached across to the bedside table to pick up the remote control. I pressed play. The familiar music began to fill my room, the same CD playing for the second time in a row.

It had become my ritual to fall asleep listening to music. There had been a time, shortly after the crime, when I had to listen to music in order to drown out the dark thoughts and images before I fell asleep. Back then it was the only way I could get to sleep. Now the music was more of a comfort, it soothed me to sleep. On this particular night it wasn't working. I was wide awake. My mind was racing with questions.

I sat up and reached across the bed to switch on the lamp. I was thinking about the man. It was morning in Australia. He would be starting his day. I wondered what he was doing right that second. I wondered if he ever thought about me and Pete. About what he had done? He was out there, a free man, free to attack somebody else. Since I'd been back in the UK I had read a book about how dangerous men think. It had mentioned that offenders usually commit a similar offence within a year of committing a crime. It had been almost a year since that horrific night in July 2001. He was still free.

In my desperation, I started to think that the only way the police would catch this man was if he committed another crime. I know this is horrible, and I didn't want anybody to get seriously hurt, but I wanted this man caught.

I hated him. I hated the thought that he was free, living his life. I felt that he was laughing at me. He must have been laughing every time a media story appeared that was slanted to suggest I had been involved in the crime. He must have laughed every time insinuations were made in the media that I had contributed to Pete's disappearance, to Pete's death. When the stories became more outrageous and the implication was made that Pete had planned his own disappearance, this man must have been delighted. He had got away with it.

This man was never far from my thoughts and I hated this. My only consolation was that one day he would do it again and be caught. I was waiting for that day.

* * *

I had been planning a holiday to one of the Greek islands with Mark. Mark had been one of Pete's best friends, they had met at university. He was there for me as I tried to settle into a different life. A life without Pete. It was easy being with him and I didn't have to hide when I was having a bad day or feeling sad. He had known Pete and me for a long time so could give me practical and emotional support. I had complete trust in him and valued his advice. Mark never pitied me or felt sorry for me. He was like the big brother I never had. He used to sign all his messages to me BBM (Big Brother Mark). He looked out for me. I'll never be able to thank him enough for helping me through the hard times. But I didn't realise things were about to get much, much harder.

Five days before I was supposed to leave on that holiday I rushed into my flat to answer the phone. I'd heard it ring as I put the key in the door. I got to it before the call rang out. It was Vincent, my stepfather. As soon as he spoke I knew something was wrong. He told me that my Mum had been taken to hospital and was very ill. I don't remember what else he told me; I just knew that after years of battling ill health my Mum was gravely ill and I had to get to her.

I hung up the phone and paced around the room, biting nervously on the inside of my cheek. I sat down on the edge of the sofa and then fell backwards, sinking heavily into the cushions. Tears started rolling down my face and I stared blankly at the ceiling. I was frozen and didn't want to move because that would make what was happening real. Eventually I got up in a daze. I picked up the phone and calmly called my dentist to cancel the appointment I was due at later that day. The receptionist informed me that I would have to pay a cancellation charge. I didn't care about the charge but I wanted to scream that my Mum was dying and that was why I couldn't come. I didn't. I apologised and hung up.

I called the national train enquiries line for suitable train times. I was informed that I would have to change trains three times and that the wait between connections was long. I knew that I wouldn't feel safe waiting at a train station at night by myself so I called for a taxi to take me to the depot for the Brighton Pool Valley coach line. I knew that there would only be one connection by coach.

I sat in the cab and felt a strange emptiness. I wanted to cry but I stopped myself. My throat burned, my eyes clouded with tears. I kept clearing my throat and I felt the familiar heavy strip of pressure across my brow and temples that always strikes when I concentrate very hard. I was trying not to collapse in a heap. I had to be strong for my Mum and brother. I had to get home.

I thought of Pete and wished that he could be here with me. I had never needed him more.

I ignored the cab driver's attempt at small talk and then got on the bus still in a daze. The coach journey to London seemed endless.

When I arrived at London's Victoria Station my body ached. I hadn't booked an onward ticket so I joined the long queue at the ticket office. I didn't feel as if I was in my body. I was detached from everything that was happening around me. I felt invisible, like a ghost. When I reached the ticket booth I was told that there weren't any seats available on the next coach to Huddersfield. I enquired if there were any seats on the next coach to Leeds. The answer was 'No'. I asked about Sheffield and the answer was again 'No'. When I asked if there were any available seats on the coach to Manchester, I was told 'Yes'. I bought a ticket.

As I walked away from the counter I started to think about my Mum. I had to see her and I had to get there quickly. Vincent hadn't said anything but I just knew. I went out and waited for the Huddersfield coach. When it arrived I approached the driver and asked him if I could get on his coach if there were free seats. I didn't beg, plead or explain my circumstances. He stared back at me and something in my face must have told him that something was wrong. He agreed to let me on board.

It was a seven-hour overnight journey up the M1 to Huddersfield. Sitting in the dark inside the coach, I stared out of the window knowing that I was getting ever closer to one of the saddest moments of my life. I was calm but I felt like if anyone got in my way I didn't know what I would do. There was so much pent-up emotion inside me and even a slight trigger would have unleashed it. Luckily nobody talked to me and no one came near me.

When I got to the hospital the smell of freshly cut grass hung in the air outside. It was a hot, sunny June day, perfect weather to have a picnic in the park, play a game of tennis or sit and eat lunch at an outside cafe. All around the country, people were doing exactly those things. They were laughing and enjoying the summer. I sat at my Mum's bedside watching the sunlight stream through the slats of the blinds over the hospital window. She lay in the intensive-care ward. It was a large room with six beds in it and she was in a bed in the corner of the ward next to a window. Tubes fastened to her body and machines bleeped around her. Her eyes were closed.

Day after day I just sat and watched her. I held her hand. I fought to keep in control, suppressing my emotions. My throat and jaw ached and I struggled to speak. From time to time I whispered 'I love you' to my Mum. Those three words were all that were necessary.

Vincent would come to the hospital with me but he couldn't sit by Mum's bed too long without needing to go outside to smoke one of his roll-your-own cigarettes. I appreciated the time alone with my Mum.

My brother, Sam, found it difficult to visit the hospital. He was only sixteen and I understood it was distressing to see our Mum like that. To listen as the ventilator pushed air into her lungs and kept her breathing. It was hard enough for me to sit there watching and waiting for her to die. Sometimes as I sat there I felt angry at Sam for not being with me, but then I'd realise that I was his big sister and I had to shield him from things. I was twenty-eight and I was having a tough time coping. I couldn't expect a teenage boy to know how to deal with watching his mum die. I sat in that ward and thought about how there was no one to shield and protect me. Pete was gone. I felt so alone, and looking back I realise that the sorrow I was experiencing was mingled with the sorrow of losing Pete. I didn't know how I was going to cope with losing the other person I had loved with all my heart.

The nation was gripped by football World Cup fever while my Mum lay dying. Life continued as normal for everybody else, but it had stopped for me. I was afraid to leave her side and whenever I was away from her I felt guilty. Even when I went to the coffee machine or to the cafeteria, I was on tenterhooks, expecting to receive a call from the nurses to ask me back because she had died.

At times I started to think it would be best for her if she did slip away. She was never going to get better and I didn't know if she was in pain or not. As soon as I had this thought I regretted it. I wanted her better, I wanted her to be able to talk to me and I wanted to be able to hug her and have her smile back at me, knowing how much I loved her. But I knew this would never happen again.

I miss my Mum every day.

My Mum died on the 28th of June 2002. It was a warm summer evening. As she lay there, I held her hand. I kissed her cheek. I whispered 'I love you.' I told my Mum to tell Pete that I loved and missed him.

After a while I was taken to the visitors' room. I sat there with my head bent low as my aunt, uncle, stepfather and brother talked amongst themselves. I didn't register what they were doing or saying. It was as though I was completely alone.

I sensed someone new enter the room. I looked up and saw a nurse. She crouched down in front of me and asked if I wanted to see my Mum again, for the final time.

I didn't.

I couldn't.

I had said my final goodbye.

I shook my head and began to cry. In a shaky voice I said, 'It's so unfair.'

The nurse burst into floods of tears and ran out of the room. I had always thought that nurses remained emotionally detached from their patients. I was wrong.

I don't know how I managed to walk out of the hospital that day. I felt like all my energy was gone and I didn't think I would ever be able to smile or laugh again. I felt weighed down with sorrow, and the loss of Pete and then my Mum could very easily have damaged me forever. But the human spirit is astonishingly resilient and I focused on planning a funeral for my Mum. In doing this I remembered all the good times and how much she had meant to me. I thought about the stories she had told me about her travels, about the people she knew and who loved her. I thought about how lucky I had been that she was my Mum and about the sacrifices she had made for me.

The funeral was lovely, with so many people. I made sure there were white roses everywhere. They are the emblem of Yorkshire, and my Mum and I loved them. I chose the music for her and was determined everything would be perfect for the day we said goodbye. I was sitting listening to the service and thinking how beautiful it all was and I could hear someone sobbing as if their heart was breaking.

It was me.

12

Positive
ID

After my Mum died I kept myself busy. I didn't want to stop, to have a moment to think about my Mum or about Pete. I didn't want to accept that I would never see them again. That I couldn't call my Mum and have long talks over the phone, like we had always done. To this day I still have her telephone number in my phone. I worked long hours, and when I wasn't working I was out socialising until the early hours of the morning. I feared being on my own because I was scared of the feelings that might surface. I suppressed my sorrow and my anger at losing my Mum and Pete. I worked, partied, drank and slept only when I was exhausted. For six months I pushed myself to the limit and thought I was coping well. But I was fooling myself and, inevitably, it all caught up with me.

One day just before Christmas I was out shopping for presents. Everywhere I looked I saw daughters shopping with their mothers. All the grief I had been trying to contain hit me and I was overwhelmed with sadness. I stood there, surrounded by Christmas shoppers, and felt so incredibly lonely it was almost a physical ache. I kept drinking and tried to hide my pain but it wasn't working. Finally, as the New Year began, I allowed myself to think about losing my Mum. I realised that although my Mum was gone I could still make her proud of me, but that she wouldn't be if I kept going the way I was.

It felt like someone had switched on a light. I had to make changes in my life. I had to look after myself. I stopped going out drinking with my friends and started going to the gym instead. I would eventually give up working in the travel agent and instead dedicate myself to doing support work with vulnerable adults. Six months later I was much healthier, though perhaps not all that happier. I was still lonely and missing having someone to love. In July 2003 I met Miad.

Miad came into my life like a breath of fresh air and introduced me to new places, experiences and a different culture. He lived in London and I was still living in Brighton so we had a weekend relationship. We were very different people and it was inevitable that this relationship wouldn't last, but Miad was into health and fitness and so he was just what I needed as I started to find my way again. Miad's family were so welcoming and open and made me feel comfortable and accepted from the first time he introduced me to them. Their friendship, love and support also helped me move forward. On and off for just over two years Miad was part of my life, but in September 2005 we finally admitted we wanted different things and that we were heading in different directions. Our relationship probably lasted longer than it should have, but it helped me at a time I really needed to move outside my old patterns and I am forever grateful to Miad and his family.

* * *

It was hard to push myself to keep focused on the good in my life when there was a huge black hole always there. I was always waiting to hear that the police had caught someone, that they knew what had happened to Pete. Three months after my Mum's death, in September 2002, news came through from the Northern Territory Police. They had a suspect. I wasn't told everything but I was informed that he was refusing to allow his DNA to be tested. Unidentified DNA had been found on the T-shirt I had been wearing during the attack. The police were going through the processes to make this happen. There was also legal wrangling occurring to allow for the transfer of any information regarding this man's DNA from South Australia (where he was being accused of a separate crime) to the Northern Territory. At the time there was no national or country-wide sharing agreement for the exchange of information, and if there was an issue it was determined on a case-by-case basis.

I had to be patient and wait so I decided to go on a week's holiday with Lisa, my friend who Pete and I had met at the start of our trip. I booked a cheap holiday through work. I needed to get away from the unwanted media attention. I was living alone in my studio flat and often when I arrived home from work there would be a journalist parked outside. Often I would be chased up the path to my front door.

When I arrived back from my holiday with Lisa the situation hadn't changed. The DNA test had still not been done. Journalists continued to sit outside my flat and followed me to and from work. Everyone around me was aware of the intrusion into my life. My manager at Thomas Cook offered me a week working in Sicily. We both agreed that the timing was perfect.

Somehow I knew the police had the right man. In my heart I knew that his DNA would match that found on my T-shirt. I don't know why I felt this so strongly, but I did. It took weeks until the DNA tests were done but on the 9th of October 2002 the Northern Territory Police announced that DNA tests had identified a man who would be charged with Pete's murder. I was in Sicily when I found out.

I had so many calls from my friends and family telling me the news had broken. Mark called to tell me there was a story on the front page of the London *Daily Mirror*. The headline read 'SHE TOLD THE TRUTH'.

Apparently the man had been arrested in late August by South Australian Police and charged with the rape of a twelve-year-old girl and her mother. According to the details of the charge he said to the young girl when he raped her, 'If you move I will give you brain damage.' He allegedly kept them captive for twenty-five hours and handcuffed and chained them in the back of his ute. He didn't want them to get away from him.

I was told his name. The man who had stopped us, the man who had killed Pete and attacked me, was Bradley John Murdoch. He had been arrested in respect of an alleged crime in South Australia. He had been caught.

* * *

A few weeks after Murdoch's DNA match, two Northern Territory police officers flew to England to interview me. Superintendent Colleen Gwynne and Sergeant Megan Rowe arranged for me to meet them at Hove Police Station. I asked my manager at the travel agency if I could take this day as my rostered day off that week. I didn't explain the reason why. I didn't want to tell anyone that I was going to sit in a police station, meet two Australian detectives and ID my boyfriend's killer. Talking about it would only remind people of what had happened to me and I didn't want to be pitied or to be treated differently.

I sat opposite Superintendent Gwynne and Sergeant Rowe in a small office inside Hove Police Station. They made small talk about the cold weather but I couldn't focus on trivial things. Two English police officers were also in the room; one was going to witness the interview and the other was going to film it. Sitting there, looking across the table at the two Northern Territory policewomen, brought back painful memories of the last police interview I had given with Detectives Kerr and Henrys. I began to cry. I tried really hard not to but I couldn't stop myself.

They had caught the man who had attacked me. They had a positive DNA match. There were times when I'd thought that they never would. There were times when I'd thought that they weren't even looking for the man. There were times when I'd felt sure the police thought I had murdered Pete. All the feelings welled up and there was no way I could control my emotions. I sat and cried.

The two English policemen backed out of the room, allowing me some privacy. The Northern Territory investigators stayed where they were. I felt embarrassed and humiliated. I had only just met them. They were strangers to me. I turned to look at the two women sitting across the table and said, 'I don't even know you'. They explained their roles in more detail and their involvement in the investigation. I will always remember Superintendent Gwynne saying, 'You can trust me.' I immediately didn't. Once I would have taken her at her word, but not anymore. People have to earn my trust nowadays.

The two English policemen re-entered the room and they were all ready to start. I hadn't given any thought to how the interview would be conducted. I had never considered that it would be filmed and that one day this interview would be screened to a full courtroom.

A piece of paper was placed in front of me. On the paper were pictures of many similar male faces. I was asked if I recognised the man who had attacked me and Pete on the 14th of July 2001. I looked down at the faces on the page. I recognised him instantly. I was told to take my time. So I did. I looked at each individual face, one at a time. When I had finished I said, 'I think it's number ten', but there was no doubt in my mind. It was him.

The film camera was turned off and the two English policemen left the room. Superintendent Gwynne and Sergeant Rowe had a book, which was handed to me. They called it a dogalogue, a play on catalogue. The book contained various breeds of dogs. I was asked to pick one out that looked like the dog that I had seen in the man's utility. This was actually more difficult than it suggests. Like human beings, dogs are unique. Dogs can be of mixed breed. One dog of a particular breed can look different to another dog of the same breed. I had already identified a dog at Barrow Creek as being very similar to the man's dog. Feeling frustrated, I flicked through the book and picked out a dog that was similar; the dog's colouring wasn't the same but its size and shape looked similar. A description was given in the book next to the picture of the dog. It described the Australian cattle dog and mentioned 'blue heeler'. I had been told by the girl at Barrow Creek that her dog was a blue heeler when I had asked her what breed it was.

I was relieved when the interview ended and then it was suggested by the policewomen that we have lunch together. I was dubious but thought that it would give me the opportunity to learn about the welfare of the two women who had allegedly been raped by Murdoch. I felt extremely guilty about what had happened to them. I had been praying that he would commit a similar crime, so he would be caught and arrested. This is allegedly what happened, but I felt sick to think that a young girl and her mother had been raped. I never wanted him to hurt anyone else.

We walked from the police station along the main street in Hove. Restaurants lined both sides of the street and we chose a small Italian one. Once we sat down I asked about the mother and daughter. Superintendent Gwynne didn't give me any information but told me not to worry about them. I couldn't put them entirely out of my mind, but the truth was I needed to for my own sanity. I couldn't carry that guilt; that belongs to Murdoch. He is the cause of all our pain.

You would think the fact the police had charged someone would have meant the media backed off and the doubters would have been blown away. The headlines announced 'The Vindication of Joanne Lees'. But after fifteen months I was bruised and battered and beyond caring what the media wrote. Over the years I had tried not to read what was being said about me, or pay attention to the hurtful theories that circulated, but I knew they impacted on both our families and our friends.

I had to ignore everything and keep going. I had to help put Pete's murderer in jail. Pete deserved justice and I was determined to get it for him.

13

Swimming

As someone who had never before been involved with the police or the processes of taking someone to trial, I struggled to understand the length of time it took to bring Murdoch before a judge and jury. From his initial arrest it would be well over two years before I could do anything. It was decided that he should face trial for the rapes he had allegedly committed in South Australia before being extradited to the Northern Territory. I was in shock when I heard he was found not guilty. It rocked me to my core to think that could happen again.

I had always thought that the only time I would have to face Murdoch was at his trial. Nobody explained to me or to Joan and Luciano that before there could even be a trial there had to be a committal hearing. The committal hearing process is where a magistrate decides whether or not there is enough evidence for a person to stand trial in the Supreme Court – there is no jury at a committal hearing. It was never explained how important the committal was. To my knowledge, we didn't have this style of committal hearings in the UK, with witnesses present, so when the police requested I attend the committal I told them I wouldn't fly out for that. I told them they could use my statements as evidence and that I wanted to put all my energy into the trial – I wanted to concentrate on the one time that really mattered. It was only when I made some enquiries that I became aware there would not be a trial unless the committal hearing decided there should be and how crucial it was for me to be there. I was the key witness.

In February 2004 I started to become very anxious about giving evidence at the committal hearing. I had never even stepped inside a courtroom before. The thought of describing the most harrowing experience of my life to a roomful of strangers was daunting, but being in the same room as Murdoch was terrifying. I wanted to prepare myself. My only knowledge of the judicial system came from watching TV. I decided that I needed to visit a court. I hoped that if I familiarised myself with the environment it would at least prepare me in some small way. It was the only thing that I could think of that I could do for myself.

I called the Victim Support Agency in Brighton and explained to the woman who answered the phone that I was a victim of a crime that had taken place in Australia and was required to give evidence there. I asked if they could arrange for me to visit a local court. I was abruptly refused. The woman explained that she was unable to help me because the crime had taken place in Australia.

I felt totally dispirited as I hung up. It had taken a lot of courage to pick up the phone and ask for help. Asking for help is something I rarely do. I sat, stunned, for a moment but when I thought about what that woman had said I wasn't convinced that victim support agencies couldn't help me. I was a victim of a crime.

Feeling determined, I looked up the number of a different victim support agency. I explained that I had to appear as a witness in court. I didn't say where that court was and I wasn't asked. They were happy to help me.

It was arranged that I could visit a court in Lewes. I was accompanied by a young woman called Kate. As we entered the court building we were both searched by security. We were then greeted by a stern woman from the witness service who introduced herself and explained her role, describing her many years of experience. She showed me around.

The courtroom was very traditional and as soon as I entered I felt like I was in a scene from 'Rumpole of the Bailey'. Everything was built of dark wood. I wandered around the room and even though it was empty it felt so alien and intimidating. The woman suggested that I stand in the witness box so I forced myself to do this. I told myself I needed all the practice that I could get. Standing up there in the witness box, I was elevated and the centre of attention. I am not comfortable in that position. I was shocked at how frighteningly close the witness box was to all the other seats, and to the dock.

The woman from the witness service suggested I practise speaking out loud from where I stood. I hadn't expected this. Even though there were only two other people in the room I stumbled to think of something to say. I was self-conscious. If I couldn't cope here, I wondered how I would cope sitting in the witness box in front of a full courtroom. I finally decided to recite the oath. 'I do solemnly declare to tell the truth, the whole truth and nothing but the truth. So help me God.' I know, not very original.

The witness service woman did not know my history or which case I would be giving evidence in. She obviously assumed that it was nothing too severe as from time to time she would say, 'But that only happens in serious cases, like murder trials. It won't apply to you.' I didn't correct her but thought to myself, 'Fantastic, something to look forward to'.

* * *

One day I was looking for some information on one of the Northern Territory government websites and I came across a virtual tour of the Supreme Court in Darwin so I accessed this. Normally a committal hearing would not have been heard in the Supreme Court, but because of the intense media interest the Northern Territory authorities spent eight weeks and nearly a million dollars refurbishing courtroom six before Murdoch's committal to create a completely modern electronic court that is one of the most technologically advanced in the world.

Individual screens had been installed for jurors to view exhibits and a big screen had been placed in the courtroom next door to serve as a public gallery. Exhibits could be placed under a camera by court assistants and scanned and displayed on the screens. It was daunting to learn of the preparations.

I also searched for any information about Darwin. I had never been there so I wanted to prepare myself as much as possible.

As much as I told myself I wanted to move forward and look to the future, the fact was until the committal and trial were over I was constantly looking back. I couldn't make any long-term plans as I didn't know when I would be needed to fly to Australia. I was given a rough idea of how long the committal and trial would go on for, but I was also told that it could be longer.

In May 2004 I arrived in Darwin very bleary-eyed after a long flight. Mark came with me from the UK. I could talk to Mark about anything. Having him around was a great help, as he talked to me about Pete. He was one of the few who did. I think most people thought that they would upset me by mentioning his name. I wanted to talk about Pete. I never want to forget who he was.

I was greeted by a line-up of people, including members of the Tactical Response Section (TRS), the police and representatives from the Director of Public Prosecutions (DPP). It was very strange and quite a spectacle as I stood near customs listening to their introductions. Other passengers couldn't help but stare at the odd scene in such a public place.

I had been told that the TRS would be in charge of my security. The TRS are a special section of the police. They are trained and equipped to deal with any emergency that requires an armed response. At first I was alarmed to hear the TRS would be guarding me, but it was explained that this was normal procedure. I was the key witness in a very high-profile murder trial and the DPP needed to be sure that their evidence was safe. That evidence was me.

As I walked through the airport towards the exit, a single photographer came close up and took my photo. The TRS brushed him to one side and I was ushered to a waiting car. Mark and I were driven to the apartment block where we would be staying. We were sharing a two-bedroom apartment, which was on the same floor and directly opposite an apartment occupied by the TRS. The apartment block was very secure. You needed a swipe-card to access the lift and you couldn't access any other floor except the one you were staying on. I never saw the front of the building or the reception area because I was always driven in and out from the basement car park.

I had only been in Darwin a couple of days when rumours started circulating through the media that Mark was my boyfriend. I didn't know about this until Jane Munday, a court-appointed media liaison officer, came to my apartment to take a media statement from me. She told me that Rex Wild, the QC representing the prosecution team, thought it important to address this issue, set the record straight and stop the speculation, but it saddened me that it was necessary to explain to the media who my friends were. I still hadn't grasped the fact that as far as some of the media were concerned, it was me who was on trial. I asked Mark for his permission to release his name to the media and he agreed. This is the statement that went out:

9 May, 2004

I am in Darwin to prepare for the committal in which I will be giving evidence.

Accompanying me is Mark Sanders. He is not my boyfriend but one of Pete's best friends who studied with him at Brighton University.

I have been requested by the Director of Public Prosecutions not to do interviews while the matter is before the court and I intend to follow that advice.

I want Bradley Murdoch to receive a fair committal hearing as I believe this is the only way justice can prevail.

I wish that I was here under different circumstances as I still have many friends here and I have very happy memories of Australia...

* * *

In the week leading up to the start of the committal hearing I had to conquer some emotionally difficult tasks. Each time I had to face something difficult I told myself it was necessary and part of my preparations to appear in court.

One day I asked to see our Kombi. The last time I had seen it was three years before in Alice Springs. I had been with Paul Falconio and had become very upset when I saw gridlines had been drawn in black around the exhaust area. Back then, seeing the forensic investigation tools had brought the events of the night vividly to life and I had reacted strongly. This time was very different. Seeing Taz was like visiting an old friend.

Sergeant Megan Rowe, who I had first met in the UK at the time of the positive DNA match, accompanied me to the forensic building where the Kombi was being stored. Mark came with us. I wanted Mark there because Pete had been so proud of the work he had done on Taz and I knew he would have liked to show Mark.

As soon as I saw the Kombi I was struck by its dilapidated condition. It stood alone in the centre of a room, which was like a garage, coated in dirt and dust. I climbed inside and the interior was dusty too. I sat in the driver's seat and looked out of the windows as I had done on that night. I didn't feel frightened like the first time I'd done this with Paul. I felt a strange sense of peacefulness.

I stood there looking around at the small fridge, sink and table. I remembered all the happy times Pete and I had shared together while we were travelling around Australia in that vehicle. It sounds a bit weird now, as I write this, but I wanted to lie down, curl up and go to sleep right there and then as if I was still travelling with Pete. Instead, I pointed out to Mark all the work that Pete had done. As I left the building I said my private goodbye to Taz. I was pleased that I had come.

Not all the tasks I had to do were as comforting. One day I sat in a room on the upper floor at the DPP. I sat facing a window and went through my evidence with Rex Wild. Josephine Down, a solicitor, sat opposite taking notes. It was emotionally difficult to talk about the crime. I hadn't spoken about it in detail since giving my police interviews. The manner in which Rex led me through the events meant that I wasn't in control of the pace. I had to stop myself from crying at points and I kept clearing my throat to make my voice audible. I do this when I am nervous or distressed. I thought it would do no good to break down and cry, to become emotional. I fought to stop myself, telling myself that I was a strong person, to pull myself together, that I could do this.

I glanced out of the window and noticed a sign for a bar hanging outside. It had a picture of a dog with the bar's name written above it. The sign read 'The Blue Heeler Bar'.

Rex Wild followed my gaze and said to me, 'You probably think we deliberately put that there.' I hadn't thought that, though seeing it had made me immediately think of Murdoch's dog. It was a strange coincidence.

Once Rex had finished going over my evidence with me I was asked to sit and watch some videos in a room next door. I was told that Rex would now be going over Vince Millar's evidence with him. Vince was the truck driver who took me to safety on that night. I felt shocked when I heard his name again. I had wanted to contact Vince many times over the years but had stopped myself, fearing it may in some way jeopardise the reliability of my evidence. I didn't want to give the defence any opportunity to say that my recollection had been contaminated.

I told Josephine Down that I would like to be allowed to see Vince and Josephine said that if Vince agreed, I could, after he had finished with Rex.

We went to that other room and I sat on a black leather sofa and watched the video of the police re-enactment. I had never seen it before. As I watched I became angry because there were things that I could have corrected had I been given the opportunity during the filming. When the video finished I didn't know what to say. The whole process seemed half-hearted, and seeing myself days after the attack was almost like looking at a stranger. I looked so lost and vulnerable.

The next video that Josephine offered for me to watch was of the Martin Bashir interview that I had given. As I have said earlier, I regretted doing this interview and felt that I had been manipulated by Martin Bashir. I told Josephine I would rather not see this and she agreed that it was not necessary. Instead I watched my final interview with Detectives Kerr and Henrys, which was conducted on my last night in Alice Springs.

I had never seen this before as it had never been made available to me prior to this. As I watched the interview I picked up on Josephine Down's reactions. She had watched it previously with other members of the prosecution team. Josephine praised me for being able to remain calm throughout. I know it is part of the prosecution team's job to watch these videos but I couldn't help feeling resentful because they had seen them before me. The crime had been committed against me, it was my re-enactment, it was my final police interview and it felt like I was the last person to see them.

It was extremely difficult to watch and listen to myself being interviewed. Except for the Martin Bashir program, I'd never seen myself on screen before. I sat and watched this young, inexperienced girl being questioned in a small room by two police officers. I felt like I was watching someone else. She was struggling not to break down and cry. I felt sorry for that girl. I wanted to give her a hug. Taking my eyes away from the television screen I shook my head in disbelief and stared at the floor. I could hardly believe that girl was me. I vowed I would never let anyone treat me like that again.

As I continued to watch I started to feel proud of how I had conducted myself throughout the interview. I remained calm. I didn't raise my voice or swear despite the insensitive and plain deceitful line of questioning. It hurt to see how they were playing me. I was trying to help the investigation and they were just trying to grind me down and get me to confess to something I had no involvement in. I was the victim. Where was the victim care?

As the video finished, Nannette Hunter, the witness assistance service coordinator, walked into the room. She told me that Vince was free to see me now. All of a sudden I felt very nervous. Someone mentioned that they would leave us alone for a few minutes to give us some privacy. It was suggested by someone else that we may want to hug each other. I didn't think that I would and dismissed the idea.

I was taken back to that first room and as I entered I saw Vince seated at the table. He turned as I made my way towards him. Since that night when he had helped me, Vince had been in a workplace accident. One day he'd been unloading his truck and some pallets had fallen on him. He had lost the use of his legs and was now in a wheelchair. He looked older and weaker than when I had first met him. I was saddened to see him like this. I wished Vince all the happiness in the world and he didn't deserve this.

I sat down in a chair next to Vince and smiled as I stared into his eyes. Surprising myself, I suddenly reached out and hugged him. Vince hugged me back. I sensed people leaving the room but I didn't want to break free from our hug. Finally I did and I sat back in my chair feeling content. I hadn't realised how much I had wanted to do that.

Vince and I talked like long-lost friends during the short time we had together. I will always remember Vince saying, 'It's him, isn't it!' I didn't say a word. I didn't have to. I stared back into Vince's eyes and he knew.

The door opened and Rex and Nannette entered the room. I realised they wanted me to leave so Rex could continue his meeting with Vince. I stood up and leaned forward to kiss Vince on the cheek. Then I left the room.

* * *

On the first day that I was due to give evidence, I left the Marrakai apartments through the basement car park with the TRS. Mark had gone to court earlier with Nick and Paul Falconio to listen to the legal arguments. As the car drove up to the courthouse I ducked down in my seat. I didn't want a photograph of me in all the papers. In retrospect it wasn't the best thing to do.

The media hypothesised that I had something to hide and suggested I was behaving more like the accused than the victim. The truth was that I simply wanted to give evidence in Darwin and then return to the UK and resume my everyday life. My life had just started to regain some normality and I didn't want to have to face the stares and whispering from the public again. The TRS drove us into the underground car park of the court. We took the lift to the upper foyer and I was led into an unused jury room to wait until I was called.

In the days that followed I would wait and wait in that room. From time to time Mark, Nick and Paul would come in to check on me. They were sitting in court listening to the legal arguments and disputes with the media. The media were appealing against the magistrate's decision to suppress certain parts of Rex Wild's opening address.

Media outlets wanted the suppression orders lifted so they were free to write about the entire proceedings. The magistrate, prosecution and defence all agreed that this may, in the future, prejudice the small jury pool that Darwin had to call upon. Murdoch's defence was led by Grant Algie and he was arguing that his client wouldn't be able to receive a fair trial if the opening address was published. I wanted Murdoch to receive a fair trial; I didn't want there to be any technical loopholes that would see him walk free. I knew if he had a fair trial he would be found guilty, because he is.

I sat for hours in that windowless room. It was agonising and it was made worse by the fact that I didn't know what was being said in the courtroom. I wasn't allowed to sit in the courtroom because I was a witness. Witnesses are not permitted to listen to other evidence, until they have completed giving their own. The reason for this is so that a witness's evidence doesn't become influenced by the things they hear.

Every time someone entered the room my heart raced. I thought that it was someone coming to tell me that I had been called. I spent the entire day trying to occupy myself by doing word puzzles that Nannette had brought with her.

I waited for seven hours. I wasn't called to give evidence that day.

I was taken back to the Marrakai by the TRS. I picked up my swimming things and then went with the TRS to their headquarters to use the police outdoor swimming pool. The pool was large and was ideal for swimming laps. It was quiet and private. The only people around were members of the police. I felt safe from intrusion by the media and was able to de-stress, slightly. On my first visit I did twenty laps. Due to the media and court delays, by the end of the committal I was swimming eighty laps.

On the way back to the apartment from the pool, one of the TRS guys pointed out Berrimah Prison. Bradley Murdoch was somewhere behind those prison gates.

* * *

The next day I was back in the jury room waiting to give evidence. Since arriving in Darwin, giving evidence was constantly in my thoughts. I was unable to think of anything else; even though people tried to take my mind off the committal hearing it was always there. I felt sick, I was unable to sleep and I had no appetite. I would later discover that the anticipation was far more nerve-racking than actually sitting in the witness box giving evidence or being cross-examined. As far as I was concerned, cross-examination was a breeze in comparison to the waiting. While I waited I would look around and every face I saw had a look of concern, everyone was serious and grave. I probably looked the same. My anxiety heightened.

To enter the jury room, where I was waiting, you first entered one door then went through a small passageway and then through a second door, which opened into the room.

I heard the first jury-room door open and then close. The noise echoed around me. Everyone turned to look at the door that opened into the room. Someone declared that I had been called.

I felt a sense of relief to be able to start doing the job that I had travelled to Darwin to do. The sooner I began, the sooner it could be over.

I walked proudly through the hallway to the courtroom. I felt that my Mum and Pete were with me. My nerves and anxiety were diminishing. I felt a surge of enthusiasm. I felt confident and ready for action.

The huge hall was silent; small clusters of people stood staring at me as I walked past them. I followed a court officer towards the courtroom door. A large group of people were gathered outside. They had not been able to get a seat inside the courtroom. As I drew nearer I was conscious that these people were waiting to see me. I'm not sure why, just like I'm not sure why the media are so intent on writing stories about me. As they stared I politely smiled back at them and said hi as I passed by.

Following the court officer, I went through the first door of the court's double doors; like the entrance to the jury room, they were linked by a small passageway. As I went through the second door, I felt like I had just stepped onto a theatre stage. I anxiously glanced around the courtroom; it was packed – mostly with the media. Every head turned towards me and watched me move towards my seat.

The media's and public's presence seemed to disappear into insignificance. I normally feel very self-conscious when people are looking at me, but right then I didn't care. Seeing Murdoch for the first time since that night overpowered everything around me. It felt like it was just me and him in the room.

My eyes were immediately drawn to him. He sat in the dock directly in front of me. He was behind a Perspex screen and he was flanked by two security guards. I recognised him instantly. He didn't look at me. He was the only person in the room who didn't. He was the only person in the room who I wanted to look at me. He stared down at what looked to me like a file, pretending to be preoccupied.

I stared intensely at him. He must have felt my gaze burning on him, but still he did not look up. Walking past the jury box I smiled at Nannette, then again as I passed Mark, Paul and Nick who were also sitting in the jury box. The media filled the remaining seats.

I stood in the witness box and held the Bible in my right hand. I kept staring at Murdoch's lowered head as I listened to the court officer read the oath. I repeated it after them, 'So help me God'. Sitting down in the chair, I continued to watch Murdoch from across the court. The piece of shit didn't look at me. He didn't have the nerve to look me in the eye. I was the only person in that room who knew exactly what he had done and he knew it.

While I was focusing on giving my evidence, Paul and Nick were sitting in the jury box opposite Murdoch, staring at him. I believe they had every right to. They, like me, had waited almost three years to see the man who had killed Pete. When court was adjourned for lunch, Nick watched Murdoch talk to his lawyer through the glass partition that separated him from the rest of the court. He saw Murdoch gesticulate towards him.

A little later we found out that the defence had complained to the prosecution team on behalf of Murdoch. Anthony Elliott, who was part of the prosecution team, asked Paul and Nick to refrain from staring at Murdoch because Murdoch claimed they were intimidating him. Nick and Paul were told that if they persisted they would not be allowed in court.

I couldn't believe what I was hearing. It frustrated and infuriated me. The whole courtroom was staring at me and I couldn't ask them not to. How Murdoch was feeling because Paul and Nick were staring at him was nothing compared to how Murdoch had made me feel on that night. He murdered Pete and threatened my life. People can stare at the victim but not at the defendant. How ridiculous.

* * *

The next day I was due to continue giving evidence, but was delayed for a week due to legal arguments brought about by the media. During the days that the committal hearing was held up I filled my time by swimming laps in the police pool. One day Mark and I went to a crocodile park called Crocadillas with two members of the TRS. We joined a group of people being shown around by one of the park keepers. I was selected to feed some of the crocodiles by dangling a fishing rod with a piece of meat on the end over the crocodiles' enclosure. The crocodiles jumped up out of the water, snapping the meat before I had time to blink.

Another day I walked around Darwin's museum, learning all about the local history including the destruction of Darwin by Cyclone Tracy. As the weekend approached it was suggested to me by the prosecution that I should go away somewhere for the weekend. They thought getting out of town would take my mind off the committal. Someone suggested I go to Bali, but two members of the TRS, Shane and Scott (everyone called him Rosey), offered to take me and Mark 'out bush'. They talked passionately about their adventures and of wild pig shooting. Although I didn't share their enthusiasm for the wild pig shooting, I felt that I should seize the opportunity to see as much of the Northern Territory as possible. I was in Australia, I didn't want to go to Bali. After waiting around all this time I was ready for an adventure. I knew I'd be safe with the TRS. They arranged everything. They had a friend who owned a private cattle station with thousands of acres of land. I thought it would be good to stop thinking about Murdoch and the committal so I agreed to go.

* * *

It was early Saturday morning and still dark as we set off on our adventure. Rosey was driving a four-wheel drive and Shane sat beside him in the passenger seat. Mark and I sat behind them in the back. I stared out of the window at the scenery and watched the sun come up. We stopped for breakfast at a roadhouse and a couple of hours later we arrived at a wooden cabin in the middle of 320-square kilometres of private land. Rosey pulled up next to the cabin and we all got out.

We walked over to the cabin, climbing wooden stairs up to the huge elevated verandah. Inside the cabin was a huge empty room with a small kitchen. It was pretty basic but it was clean, and I felt comfortable with the thought that this was where we were going to be staying. Shane and Rosey began to unload one of the quad bikes that we had brought with us. I sat on the verandah in the shade and took in my surroundings. It was still and quiet. The only sound came from birds flying around among the trees in front of me and the constant humming sound of crickets and mosquitoes.

Once the quad bike was unloaded Shane rode off through a gap between the trees in front of the cabin. He came back shortly after and told me to get on the back of his quad bike so he could show me some water buffalo and wild pigs. I had no idea what I was letting myself in for. I hopped on the back and held on to Shane. He drove through the trees and into what I can only describe as marshlands. We sped across the mud and water buffalo ran along beside us. It was exhilarating. Shane was looking out for wild pigs. He could see a group running away from us and sped up in chase, steering into denser trees. Weaving in and out between trees and bushes we chased after the pigs. I found it strangely exciting, I can't exactly explain why. I have stopped and questioned myself and the only explanation is that it was totally different to anything I had ever done. I felt a real sense of freedom and I did not once think about the committal.

Our quad bike began to chug, slow down and then came to a halt, slowly sinking into the mud. Shane jumped off and announced that we were bogged. He lifted me across to a drier piece of land, then pulled the quad bike out of the mud. I watched as he managed to free the bike easily – I could tell he'd done it before. We were soon off again, weaving between trees, ducking down to pass under low branches and spider's webs, searching for pigs.

We soon got bogged again. This time Shane didn't lift me to drier land. There probably wasn't any, but I suspect his gentlemanly conduct only extended to the one time – and I say this with good humour; I can rough it with the best of them. I climbed off the bike, stepped onto the mud and straightaway began to sink. Water buffalo were standing nearby curiously watching me. I'd arrived there less than an hour before and I was already caked in mud. I didn't care and I helped Shane to free our quad bike.

We drove back to the cabin. When we got there we had some lunch that Rosey and Shane had brought with them. After we'd eaten, Shane and Rosey began to pack away, declaring that we should head off to the place where we were spending the night before it got late.

I had thought that this was where we were going to be staying. Climbing into the back of the four-wheel drive I assumed we must be going to stay in an even better cabin. I felt slightly relieved because the cabin we were leaving behind was very basic. I should have known better; after all, I was with Rosey and Shane.

When we pulled up in front of a run-down shed I was horrified. I wished we'd stayed in the wooden cabin we'd first stopped at. When we went inside the shabby building there was a small kitchen covered in a layer of dust and spider's webs everywhere. I wondered where the spiders were. There was a small bathroom, also covered in cobwebs. I wasn't feeling ungrateful; it just wasn't what I was expecting.

Outside the shed, Shane and Rosey set up two mosquito-dome tents, which are made from fine mesh material, and laid our swags inside. I was sure nobody had told me we were camping!

Once we were set up, I pictured myself sleeping outside underneath the stars, and waking up to the sun rising. I was looking forward to it. It was far better than sleeping inside any cabin.

With our sleeping arrangements sorted, Mark and I got on the back of the two quad bikes driven by Shane and Rosey. They took us into the centre of a flat savannah. Flocks of magpie geese flew across the milky pink and lilac sky. We stopped and Shane handed out some beers from a small esky that was strapped to the back of one of the bikes. We leaned against the bikes, breathing in the warm air and taking in the view, and we stayed there until the sun set.

I had a great time on that trip (it was worth the mosquito bites) and the wonderful thing was I didn't think about the hearing; well, hardly ever.

The night after we got back to Darwin I asked Mark to take Vince Millar and his family out for dinner on my behalf. I would have loved to have taken them myself but I didn't think that it was appropriate. Perhaps I was being over-cautious but I didn't want to be criticised for speaking with another witness. I didn't want to jeopardise the committal in any way.

When Mark came back we sat around the table discussing the following day. The confidence I had been feeling had evaporated when I thought about being cross-examined by Grant Algie. Because the defence had access to all my statements and interviews I knew where Algie would go. I suspected he would ask me about Nick Reilly in an attempt to discredit me. In my eyes it was irrelevant to the case, but I knew that the media would make something of it. Someone once told me that the defence would be hard on me at the committal, as there wasn't a jury to get offside. They would hope that I wouldn't come back.

Mark was supportive. He told me to answer Algie's questions by simply replying 'Yes', 'No' or 'Don't know'. He reminded me I didn't need to expand my answers unless I was asked to do so.

The next day, as I sat in the witness box answering Grant Algie's questions, I looked across the courtroom. Paul and Mark were sitting in the back. Murdoch would not be able to criticise them for staring and intimidating him now. I was glad the boys were sitting there because they were facing me and always in my line of vision. When they had been sitting in the jury box I felt comforted that they were very close by, but I had to turn my head to look at them, and in doing so turn my head away from the person questioning me.

From where I was I could see the faces of the media. Their expressions were serious as they listened intently to what I was saying. As far as I was concerned they were parasites living off other people's tragedies. They didn't care about the outcome of the trial, they had made that quite obvious throughout the last couple of weeks. The media just wanted a story, a drama, and headlines to sell their newspapers. Amongst all the expressionless and serious faces, one person shone out, sitting upright, his arms folded while he stared straight at me, smiling proudly. It was Mark. He stood out like a beam of light. I instantly knew that there was nothing that anyone could say or do that would change my friend's opinion of me. Mark was proud of me. I'm sure that Pete and my Mum were too. I returned Mark's smile.

Grant Algie picked his moment to question me about Nick Reilly. I held his gaze and answered clearly and concisely. Algie had given the media the story they wanted. I just wished that the media would report the facts and not sensationalise everything.

I had realised I could stand anything Algie could throw at me when the magistrate told me that I was free to go. I practically skipped down from the witness box and made my way back to the room I had waited in for so long.

Once there, I was joined by many people. The police, the TRS, the prosecution team and Paul, Nannette and Mark. Everyone told me how well I had done. The room felt crowded and busy and I felt disorientated and dizzy. Mark came over to me and gave me a hug. I began to cry and everyone looked at me with concern. I apologised to them for my tears and explained to them that I wasn't upset. I was relieved that it was all over and I was leaving. Someone pointed out that I would be coming back next year, to do it all over again. That prospect hung over me like a dark cloud. The prosecution team said hurried goodbyes and then rushed back into court for the next witness.

I was ready to leave. As I was standing by the door, Sergeant Megan Rowe handed me a book. It was the Lonely Planet guide to Thailand. It was just what I needed. Megan told me that she had won it and thought that I could make use of it. I leaned forward and hugged her. When we broke away from each other I stood and looked deep into her eyes. I hoped she realised how grateful I was to her. Since I had first met her, she had always treated me with respect and had won my trust. She seemed to understand. The older I get, the more I find that often words are unnecessary and sometimes they are just completely inadequate.

14

Friends indeed

After the tension of the committal hearing, Mark and I decided to travel on to Thailand. Diane was going to meet us there. Mark and I arrived in Bangkok late in the evening. It was dark as we caught a taxi to a guesthouse on Khao San Road, where I'd been with Pete.

As I walked down Khao San Road with Mark, I couldn't help thinking of the dramatic contrast between the bustling street full of life and the cold solemnity of the courtroom I had been sitting in less than twenty-four hours earlier. Slowly I was starting to feel like myself again. I had felt so cooped up in Darwin; now I was enjoying my freedom and was looking forward to meeting up with one of my closest friends, Diane, on the island of Koh Samui.

One afternoon, Diane and I were on the wooden verandah outside our beach bungalow, reading quietly. The heavens opened and warm tropical rain poured from the sky. Looking up from my page, I could see people running out of the sea, shrieking as they raced up the beach to take shelter. The beach was deserted in minutes.

I turned to Diane and she was looking at me too. I acknowledged her mischievous smile and we both jumped to our feet at the same time. I raced her down to the beach. The rain fell heavily, running down my face, hair and body. I felt so alive. When I reached the sea I ran into it, taking big strides, the water splashing up. I turned around to see Diane laughing. I fell backwards into the sea and the waves washed over me.

As I lifted my head I was coughing and spluttering out the sea water that I had swallowed. This is what happens when you laugh underwater. I realised that I'd never laughed underwater before and this thought made me laugh even more. For the first time in years my mind was free to think about silly insignificant things like this.

Diane and I turned and looked out to the horizon. All we could see were bobbing waves and the dark blue sea. We turned back around to face the beach and it was empty, there was not a single person in sight. Diane and I stayed there for a long time, splashing each other, singing and swimming in the rain. I've included this memory because it is one of my happiest. Whenever either of us feels down, we remind each other of this time. The strong feelings of exhilaration come rushing back and I can't help but smile.

While I was in Thailand I received an email letting me know that a member of the Sussex Police was offering to be of assistance to me. It had been suggested that a member of the police could meet me at the airport on my return to the UK in case there were any journalists waiting there. This email and the proposal were a surprise and completely out of the blue. I'd had no contact with any UK police prior to this and they had never offered assistance before. I had been hardened by years of standing alone so I couldn't help but feel sceptical. Why were the British police offering me assistance now? The thought ran through my mind that it could be a journalist offering assistance in order to find out my flight details. It wouldn't be the first time that a journalist had pretended to be somebody else in order to get information. Journalists had telephoned my Mum pretending to be someone from the tax office asking for my address, or had called her saying they had found my wallet (which I had never lost). One journalist somehow obtained my mobile phone number and rang me claiming to work for the post office. He told me he had a parcel to deliver to me and asked me to confirm my address.

I replied to the email and asked that the police officer's identity be authenticated and said that if it checked out I would accept his assistance. I resented the fact that help was being offered to me so late, but decided that if he could help I shouldn't knock it back. If it made my life easier, even in a small way, it would be a good thing.

Mark and I arrived in the UK on an early morning flight that landed at Heathrow. We had said goodbye to Diane in Thailand. Walking through the airport towards Arrivals, I could see a rose glow outside through the windows: a pink sun was rising. It was going to be a beautiful sunny day. I was happy to be home.

Through the crowd of passengers queuing to go through immigration I could see Kate from the victim support office standing next to three tall men. Mark and I weaved our way through the crowd of people towards them. Kate introduced me to Detective Sergeant Phil Banton from Sussex Police.

Phil was a tall man and looked to be in his mid-forties. He had a wide grin and seemed genuinely happy to be meeting me. The two other men were from airport security and they managed to get Mark and me swiftly through immigration. Together we all walked over to retrieve our luggage. Standing beside the carousel I said goodbye to Mark. He was returning home to Plymouth. It felt strange to be parting from him after six weeks of spending so much time together. He had helped me through a very confronting time and shared the journey with me. I was going to miss him.

* * *

I returned to work almost immediately. I had been away for six weeks and I had a lot of catching up to do. I didn't mind because I enjoyed my job. I was happy to be back at work. It was summertime and I found the long, warm days energising.

On my first day off since arriving back from Thailand, I walked the five kilometres from my flat in Hove into the centre of Brighton. Walking the long continuous road stretching to Brighton I passed the many cafes, shops and restaurants that lined the streets. In between the blocks I looked down the wide roads at the sea. I breathed in the fresh sea air. The five kilometres felt like a gentle stroll. I arrived in the city centre in a short time completely unaware that I was being followed. I needed to buy a birthday present for a friend, but of course I got sidetracked. I stopped to look at digital cameras for myself, went into shoe shops, visited Marks and Spencer's, and spent an hour browsing through the bookshelves inside Borders bookshop.

As I shopped I periodically received calls from friends and made arrangements to meet up later. After a few hours I walked home to my flat.

A few days later a friend showed me an article in a newspaper. The headline was something along the lines of 'Joanne Lees comes out of hiding'. There was a full-page photograph accompanying the article. I read the text in silence and felt sick. The journalist had written that I'd been hiding out at home since returning from Darwin after the committal hearing. There was no mention of me holidaying in Thailand or working long hours once I got home. The article went on to describe my recent shopping spree and catalogued the various shops that I had visited.

My blood ran cold.

I had no idea that someone had been watching my every move. They must have kept watch for hours and I had never picked up on it. This wasn't the first time that this had happened.

One day I was on Brighton Pier with a group of friends and the next day a photograph of us appeared in a newspaper next to a story saying I appeared melancholy. The truth wasn't as newsworthy. The reality was I had enjoyed myself and had a nice time with my friends.

I don't consider either of these outings newsworthy. There are some journalists who I have respect and admiration for. These journalists endeavour to report the truth, research the facts, and want to inform and educate others about important issues and forgotten causes. They use their powers responsibly and respectfully. I understand the need for them and the job that they do.

Then there are the hacks who follow me, who conned my Mum, who distort and twist any fact to make it more sensational, and report complete rubbish. I try to ignore them, but it is very hard to maintain any sense of normality when you are never sure who is watching you and what conclusions they will jump to.

The studio flat I had been so happy in stopped being my sanctuary. I no longer felt secure there. Journalists often rang my doorbell, or waited for me on my doorstep. I became suspicious of people sitting in parked cars outside my flat. Because of this I decided to move again – for the fifth time since my return. A friend of a friend invited me to share a cottage with her. It was in Hove, still close to the sea, my friends and work. I moved in.

Around this time Detective Sergeant Phil Banton became an important person in my life. Since first being introduced at the airport I had met with him regularly. Our first meeting took place at the victim support office in Hove. Phil sincerely apologised to me on behalf of the Sussex Police for not identifying or offering me assistance earlier. He said that I should have been flagged for immediate attention when Superintendent Gwynne and Sergeant Rowe had visited the UK with the identity board. I was surprised when Phil said this as I had never expected any support from the Sussex Police or the UK police in general. I never thought that it was an option for me because the crime had happened in Australia.

Phil rubbed his hands together and grinned at me as he said, 'Well, we're here to help now.' I couldn't help thinking I had made it this far on my own and I didn't know how he could help. However, I accepted Phil and the Sussex Police's apology. I appreciated it.

Apart from Libby, Phil was the first professional to offer me any kind of *real* help. His official role was to become my family liaison officer. At first we just had monthly meetings but then, as the date for the trial was set and drew nearer, our meetings and contact became more frequent.

Phil was straight-talking, honest and upfront. He could have come from Yorkshire! I appreciated his honesty, and without sounding overly dramatic, he restored my faith in the police and the justice system. Phil did not train or coach me; what he did was more powerful than that. He made me feel good about myself; he made me feel proud of myself. In some of our earlier meetings he would often remind me that I was not the person on trial.

During one of our meetings, Phil asked if I thought it would help if he travelled to Darwin for the trial to support me during the week that I gave evidence. This offer came as a complete surprise. I said that I would think about it. In the past I have found it difficult to accept help when offered. I can't explain why. Perhaps it is because I became independent from a young age and got used to doing things for myself. Or maybe it's because of my career. As a support worker, I am the one who helps others. I remember Marelle, who I worked with at Dymocks, telling me shortly after the crime that the best person to take care of you – is you.

I thought hard about Phil's offer and decided that I needed him. He seemed far more experienced than anyone I had come across in the Northern Territory Police. I am so glad that I made this decision.

The trial was set to start at the beginning of May 2005. I had a lot to organise before then. First, I had to arrange with my employers for two months' leave from work. My manager, Tony, freely granted me this, which I appreciated. I'd always been upfront with him and he knew that one day I would need extended time off work to attend the trial. Arrangements were made for a relief member of staff to cover my shifts.

After the furore over what I wore previously, I knew there would probably be comments on my clothes. I wore casual clothes to work and didn't own anything that I thought was suitable for the trial. I still had some things I had worn at the committal hearing stored away under my bed, but with the trial expected to last eight weeks I would need more clothes than I had. I went shopping with a friend. Ordinarily I would have relished a day out shopping with a girlfriend, but this shopping trip was not enjoyable.

I was right about the media commenting on my clothes. Over the years I have become more experienced in how the media report and what their focus is. I feel that people shouldn't be judged on their dress but the reality is they so often are, especially women. During the first week of the trial I received an email from my aunt that read: 'Saddam Hussein has taken your place on the front pages of the newspapers now, and also the Tory leadership – but the media are not reporting what *they* are both wearing. Shame!'

That day I bought plain black and navy skirts and white shirts. This was to be my court uniform. I was pleased when one day during the trial I was told about an article written by a journalist called Paul Toohey in *The Bulletin* magazine. Toohey commented that my dress was 'two-tone and lacked personality'. I smiled, feeling satisfied. Even though I thought it was ridiculous that there was any comment at all about what I was wearing, I'd achieved what I'd set out to do. I had not given the media anything to 'interpret'.

* * *

Three of my friends were coming out to Darwin at separate times to provide me with support, company and a little normality. If the trial had been taking place in England all my friends and family would have been able to attend and support me. If it had been in England I would have been able to go home at the end of each day. But the trial was on the other side of the world and I could not have that support or go home at the end of each day. All I could take was a suitcase and one friend at a time. I was and continue to be very appreciative of the efforts of my friends. Their personal sacrifices were significant and I am forever grateful to have had their support.

Thinking practically and taking into account my friends' work and personal lives, I decided that it would be best if they staggered their support visits. They would be like a relay team. They each arranged time off from their work and their flights were booked.

Then, five days before I was due to fly to Darwin for the trial, I answered a phone call. On the other end were Nannette Hunter, the witness coordinator from victim support, and the prosecution team's Anthony Elliott and Rex Wild. They had me on speaker phone. Anthony Elliott spoke first and asked me if I had heard the news. I hadn't. It was early morning in England. Anthony replied that he had some good news and some bad news. He said the bad news was the trial had been postponed, probably until October but he wasn't quite sure.

I couldn't believe what I was hearing. I had spent weeks preparing for this; the start day of the trial had been written in my diary for almost a year. Before I could tell them how dismayed I was, Anthony told me the good news. They had some new evidence. I was told they'd found DNA on the cable ties. I was amazed. The cable ties had been in the custody of the police since the morning of the 15th of July 2001. It was now April 2005.

Even hearing the good news, I could not hide my disappointment that we would have to wait a further six months to obtain justice for Pete. My life would have to be put on hold for another six months. Joan and Luciano would have to wait longer to see their son's murderer brought to justice.

Anthony Elliott asked me to give a thought for poor Murdoch because he too had to wait a further six months. This comment infuriated me. So did his next. Anthony Elliott reminded me that there were another eighty or so witnesses who were also being inconvenienced. I agreed that they would have been, but they were not the victim.

I asked Anthony if a postponement could happen again in the future and he replied that he did not have a crystal ball, so could not answer that question. After putting the phone down I decided that I wouldn't speak to these people over the phone again; it was too frustrating and upsetting for me. I knew that Anthony was just doing his job, but I found it too distressing to hear the trial spoken about so matter-of-factly. I knew there were other people who would be affected by the trial's postponement but I honestly didn't think it was going to be as emotionally devastating for them as it was for the Falconios and for me. Rightly or wrongly I sensed that I had been judged because I expressed my anger about the delay. I decided all communication from now on could go through Phil. I also decided that the time had come to make a formal complaint.

I was determined to express how emotionally devastating the continual indifference to my psychological wellbeing was. I wasn't doing it only for myself. I had managed to get to a point where I was able to look after myself. But I didn't want anyone else to ever have to endure the lack of concern for a victim's welfare that the police and the prosecution had shown to me.

It was a big step to take but I hoped my letter would mean future victims of violent crime would not be so isolated and poorly looked after. I hoped to make a difference.

I carefully listed sixteen points, detailing some of the ways the police had failed in their duty of care. These points ranged from: the fact the police took approximately six hours to arrive at Barrow Creek and why I was left in the care of a complete stranger (Helen Jones, Barrow Creek Roadhouse landlady); to the 'freeze' that had been put on my passport by the NT police and the insensitivity shown when telling me of the delayed trial.

As I wrote the letter I became angrier and angrier at the catalogue of errors and the way the police had contributed to the psychological trauma that I had suffered. I offered to work with the police to address the problems and give them feedback on what could have helped make a harrowing ordeal less traumatic. I also asked for a written acknowledgment and requested an apology from certain police officers. I didn't back away from anything and made it clear I was going to pursue the issues I had raised further.

I sent off that letter feeling disappointed that I had been forced to act. But I knew if I didn't speak up then things would not change. I hoped no one ever again would be made to feel as I had.

I received a letter of response from the Ombudsman telling me that the Northern Territory imposes a time restraint of twelve months between the conduct complained about and the time when a complaint can be made and action taken. After that the issue could not be investigated. In other words, I had waited too long and nothing could be done. That was basically all that was said.

I replied, detailing the many reasons to vary the twelve-month limit and outlining again that my reasons for complaint were ongoing.

On the 22nd of November 2005 I received an email from the Ombudsman. Not one of my sixteen points of complaint were addressed and nor did they take up my offer of assistance.

I was simply informed of the developments put in place since 2001 to assist victims of crime. They were:

- A recruitment drive for new officers and the force increased by 28 per cent.
- A new training college and facility put in place with an emphasis on increasing the professionalism of the force generally.
- The establishment of a continuous improvement program for the NT police in all its operational areas.
- The injection of an additional $72 million for the recruitment, training and development of NT police.
- An independent review of the NT police resources and operations was conducted. (Spookily, this was not attached.)

I was shattered reading this reply. I felt totally disheartened. They had completely missed my point and their response only confirmed to me that no changes and improvements had been made towards the lack of victim care. Any hope I had in instigating change was dashed. It is my hope that by writing about my journey the people that have the power to address the issues will realise that problems exist and something will be done.

* * *

After I had heard about the trial postponement I visited my friend Sharon who lived only a few streets away. Sharon had arranged time off work to travel to Australia to support me at the trial, so she was also directly affected. We spent the morning sitting at her kitchen table devising an action plan. I had to contact Phil, Martin and Diane (who were the other two friends coming to Darwin to support me). I also had to speak to work and see if it was too late to keep my shifts. I thought I might have to get a temporary job for the two months I'd told Tony I'd be away. I didn't want to cause problems for the people who were counting on the income from filling in on my shifts.

Tony kindly went out of his way to find shifts for me. I work for a non-profit-making organisation, which doesn't have a budget to pay for extra workers. I felt humiliated having to ask and frustrated that I had no control over the rescheduling of the trial.

* * *

After learning the trial had been delayed I thought there was nothing that could bother me as much. But a friend warned me that a program was going to air on television about me and the trial. It was made by IWC Media and entitled 'Murder in the Outback'. It was broadcast at 10.00 pm on Monday, the 2nd of May 2005. I chose not to watch but my friends did. In the days immediately after the program aired, people I knew would come up to me and offer sympathy. Other friends told me how angry they had been as they watched. I decided I had no choice but to see for myself what they were talking about. Because of the trial I thought I should be aware of what was being reported.

Phil arranged for me to see the program at the Hove Police Station. I sat in front of a television and watched in silent disbelief. I still get shocked at how some media twist, sensationalise and report untruths. As we watched Phil would occasionally smile at me and ask, 'Alright, mate?'

It is painful to watch people exploit my and the Falconios' tragedy. It seemed the way for an author to sell his or her book was to create doubt about the validity of my evidence so they could create an outback mystery. An example was when Robin Bowles, an author who was proclaiming about her access to Murdoch, described how she had re-enacted my escape from Murdoch's ute. She stated that what I had done and how I had hidden in the bush for five hours was impossible. I could barely contain my anger as I listened to her. She was claiming that everything I knew was the truth was a lie.

I was lucky to have Phil with me. He encouraged me to take my anger about this program and use it positively. The program had used film footage of me entering the court during the committal and ducking down in a car. There were a lot of negative comments made about me and Phil told me to use them and to be strong. It was becoming very clear that the media attention wasn't going to go away.

I went straight to work from the police station, but I struggled to concentrate. Watching that program had put me in a very bad mood and I felt very low. I was really daunted by the trial and it frightened me that people could think that Murdoch was innocent and could judge me so harshly without ever meeting me.

No matter how much I tried to keep the media focus and that program in perspective, I have to admit it hurt. I may seem tough but how I appear on the surface is definitely not how I feel inside. Normally I can shake off feeling depressed and anxious but this time it was much, much harder.

Within my small circle of Yorkshire friends we have a tradition we call 'Mercy Missions'. We all look after each other and pull each other out of tough times. After hearing about the postponement of the trial and then watching a television program that professed to 'document' the crime and in doing so effectively labelled me a liar, I was struggling. Diane knew I was having a tough time and she sent me a text message saying 'Get here to me in Berlin now!'

I must have been feeling intense pressure because what I did next was very out of character for me. I went and spoke to my deputy manager. I told him that although they had kindly reinstated my shifts I now needed one week's emergency annual leave to go and visit my best friend who lives in Berlin. I apologised to him but told him if he didn't give me the time off work then he could fire me because I was going anyway. He gave me the time off.

In retrospect it *was* the most responsible thing to do, though I could perhaps have phrased it better. But that was how I felt at the time. I was in no shape to support anyone else. I needed to help myself for once. I'm proud of admitting that I needed time out and of doing something about it, instead of struggling on. I am also very grateful to my work colleagues for their understanding. Until that point I had never asked for special treatment and I had never received any. I had been dedicated to my job and to empowering people with learning difficulties to live as independently as possible. Perhaps helping others was the way I escaped from my own life. I could make a difference for them, whereas every time I tried to move forward myself, something happened to knock me back down.

I spent a lovely week with Diane in Berlin. We talked, ate, walked, bicycled around the city, talked some more, ate, drank, sat in the park, laughed, and cried a bit. As another tradition has it, we discuss, compare and constructively criticise our personal as well as professional plans and dreams. It is incredibly good for my soul and my mental health. I suppose some people have expensive therapists. I just have a few good friends. After that week I felt much stronger.

I needed to, because I was about to face the man who had changed my life forever. There would be only one chance to find justice for Pete and for myself.

15

Because of him...

After four and a half years of waiting, after all the delays and uncertainty, the trial of Bradley John Murdoch was set to begin.

My stepfather, Vincent, drove me to the Huddersfield train station on the 12th of October 2005 for the first leg of my journey to the other side of the world. I wasn't daunted by the distance I had to travel; it was what was waiting at the other end in Darwin that I was concerned about. After the committal, I had some idea of what was in store for me and the possible media attention the trial would generate. But my overriding worry was that I wouldn't be able to stand up in court and convey to the jury the truth adequately enough. This was the only time that really mattered. The only people I cared about were the jury and if they didn't believe me...

As the train approached I hugged Vincent and said goodbye. He helped to put my suitcase onto the train and I stepped on. I turned back round just as the train doors began to close and looked out through the window. Vincent was standing there waving, watching me go. He looked so vulnerable, tired and lonely. I couldn't help worrying about him and was sorry to have to leave. The last few years had impacted on so many people in my and Pete's lives and it made me feel sad for all of us. As my train pulled away from the platform I knew it would be some time before I saw my hometown again.

I stood balancing in a doorway between two carriages with my heavy suitcase and sports bag and looked around for a seat. I could see both carriages were full. An army of rowdy Manchester United fans, singing loudly and clutching beer cans, filled them both. They were obviously on their way to a match.

The train was bound for Manchester airport, via Manchester Piccadilly. I had arranged to meet my friend Martin Jaffier (Jaffa) onboard. He was coming with me to Australia to support me. Martin lives in Leeds and had boarded the train there. I was too intimidated to walk past all the football fans to look for him.

There were two fold-down seats in the passage and I sat down on an empty seat next to a young girl who looked to be about eighteen years old. We were the only two people in the passageway. I hadn't been sitting down for very long when a train guard passed by on his way through to another carriage. He stopped in front of us and asked if we would like to move into the first-class carriage. He told us there were free seats and we would be safer there. Though I'd been wary I hadn't really felt at risk, but the guard thought otherwise. We stood up and followed him. The girl kindly offered to push my suitcase through the carriage while I followed behind her carrying my sports bag. My bag weighed a ton and was loaded up with records of my police statements and interviews. I stared straight ahead and avoided eye contact with the football fans as we passed by. The calm atmosphere of the first-class carriage was just what I needed.

The young girl and I sat down next to each other and began chatting. She asked me where I was travelling to. I hesitated for a moment before answering. I don't like lying but it is often easier to tell a stranger a white lie rather than drop a bombshell and explain that you're travelling to Australia to be the key witness in your boyfriend's murder trial. Lying would have shielded both of us but I decided I would be truthful. I told her that I was travelling to Australia. Her eyes lit up and she told me that she had just got back from Australia five days before. She asked me what my plans were. I hesitated before telling her I was going there for a trial. She looked at me in surprise and then asked what sport I did.

I almost laughed out loud. She was so innocent and it was lovely. I remembered back to when I was so carefree. We spent the rest of the journey together and I finally met Martin inside the airport entrance.

Inside Manchester airport, Martin and I crossed our fingers as we checked in our luggage, hoping that our suitcases would make it all the way to Darwin. Together we caught a flight to Heathrow airport and it was nice to catch up with each other's news in person as all our travel arrangements had been made over the phone or via email. At Heathrow we met up with Phil, who had travelled to the airport from Brighton. I slept nearly all the way to Singapore, and then on the connecting flight to Darwin I was wide awake and felt restless and anxious. Our destination was getting closer. I would have been quite happy to keep travelling. From time to time I glanced across at Martin and Phil. They were both wearing headphones and watching a movie. I didn't want to disturb them so I distractedly flicked through the various movie channels, always returning to the flight-path channel to check our progress.

We were given the usual meals on the plane, plus a bag containing fruit and other snacks. I couldn't eat anything because I was feeling anxious. The three of us were all conscious that there may have been members of the media on board and Phil kept watch.

Once the plane landed and the cabin lights came on, the passengers began to rise to their feet and reach up to retrieve their hand luggage from the overhead lockers. When I stood up to do the same I noticed a man staring at me. I looked at him and he kept staring. I immediately thought that he must be a journalist. I was tired after my long journey and not ready for any questions. I stared hard at him and he held my gaze for a moment and then he said, 'Why are you staring at me?' I was embarrassed and apologised quickly. He was clearly not a member of the media. I was angry with myself for becoming so paranoid.

Walking into the small arrivals hall at approximately 4.00 am on Friday the 14th of October, I immediately noticed Superintendent Colleen Gwynne and a small group of other officials waiting to greet us.

I walked towards them with Phil and Martin and was introduced to Lorelei Fong Lim, the Director of Public Prosecutions' appointed media liaison officer. I had spoken to Lorelei over the phone on a few occasions and was pleased to finally meet her and put a face to her voice. She greeted me with a bright smile and I instantly warmed to her.

Lorelei and I moved away from the others and sat down on two chairs at the side of the luggage carousel. It was the most private place that we could find. We spoke in low voices because we didn't want to draw any attention to ourselves as the other passengers collected their luggage. Lorelei told me that a media pool was waiting at the other side of the arrival doors to photograph and film me. This was part of the media strategy that we had devised in the lead-up to the trial. In the past my reticence to have any contact with the media had only intensified their curiosity about me. I wanted to give them the opportunity to film and photograph me in the hope that they would allow me some space and privacy at other times. Even though I wasn't at ease 'putting on a show' I thought it would be worthwhile in the long run.

Martin, Phil and I had to go through the usual immigration channels and we were all asked to fill out an Arrival's form. The form required details about the reasons for my visit to Australia, where I was staying and the intended duration of my stay. Superintendent Gwynne helped me to answer some of these questions as I didn't know how long the trial would go for.

When we were asked if we had anything to declare all three of us answered 'No'. But the small dog that customs officers use to sniff out undeclared food didn't think we'd given the correct answer. It stood stock-still staring at Phil and Martin's luggage. The customs officer asked again if we had anything to declare and once again we answered 'No'. We were then asked to walk towards two immigration officers standing nearby. I followed closely behind Phil and Martin and the officers started with Martin's suitcase and meticulously searched through it. They came up with nothing.

They then turned their attention to Phil and requested that he open up his small rucksack. He did and they discovered the fruit that Phil had been given on the plane. None of us had realised this should have been thrown away. Even after finding the fruit, the dog was not satisfied and kept staring at Phil's suitcase. Phil was asked again if he had any food to declare and he categorically said that he did not. Lifting Phil's case up onto the table, an officer began to search it. To Phil's extreme embarrassment, and everyone else's amusement, the officer produced a sealed bag containing Phil's favourite nuts. It was one very red-faced Sussex policeman who realised he was holding us up. It became an ongoing joke for the next week.

As we walked towards the exit I caught a glimpse of the cameramen waiting out there each time the automatic sliding doors opened for a passenger in front of us. They saw me too, just before the doors slid shut again. I felt silly; it was like a game of peek-a-boo. I was tired and wanted to get to my apartment so I walked through the arrival doors with my head high and stared straight ahead. Even though I had anticipated it, nothing can fully prepare you for getting off a plane after a thirty-hour journey and stepping straight into such a spotlight.

I'd been told that a car was waiting outside for me, so I turned to my left and headed towards a side exit. It felt very surreal to be receiving this amount of attention.

Lorelei had told me I wouldn't be asked any questions but one female journalist fired some at me. I appropriately ignored her. I was in Australia to appear as a witness in a trial and witnesses aren't supposed to answer media questions. I didn't expect to be treated any differently from any other witness. The woman sidled up close to me and asked in a condescending tone, 'Haven't you got *anything* to say, Joanne?' I felt my blood boil. I was tired and emotional and found her rude and intrusive. I would have liked to reply that I had plenty to say, but had nothing to say to *her*. Instead, I calmly walked away from her, exited the airport and climbed into the waiting vehicle.

Photographers followed close behind and kept photographing me through the car windows. I was sitting there by myself, with the flashes illuminating everything, wondering where Phil and Martin had got to. They had been asked by the media via Lorelei to walk a few paces behind me so that they wouldn't be in the camera shot.

As they had been during the committal, the TRS were once again in charge of my security, and I was once again staying at the Marrakai apartments. The TRS drove Phil and me to the Marrakai. Martin was in another car.

A member of the TRS, Sergeant Shaun Gill, who I had never met before, took us up to my apartment on the fifteenth floor. I followed him out of the lift and he pointed out the open door across from mine. The TRS were occupying that room as added security and I was told I would be introduced to everyone later.

As we entered my room, Sergeant Gill told me that Phil was staying in a different apartment building. I was disappointed as I would have liked him close, but was assured that he would be nearby. Sergeant Gill said he would drive Phil to his apartment once I had settled in.

All I really wanted to do was go to sleep but I couldn't. I had to sit down with Phil and listen to what the TRS had to say. I made us all a cup of tea. The sergeant explained to me the role of the TRS and handed me his contact details on a card. While he was filling us in on what would happen, Martin arrived.

Finished with his briefing, Sergeant Gill asked Phil, Martin and me to follow him to the opposite apartment, so he could introduce us to the TRS officers who would be acting as security for me. There were six members to meet, which I couldn't help thinking was slight overkill.

Introductions over, I walked back to my apartment with Martin, and Phil left to check into his accommodation. We arranged to meet up in the afternoon, when we had all had some sleep. I needed some rest but wanted to try and adjust my body clock to Australian time so didn't plan to sleep for very long. I wanted to be able to sleep during the night.

I gave Martin a tour of the apartment and showed him his room. I was relieved to have some time away from police officers, to clear my head and try to relax. Martin and I decided that we would both go to our rooms to unpack, and then sit on the balcony and watch the sunrise together before trying to go to sleep. I would see a lot of sunrises over the next few weeks.

* * *

On Sunday the 16th of October 2005, Phil and I were driven by TRS officers to the DPP building. Here, we met with Rex Wild and Josephine Down. We were there for Rex to lead me through my evidence, just as he had done in May 2004 before the committal hearing. We were in the same room and sat around the exact same table as we had eighteen months before. Looking out the window I noticed that the Blue Heeler bar sign was no longer there, a new sign hung in its place. It said 'Kitty O'Shea's'. It was the only thing indicating time had passed.

People often say to me, 'You must have told your story a thousand times?' I haven't. Excluding my police statements and police interviews I had only ever described in full the events of that night three times. Once to Amanda and Lisa, once to Joan Falconio, and once at the committal hearing. My friends never asked me what happened. People don't know what to say or how to deal with Pete's death. To get through I had to shut down and, because no one asked, I didn't talk about what had occurred. It was strange because there were times when I would have liked to open up, when I wanted to talk about the attack and my escape to those close to me, but after so long keeping my emotions to myself, I couldn't.

That day I spent four hours sitting in that room, staring out the window and reliving the night of the 14th of July 2001. At one point the image of the man standing outside the Kombi's window returned so vividly that I stopped speaking. Rex Wild prompted me, asking, 'And then what happened?' I wanted to tell him so that I could end this ordeal, but the words I spoke were barely a whisper and tears began to fill my eyes.

I needed a break so I stood up and left the room. Phil followed me out. I walked down a corridor looking for somewhere private to sit and found a small kitchen area which looked like a staff room. I sat down at a table and Phil made us both a cup of tea. I apologised for becoming so emotional. I was shocked that I had been so overwhelmed and hadn't been able to control myself. I had to be strong. Phil was his usual professional self and talked to me calmly before giving me some advice. I had heard the words before but they had never resonated. Because it was Phil, and I respected him and his wisdom, I took note. He simply said, 'Just be yourself.'

I went back and finished our preparation. Before I left, Josephine Down told me that the prosecution was going to approach the judge and request that I be permitted to start giving my evidence on Tuesday morning. They had estimated that the prosecution's opening address and other matters would take up most of the first day in court, and both Rex and Josephine thought it would be easier on me if I started giving my evidence at the definite time of 10.00 am Tuesday as opposed to late on Monday. I liked the idea because it meant I wouldn't have to spend the whole of Monday nervously waiting to be called. During the committal hearing I had experienced many long hours anxiously waiting. Josephine said it was not guaranteed that the request would be approved as it was up to the Chief Justice to decide, but she was confident that he would agree.

I was driven back to my apartment by the TRS and Phil went with Shaun Gill to the Supreme Court to be present at a media briefing, which was taking place at 4.00 pm. The purpose of the media briefing was to allow photographs to be taken of the inside of the courtroom and to give clear instruction to the media about what was acceptable, and where the boundaries lay.

I waited in the apartment with Martin for Phil to get back. I was interested in finding out just how big the media presence would be. Many people had speculated and their estimates differed greatly.

While I waited I tried to read through the hundreds of pages of my statements and interviews, which I had brought with me from home. I had been given them before the committal hearing and I hadn't read them since then. They contaminated my soul. Now added to the pile of pages were transcripts of my evidence taken during the committal hearing.

When Phil and Shaun arrived back from the media briefing they sat down at the long oak dining table, which now resembled a boardroom table during an audit. There were papers spread out everywhere and I piled them up to create some space.

Phil let me know of two outcomes from that briefing that directly impacted on me. Firstly, it seemed there weren't enough seats in the courtroom. The media had been allocated most of the seats and Phil and Martin were told they would be sitting in another room that would have a live TV feed to a large screen. I couldn't believe it. If the case had been happening in England my whole family would have been there to support me. At least there were seats for Joan, Luciano, Paul and Nick Falconio but the other two people there to support me were being excluded. The whole reason they had come to Darwin was to be in the courtroom for me. To make it worse, Phil told me that Murdoch's girlfriend, Jan Pittman, would be sitting just a few seats away from where I would be sitting once I had finished giving evidence. I was dismayed and Phil knew it. He promised me he would sort it out.

Phil started to sketch a drawing of the Supreme Court steps to show me where the media would be standing and how I would enter the building. Shaun suggested that we drive over there and have a practice run. Martin had been quiet up to that point. I told them all that I was worried I wouldn't be able to move once I saw all the media, that I was scared I'd panic and freeze as we drove up to the courthouse. I jokingly queried if they could drive around the block so I could get myself together. Phil insisted that wasn't going to happen, that I would be fine. Martin said, in that deadpan way only true friends can, that he would push me out of the car if I refused to move. I was so glad I had someone there who knew me so well and to tease me occasionally. It made a very strange situation slightly more normal.

We decided that Phil would stand at the top of the steps waiting to greet me when I pulled up. We set up our plans and everyone had a role to play.

That evening I stayed in the apartment and watched an episode of 'The Sopranos' on DVD. I couldn't concentrate, my mind kept drifting to the trial, and when the episode ended I replayed it because I hadn't taken in a single word.

I went to bed around 1.00 am but lay awake all night. I was feeling the pressure and was incredibly anxious. As the clock ticked down the minutes and the hours till sunrise I ran through all the worst-case scenarios I could think of. *What if I froze? What if I couldn't remember things? What if the jury didn't believe me? What if Murdoch got off?*

I got up feeling dreadful. I sat outside on the balcony and watched the sunrise. It was very early and there were no cars or people in sight. It was quiet and peaceful. The only occasional movement was that of a colourful bird flying into the trees below. I was relieved that I probably wouldn't be giving evidence until the next day. I decided that I would spend the day at the DPP reading through my statements. Sometime later the phone rang. It was Josephine Down telling me that their request that I begin giving evidence the following day had been denied. I would be giving evidence that day and would have to wait inside the courthouse from two o'clock onwards until I was called.

I felt terrible, completely unprepared and thought I was going to be sick. Before I had a chance to move, the phone rang again and this time it was Superintendent Colleen Gwynne. She said she had something that she wanted to tell me before I began giving evidence and asked if she could drop by at lunchtime to talk to me. I told her that was fine.

Colleen Gwynne arrived at my apartment on time. I still didn't feel any better and, in fact, I was probably getting worse. I felt ill with anxiety, I was nauseous and I hadn't been able to eat anything. We both sat down at the table and she looked very serious.

She told me that while I had been staying in Alice Springs helping the police in the very early stages of the investigation, listening devices had been put in my room. I wasn't sure I'd heard properly at first, and then when I realised what she had said, I was stunned. Colleen then added that after I had left Alice Springs and gone back to Sydney I had been under police surveillance. She told me this was standard procedure in case the offender tried to make contact.

I felt like saying, 'I am not an idiot,' but I stayed calm and listened. Colleen went on to say that she had not been part of the investigation at that time and had only recently found out herself that this had happened. She said that she was telling me all this now, because she didn't want me to first hear of it if it came up in court.

I was calm and polite as I thanked Colleen for informing me and she left. I sat there at the dining-room table absolutely furious. I was so angry and I felt violated. What I had just been told underlined the fact that some of the police hadn't believed what I had told them. I started to calculate the valuable time, money and resources wasted trying to catch me when they could have been looking for Pete and his killer. I felt insulted by Colleen's justification. Just in case the offender tried to make contact with me! How stupid must they think I am? Did they think I had exchanged telephone numbers or contact details with the man who'd murdered my boyfriend and who seemed intent on raping and murdering me? In the early days I had always felt deep down that some of the police didn't believe me, but I had pushed the thought away and concentrated on trying to give them as much detail, as much information, as I could to help them find Pete and catch the man. I knew one detective had asked Paul Falconio outright if he thought that I could have been capable of murdering his brother. I couldn't help thinking that the suspicion of me by some police had somehow influenced the media's reporting of the attack.

I paced around the room, swearing and crying, and then, all of a sudden, the focus of my anger shifted. All my anxiety and frustration crystallised and centred on the man who had set this all in motion: Bradley John Murdoch. At that moment I knew I could sit through anything in court because I was going to make sure that justice was done. I wanted to see this man found guilty of murdering Pete and it was my job to make sure the truth was revealed. I couldn't let myself crumble. He was the one who had caused all this. It was because of him...

My anxieties turned to defiance. I knew what I had to do and I was ready to do it.

16

Just being myself

On Monday the 17th of October the trial began in Darwin Supreme Court. At 1.45 pm I steeled myself and set off to the courthouse accompanied by Jaffa and the TRS. The journey was short as nothing is far away in Darwin. As we approached the courthouse I could see the media pack through the car window. I'd mentally prepared myself for this moment, but it still took my breath away. Seeing the rows of news channels' white tents, vans with satellite dishes on top taking up half the car park and crowds of journalists was like a scene from a movie – not a scene from my life. Unconsciously I said, 'Holy shit!' out loud. I laughed and wondered to myself when I had started talking like an American.

As we had planned, the car stopped outside the Supreme Court steps and a member of the TRS opened the door for me. As soon as I stepped out of the car I was hit by flashes of light and the sound of camera shutters in rapid fire. Reporters and cameramen lined both sides of the steps. I walked steadily through the centre of them and up the stairs. I stared straight ahead and focused on

Phil's reassuring face. He was standing at the top of the stairs waiting to greet me. Once I reached him we walked through the automatic doors together and they closed behind us. At least inside the building no one was allowed to take photographs.

I was taken to a small witness room to wait until I was called to the stand. The room was usually used for children. It was colourfully decorated, with a bright rug and red chairs. Though the room was small, there was a window and I appreciated the natural light. It was much brighter than the jury room I had been asked to sit and wait in throughout the committal hearing. The Falconio family were in that room, just across the hallway. I saw them when I went to use the bathroom but I needed to be alone so I didn't join them. I didn't want to speak to anyone. I needed to hold my resolve and keep my focus. They completely understood. Because they knew me so well, I am sure Joan and Luciano recognised the anguish on my face. You know when you are very upset but are managing to hold it together until someone says, 'Are you alright?' That was what I was afraid of. Just a small act of kindness could have unleashed all my emotions. I just wanted to sit in silence and keep myself together.

I waited in that room for two hours. Phil and Martin were with me but I was completely incapable of making small-talk. At 4.00 pm my name was called. As I walked out of the witness room, Phil, Martin, Nannette Hunter and Colleen Gwynne gathered around me. I thought they were about to wish me good luck, but before they could say anything I reassured them, saying that everything would be okay. Superintendent Gwynne laughed and replied that she should be saying that to me.

* * *

I deliberately didn't look at Murdoch as I walked into the courtroom. The room was absolutely packed but I could see the

Falconio family – Joan, Luciano, Nick and Paul. Phil had indeed made sure that he and Martin also had a seat.

To get to the witness stand I had to walk past the media scrum, Murdoch's girlfriend and then the jury. I walked up a few steps to a raised seat. Everyone was completely expressionless and silent. A small, blonde woman approached me with a Bible and I was sworn in by her. It was all suddenly happening and I wasn't prepared for the moment when I had to repeat 'So help me God'. I was asked to sit.

The witness stand was almost diagonally opposite Bradley John Murdoch but I positioned my body so I was looking at Rex Wild and my support team behind him rather than at Murdoch. Rex Wild QC got straight into the questioning and for the next half-hour he posed very straightforward questions and asked for details about the trip, about my friendships in Sydney and about our plans for the next part of our holiday. The prosecution's strategy differed to the one they had used at the committal hearing. This time they were going to get everything out in the open and question me about everything, including Nick Reilly, putting it all in proper context and leaving nothing for the defence to make an issue of.

The courtroom was absolutely silent and everyone was hanging on my every word. I started to feel less anxious and answered each question directly. When court finished for the day at 4.30 pm I had found a new confidence in myself and a determination to tell what happened. I was surprised that I was not more intimidated by the process. This was my chance to tell the facts and I wasn't going to let that man get away with what he had done. He'd taken Pete's life and ruined many others.

I walked out of the courtroom as I'd walked in, with all eyes on me. The media pack was outside the courthouse shouting questions. I walked swiftly past them and was escorted back to the apartment by the TRS.

I was trying to look after myself but it was hard as I still wasn't able to sleep. I couldn't eat during the day, though I forced myself to eat dinner. I am definitely not an athlete but during those four days of giving evidence I was like a disciplined sportsperson, totally fixed on one event to the exclusion of everything else. Although the trial was the leading story in the media, I deliberately avoided watching the news and reading the newspapers. Phil was collecting and saving the NT newspaper articles for me, just in case I might want to read them later. On that Monday night friends and family called me from the UK and Sydney but I couldn't speak to them. It wasn't rudeness. I just couldn't share how I felt with anyone. I had to be committed and strong to give evidence and the only way I could do that was to keep my emotions contained. On the outside I may have seemed cool, calm and collected but inside I certainly wasn't.

* * *

On Tuesday morning I was ready early and was taken to the courtroom by the TRS. Again there was a huge crowd waiting for us when we arrived and some well-wishers greeted me with a cheery good morning. Reporters shouted questions.

Most of that day was spent with Rex Wild asking me about the details of that night. I struggled to hold back my emotions. I tried not to look at Joan and Luciano or anyone I knew. I focused on clearly and concisely informing the jury of the details of the attack on us.

REX WILD: Now as you were driving north did you become aware of another vehicle in your vicinity?

ME: Yes.

REX WILD: Was there some discussion between you and Peter about that vehicle?

ME: Yes.

REX WILD: What was said?

ME: Pete said to me he wished the vehicle behind would just overtake us.

REX WILD: You'd been aware before he said that, that there was a vehicle behind you?

ME: No, not until the headlights lit up our vehicle.

REX WILD: That's the headlights from behind you?

ME: Yes.

REX WILD: Shortly after Peter said that what happened?

ME: The vehicle behind drove alongside us.

REX WILD: And you could see that vehicle yourself?

ME: Yes.

REX WILD: You were sitting in the passenger seat?

ME: Yes.

REX WILD: What was it you saw?

ME: I saw a man.

Not long after it was established a man with a moustache had gestured for Pete and me to pull over I was asked:

REX WILD: Did you and Peter discuss what was happening?

ME: Yes.

REX WILD: And what terms?

ME: Pete was going to stop and I asked him not to.

REX WILD: Did he stop?

ME: Yes.

* * *

It was exhausting going over minute details but I knew it was important. Time passed very quickly and in the breaks I would sit in the jury room and people like Nannette Hunter and Megan Hunt, from the British Foreign Office, would fuss over me. I know they were concerned about me, but I just wanted to sit quietly with Martin and Phil. They were my support team and they were all I needed to get me through this.

On occasion I was thrown by Rex Wild's rhythm and a few odd questions but I didn't let my concentration waver. I had intense blocks of time during which I had to keep my mind on the job. Court was scheduled into distinct periods. We started at 10.00 am and broke at 12.30 pm for lunch. There was a short mid-morning break within this session. Court reconvened after lunch at 2.00 pm and went until 4.30 pm, with a short mid-afternoon break included in this period. On Fridays court went from 10.00 am until 1.00 pm. A couple of times during my testimony the judge lost track and we kept going past the scheduled finish times. This shows how riveted every single person in the courtroom was with the unfolding testimony, including the judge.

The most chilling moment for me was when Rex Wild interrupted as I was describing the man holding a silver revolver to my temple. 'Do you see that man today?' he asked.

I turned my head to the right, looked straight at Bradley John Murdoch and replied, 'Yes, I am looking at him.'

We made eye contact and Murdoch shook his head, 'No'. I didn't flinch. I nodded back to him, 'YES!' and gave him a scathing look of disgust. This was the man who had attacked me, who had killed Pete. I had absolutely no doubt.

I turned away and didn't look at Murdoch again for the rest of the trial.

* * *

On the Tuesday afternoon when the court resumed after the lunch break we were going to go into what happened at Barrow Creek. The judge interrupted and asked me, 'Can you give the jury, please, an idea of how you were feeling emotionally and what was running through your head at the time?'

I was stunned that he cared, that he wanted the jury to hear. My life was on display and very public, but up to this point I had tried desperately to keep my emotions to myself. I had been reporting the facts but not daring to feel them, at least until that moment. Turning in my seat to face the jury I started to answer and it was like opening the floodgates. All the fear, sadness, grief and anxiety welled up. I struggled with my words and then I said, 'I couldn't believe it was happening.'

Sitting there in front of all these people I realised that at one point I had accepted that I was going to die. I had screamed and struggled so much and accepted no one was coming to save me. Lying in the back of Murdoch's ute I had started to imagine what he would do to me and it had galvanised me. I had found the strength to fight – or at least to try to escape. I had not believed that my chances were good but I had to try.

I jumped out of the back of his vehicle and from somewhere I found the energy to run – and whether it was inner strength or adrenaline or a higher power, I had succeeded.

As I described all this, I looked over at the jury and started to cry. A woman juror looked back at me with tears in her eyes.

* * *

After court was dismissed on Tuesday afternoon I was again escorted back to the apartment by the TRS. That evening I went to a yoga class. The yoga teacher was all too conscious of who I was and tried to help me settle in. Unfortunately, by treating me differently from everyone else in the class she made me even more aware of how bizarre my life was. She had meant well. I continued to attend her class throughout the trial.

* * *

Wednesday morning was another blur of night to day. I felt worse than I had on the morning of my first day in the court. This was the day I expected Murdoch's defence to cross-examine me.

When Rex Wild had finished questioning me the defence lawyer, Grant Algie, stepped up. He began by asking me about the moment I noticed headlights behind us. His questions could be long and rambling and he would often ask the same question in slightly different ways so I had to listen intently to every word and not allow my mind to drift. An example of this was when he queried Murdoch's position inside the Kombi.

GRANT ALGIE: I was asking you again, before lunch, about whether this man was kneeling on the seat. Do you recall him kneeling on the seat?

ME: No.

GRANT ALGIE: Again, when you spoke to the police on 16 July 2001, did you tell them that, 'He's kneeling on the seat facing me so his right side is towards the windscreen.' Did you say that?

ME: Yes.

GRANT ALGIE: Is that correct, is that right?

ME: I didn't look at his legs, the position of them, but he was facing me. His right side was towards the windscreen.

GRANT ALGIE: So was he kneeling on the seat?

ME: As I've just said, I wasn't looking – I presume he was, I was looking at his face.

GRANT ALGIE: You see, I can understand Ms Lees . . .

HIS HONOUR: Mr Algie, we're not worried about whether you understand. Do you mind just asking the questions?

GRANT ALGIE: You've told his Honour that when you spoke to the police, certainly on the 15th and perhaps on the 16th, you'd not had a lot of sleep. That's right, isn't it?

ME: That's right.

GRANT ALGIE: So there may have been details that you don't remember, is that fair?

ME: It is fair. A person can't always remember everything, every detail. No matter how much sleep.

GRANT ALGIE: But when you appear to give to the police detail such as, 'The man was kneeling on the seat facing me,' can we rely on that?

ME: You can because you are stood up, but I can't see your legs. But I know you are standing.

I thought that everyone would think that I'd said something stupid or was being insolent. I looked across at the prosecution team to try and gauge their reaction; their faces were expressionless. I looked at Martin and Phil and they both sat upright looking grave. Later everyone would tell me that what I had said was the best one-liner of the week. Megan Hunt from the Foreign Office, who had been sitting watching me on a huge screen in the room set up for journalists and the general public who were unable to get a seat in court, said that the room had erupted with cheers.

Algie was trying to trip me up, to have me change what I had said previously. I wasn't concerned because I knew I was telling the truth and nothing could change what had happened and what Murdoch had done. No matter how many times Algie asked me.

As any defence lawyer would be, Algie was tenacious and attacked any evidence that he thought had caught the jury's attention. When cross-examining me about the handcuffs he probably wasn't expecting me to be so open.

GRANT ALGIE: It was after the second vehicle left you've told us that you moved the handcuffs from the back of you to the front of you?

ME: Yes.

GRANT ALGIE: Would that have been possible, were it not for the three loops in the middle, if your hands were tied together, would you have been able to do that?

ME: I think so. I've demonstrated to the police anyway.

GRANT ALGIE: In relation to the handcuffs that have been depicted here, with the loops between them?

ME: I think I kept my hands together, but if at any point the jury would like me to demonstrate that, just let me know.

When the court was adjourned at 4.39 pm my mind was still racing. I kept going over what I had said, what I didn't say and what I should have said. The media pack was ready and waiting and Nick and Paul could see the cameras and the reporters. Nick turned to me and gave me a supportive smile and we all walked out together.

* * *

I watched yet another spectacular Darwin sunrise on the Thursday morning. I'd given up trying to sleep. I'd lie in bed going over what had happened in court and trying to guess what this new day would bring. Once I heard noises from Martin's room, I knew he was awake. After hours of waiting in silence it was good to have someone to talk to. When I was ready, the TRS officers escorted me back to the court and after the usual legal arguments I was called back to the stand.

Algie kept going through his queries and then, suddenly, it was over. I didn't even realise he was finished with me. I answered a question, he said thank you, turned and sat down. I thought he was just getting started.

Straight after Algie finished his cross-examination I went to the bathroom in the jury room that the Falconio family were using during the breaks to wait in. I felt anxious as I believed the kicking (Phil's terminology for gruelling questioning) I'd anticipated was just about to come. Standing next to the sink, I fought to compose myself. Algie had kept saying that it wasn't Murdoch, that I'd got the wrong man. I hadn't. I felt angry, frustrated, anxious. I could feel another headache coming on. I just wanted to cry. Leaning against the sink I looked up at the ceiling and thought to myself that it was incredible the things that you have to go through. I was about to burst into tears when the bathroom door flew open and in walked Nannette. I turned to her, wiping away a tear and said, 'It's started.' Nannette looked back at me in confusion and replied, 'It's over, he's finished. He sat down.' I could hardly believe it.

I let out a deep sigh of relief and Nannette left me to get undressed. While the cross-examination was over, I still had to demonstrate to the court how I had moved my bound hands from behind my back to the front. I changed out of my skirt and into my tracksuit, which I'd brought with me. After changing I went to wait out the afternoon break in the small witness room. I curled up on the sofa and began to think about the reality of demonstrating to the jury how easily I had been able to move my bound hands from behind my back to my front. I would be tied up in front of a full courtroom. In front of Murdoch. My relief at having just been told Algie had finished cross-examining me was replaced with panic. I wrapped my arms around my legs, curling up tighter, and buried my head down towards my knees. I couldn't believe I'd offered to do this, but I had to put all my feelings aside to get through it. So many people had doubted that it could be done.

Paul Falconio and I had laughed when we read in a newspaper that a trained Sydney ballet dancer had said that it couldn't be done. Paul had put the newspaper down and done it himself easily. I had to prove it was very possible in front of the jury. Taking deep breaths as I thought about it, I decided I would focus on the jury and ignore everyone else in the courtroom. I'd try to pretend that Murdoch wasn't there.

Phil and Martin entered the room. They were both calm and supportive, they reminded me that this was the last difficult hurdle to get through. I knew they were right and started to relax a little. Suddenly I was struck with the doubt, 'What if I can't do it?' I began to panic. Phil and Martin had to calm me and they suggested I have a quick practice now inside the witness room. Phil closed the door so that it was just the three of us inside. We all looked at each other wondering the same thing. What to use to fasten my hands? Phil volunteered the use of his tie. He took it off and proceeded to use it to bind my hands together. We heard someone approaching the other side of the door and Martin went over to stand guard. We had to laugh at what a strange scene this would be for anyone to walk in 'on. Phil had fastened my hands more closely together than Murdoch had done. Sitting down on the floor I performed the manoeuvre with ease.

The break was over and I was called back into the courtroom. It had been decided that the courtroom would be empty while I was tied up and then the media, public, accused and jury would be allowed in to watch. Phil tied my hands behind my back using his tie again. I was then asked to take my seat in the witness stand while everyone re-entered the room. I felt vulnerable all over again. I felt humiliated sitting up there, hands tied behind my back, being stared at.

As soon as everyone was settled, the judge asked me to step down into the court well — the space in between the dock and the jury box – to do my demonstration. I blanked everyone in the room out of my mind. I sat down on the floor facing the jury. I brought my hands from behind me to the front of my body, just as I had done that night. The judge asked that the time it took me to do this be recorded. Just under two seconds.

I immediately rose to my feet and walked over to Phil to be untied. It probably only took him a minute to untie me but it felt like an eternity. Once my hands were freed I was asked to return to the witness box.

After a short re-examination by Rex Wild I left the court to change out of my tracksuit. Vince Millar was the next witness to be called and I hurried to dress because I wanted to be there to support him and hear his evidence. Now that I had finished giving evidence, I was able to sit in the courtroom myself.

Because of the injuries from his accident, Vince was uncomfortable staying in one position for any length of time, so testifying was hard for him. I was so glad that he'd been the one I flagged down. He never wavered in his statements and I think he wanted Murdoch punished almost as much as I did. I made sure I smiled at Vince to show my gratitude. I knew what it was like on the witness stand and wanted him to know I appreciated what he was going through.

I didn't know it then but this would be one of the last days the TRS would be there to protect me. After four days the media knew as soon as the black Ford Falcon with tinted windows pulled up in front of the courthouse that it would only be moments before I appeared. I would wait in the foyer of the building until I saw it arrive. On this day, Joan, Luciano, Paul and Nick were waiting with me and they could see the huge crowd outside.

Joan said, 'Come on, we will walk out together.' I am sure they felt sorry for me but having them there gave me added strength to hold my head up. We were all united in our need to see Murdoch

The media were waiting when I arrived at Darwin airport on the 14th October 2005 for the trial of Bradley John Murdoch. I had been told that I wouldn't be asked any questions but one female reporter fired some at me. I ignored her. I was a witness in a trial and I didn't want to compromise any of my evidence. She sidled up close to me and asked, 'Haven't you got *anything* to say, Joanne?'

Because I was having trouble sleeping, I saw a great many sunrises when I was in Darwin. They were spectacular. This was a photo I took from the balcony of the Marrakai.

Courtroom six of the Darwin Supreme Court. The Northern Territory authorities spent eight weeks and nearly a million dollars creating a completely modern electronic court.

Some of the media waiting outside the court.

Every arrival and exit was made with cameras recording every movement.

Left to right: Phil, Wall, Rosey and Jaff in Kakadu. The night after our visit was the first good sleep I had managed since the start of the trial.

I know some people would think it impossible to find humour in anything while going through a murder trial. But we did. We had to. *Left to right*: Me, Diane, Joan and Nick Falconio at the Seville Hotel in Darwin.

With Phil the evening before he left Darwin to fly home to Sussex. Neither of us knew that this would be one of our last times together.

Me and Sergeant Libby Andrew. Libby couldn't stay in Darwin for the verdict so we took a photo pretending it was verdict day and Murdoch had been found guilty. We both wanted justice for Pete so badly.

After the verdict was announced the Falconio family and I stood together
to address the media.

On sentencing day I had reason to smile. We found justice for Pete.

found guilty. They walked me to the car and we arranged to meet up later.

I had finished my part in the trial and I hadn't fallen apart. The defence had tried but I didn't think they had made a dent in the prosecution's case. Though there was still a long way to go it was now okay for me to relax a little, and as the TRS guys drove away from the courthouse we decided we should all have a drink back at my apartment.

The only problem with that was I didn't have any beers in the fridge or any money on me to buy some. Sergeant Gill offered to radio Martin, who was with more TRS officers in another car. I couldn't help laughing to myself as I listened to Sergeant Gill's serious voice pass on a message to Martin in police jargon to organise delivery of the beer to 'the secure location'.

After the tension and drama of the last week it was definitely time for a beer!

17

Darwin

I hadn't realised how important my giving evidence would be to healing myself. For me, and for the Falconio family, this was our chance to see Pete's death acknowledged and the man responsible punished. We needed justice to be done. But one of the other things that kept me going was knowing that I was standing up for myself. I was determined to speak the truth, no matter what anyone thought of me or wrote about me. I had received many letters from other victims of serious crime and their words of encouragement and strength made me conscious of the many others whose lives had been affected by brutal criminal acts. I wasn't alone. One woman who had been raped sent me an angel brooch to wear, and I took strength from the thought that I could inspire others. Part of my motivation for writing this book is to show people that you can keep going even after the most horrific, life-changing events.

On the night I finished giving evidence I went to the Mindil Beach markets. I still had TRS support, though I knew that this was to be one of the last times I would. Once I was released as a witness there was no longer any need to protect me. Martin and Phil were with me and we ran into Superintendent Gwynne. We wandered around and then after a while I turned around and saw a news camera trained on me. I had no idea how long they had been following me but it was totally unexpected. I left the market almost immediately. One of Martin's friends called him from England the following day to say that he had seen Martin and me on the news walking around a market. He teased Martin about wearing a silly hat – Martin had bought an Akubra hat.

* * *

I was determined to be at court every day and I sat with Joan, Luciano, Nick and Paul. Martin was due to fly back to the UK on the 28th of October and Phil was leaving the following day, but my friend Sharon was flying in a day later as my support.

It was often frustrating to sit in that courtroom and listen as other people gave their evidence. I would learn things that I hadn't known about. On Friday the 21st of October, Pamela Nagbangardi Brown was called to the stand. She had been driving on the Stuart Highway on the 14th July 2001 with her husband, Jasper Haines. They were driving to the Antere Community in Ti Tree. Pamela testified that she saw a big white car, like a Toyota Landcruiser, pull off the bitumen onto the highway and start heading north. She then stated that she saw an orange Kombi parked on the side of the bitumen. Her husband, Jasper Haines, would later testify that he saw the four-wheel drive pull out from behind the Kombi. Mr Haines would also state that the four-wheel drive vehicle had a canopy on the back.

These two people had heard about what had happened to me and Pete on the highway the day after the attack and had gone to the police to tell them what they had seen. I was grateful that they took the time as they were supporting what I knew to be the truth. I couldn't help asking myself why the police hadn't told me and the Falconios about this key sighting at the time. It corroborated my story. If they knew this and knew about the CCTV images, why weren't the Falconios and me and the public informed? If they had informed us, maybe the investigative and media focus would have been directed to finding this man. Instead the vacuum of information fostered speculation – speculation about me – which clearly didn't help the investigation.

* * *

It was strange being so focused on court and then to have the weekend break. Rather than sit in the apartment and go crazy I tried to keep busy. On Sunday, Phil, Martin, me, Rosey and a TRS guy called Wal got right out of town and went to Kakadu National Park. We walked for miles in the heat, climbing up rocks and walking across waterfalls; that night I fell asleep as soon as my head hit the pillow. For the first time in a very long time, I slept through the night.

On the Monday it was back to court and as usual the first court business was hearing any legal arguments or issues that needed to be raised before the jury was allowed to enter the room. That day there were concerns about an article that claimed Rex Wild had called the judge by his first name. The story had appeared in *The Guardian* newspaper in the UK and also in *The Age* and the *Sydney Morning Herald* in Australia. After reviewing the transcript, the judge called for a retraction and an apology. I couldn't help thinking how seriously this inaccuracy was being treated and how so much incorrect and misleading information had been written about me over the years and yet I had never had the power to ask for a retraction or an apology.

* * *

On the day Jaff was flying home I decided I wanted to do something nice for him, to show him how much I appreciated his support. Jaffa was a constant reminder that I had friends who genuinely cared for me, who would stand by me whenever I needed them. He didn't tiptoe around me and I appreciated that. He spoke freely and honestly to me and was always cool and calm. Besides sharing my feelings with him, we were able to talk about old times, mutual friends and music. He is the only person I know who can talk passionately about gadgets and technology and not put me to sleep.

I secretly made an appointment for him to have a massage at the Seville Hotel. I arranged with the TRS for us to get a lift there. That morning after picking Phil up from his hotel, the TRS car approached the Seville. Martin thought he was going to court with me so when he saw we were going somewhere else he asked what we were doing. Everyone in the car answered him at the same time, but each person offered a different reason as to why we needed to call in at the Seville Hotel. We all laughed and then I told Martin that I was meeting Lorelei there because she had something to discuss with me before I went to court. Martin seemed satisfied with my weak explanation.

The TRS car pulled up outside the hotel entrance and Martin and I stepped out of the car and entered the hotel. Walking across the marble floor through the cool, spacious foyer I noticed a journalist standing beside the reception desk. I recognised him from the IWC documentary that had aired before the trial, casting doubt on my recollection of events. He was watching me. His head turned and I felt his eyes follow me as I walked past him on my way to the beauty salon. I thought that this journalist would presume that I had an appointment there. I could just picture the headline, 'Joanne Lees gets a manicure instead of attending the trial', or something similar. I tried not to let this spoil my mood and my surprise for Jaff.

When I reached the salon door, I opened it and stepped inside. Two ladies stood there looking very surprised. At that time my face was on every newspaper and television news and from the looks on their faces I was obviously familiar. Martin had followed me through the door and he looked equally as perplexed, though for a different reason. I turned to him and said, 'Surprise!' and then left to make sure I got to the courthouse in time. As the door closed I yelled, 'Enjoy!'

* * *

In court that morning, Tim Sandry, one of the two Northern Territory police officers who gave evidence in their capacity as crime-scene examiners, continued his evidence. He was very nervous and was physically shaking. Just watching him made me feel nervous. While he and Constable Ian Spilsbury were on the stand I found out that the police had found the remains of my lip balm and the pieces of black tape *three months* after the attack. Apparently they had returned to the crime scene on the 15th of October 2001 and Detective Kerr had found two pieces of black tape where I had been hiding. When Officer Spilsbury had scraped around in the leaf litter he had found my tube of lip balm. The irony that the very same dectective who had expressed undisguised cynicism at my explanations about the missing lip balm during my final interrogation did not escape me. Why hadn't they looked properly the first time they were there, straight after the attack?

Listening to the forensic evidence was very distressing and Joan had to leave when they started talking about the large area of blood they had found on the road. Anthony Elliott handled the questioning of these two witnesses for the prosecution.

Court finished for the day at lunchtime. I went back with Phil to my apartment to see Jaff. He told us that he had enjoyed his massage. I recorded the moment on my camcorder. I wanted to have a piece of my friend on film to watch during the times when I felt homesick and would miss him and his support.

Phil, Martin and I went to a cafe to eat lunch and afterwards I waved Jaff goodbye as he set off for the airport in a taxi. It was sad to see him leave but at the same time I was looking forward to seeing Sharon. She was arriving on Sunday morning. Having been surrounded by men for the last two and a half weeks I felt badly in need of some female company.

That evening some members of the TRS were going out to a few bars in Darwin and they invited Phil and me to join them. It was Phil's last evening in Darwin as he was heading home as well. Phil had been adamant that I should not hide away while I was in Darwin and he encouraged me to do what I would normally do if I were at home. That was why I watched 'The Sopranos' and went to yoga classes. I would also normally go out with my friends and have a few drinks on a Friday night, so that was what I did.

The TRS guys had already had a few beers and were in high spirits when we caught up with them. I had already noticed the camaraderie they shared; they weren't just colleagues but friends as well. Phil and I followed them towards the Deck Bar. As I approached the bar I could see that it was crowded. The Deck Bar is situated on a street corner opposite the law courts. I was told that it is at its busiest about this time, as people tend to drink there straight after leaving work. When we entered I could see all the seats and tables were taken, and many people were standing. I walked across the bar through the crowd and, like a Mexican wave, people's heads turned to stare at me. I could see them whispering to the person next to them. I pretended not to notice and followed Phil and the TRS boys to an outdoor area. I chatted with Phil and the others, and though I was conscious of journalists drinking in the same bar and of strangers staring, I forced myself to relax into the evening. Everyone was enjoying themselves, feeling casual, and I had as much right as anyone to be there.

A woman of about my age approached me. Phil and the TRS boys were talking among themselves. The woman walked straight up to me and said, 'Have you killed anyone lately?' Everyone nearby stopped talking. I couldn't believe what I had just heard, surely I was mistaken? I asked her to repeat what she had said. She stared straight at me and repeated, 'Have you killed anyone lately?'

I calmly replied, 'You've said enough.'

At that point the TRS stepped in and ushered her away. I was stunned. I thought she was stupid, insensitive and ignorant. I could see Shaun walking towards me with a look of concern on his face. He asked me what had happened. I began to explain to him and as I did I saw the woman return. Once again she was removed by the TRS. The boys told me afterwards that the woman had been crying and had wanted to apologise. I wasn't in a forgiving mood then and I am not now. I will never forgive her. That woman has to take responsibility for her actions. I don't know what she was thinking, but if she wanted to upset me and to hurt me, she succeeded. I tried not to show how distressed I was. Shaun told me not to worry, he said that at that moment I was the most protected person in Australia. He didn't quite grasp what had happened.

Not long after, Superintendent Gwynne came to join us for a few drinks and I asked the boys not to tell her what had just happened. I just wanted to forget about it.

Later that evening we went to a bar called the Pub Bar. Neither the TRS nor Superintendent Gwynne had been there much. I instantly loved the place. It was dark and cool inside and the décor was quirky. The bar staff and the patrons were friendly, respectful and left me alone. People didn't stare and no one came and asked me if I was a murderer.

We sat up on high stools around a table opposite the DJ, who passed around a pen and paper inviting us to write down song requests. We all took it in turns to write down what we wanted to hear. Everyone sang along to the music. We ended up staying there until the early hours of the morning.

* * *

The next morning I went to meet Phil for a coffee before he left Darwin. We walked into Darwin's shopping centre and I bought him a book and a few other souvenirs to take back with him to England. Phil protested profusely, of course, but I was forceful and insisted that he accept my gifts. They were a small token of my appreciation to him. I walked back to his hotel with him and waited while he collected his bags. Standing opposite one another in the reception area of his hotel we exchanged an awkward goodbye and a brief hug. Phil had always been the consummate professional and he didn't reveal a lot about himself to me. He was focused on empowering me. I knew he'd been battling a bad back while he'd been in Darwin but he rarely complained.

I walked out of the hotel and began walking back to my apartment. For me our goodbye had felt inadequate. I had not expressed to Phil how much he had helped me and I was disappointed in myself. I struggled not to cry. I had so much respect and admiration for Phil and I wanted him to know that. I also wanted him to be proud of me. I arrived back at the apartment feeling miserable and alone. I didn't know it then but this would be the last time I saw Phil.

I didn't know what to do with myself. I hadn't spent any time on my own in weeks. It felt strange at first.

That evening I went out to dinner with Lorelei to a Chinese restaurant. It was good to spend some time with her and get to know her better. I liked hearing about her and her family. She told me she came from a pioneering Australian–Chinese family who'd lived and worked in the Northern Territory since the gold rush days. They hadn't worked as miners, which most Chinese immigrants had, they'd been tailors, greengrocers and, later, publicans. Lorelei's father, Alec, had been Lord Mayor of Darwin while her mother's family had included the first chef at Government House in Darwin. I told Lorelei about my life and it was an opportunity for her to get to know me too. Many people had read a lot about me, but no one really knew me. The food was great and we ended up eating enough for five people, literally. A table of five people sitting next to us ordered the same.

The next morning I woke up at 3.45 am and Superintendent Gwynne drove me to the airport to meet Sharon and take her back to the Marrakai. We stayed awake watching the sunrise from our balcony, drinking Bacardi and Coke, which Sharon had bought from duty free. At 7.00 am we both went to sleep for a while.

The next day was Sharon's first day in court. I introduced her to the Falconio family, members of the police and the prosecution team. Sharon sat next to me in the courtroom. I became distressed twice during the day and had to leave the courtroom. I listened to evidence from a witness named Carmen Eckhoff, she is a forensic biologist and had been the one who tested my T-shirt for DNA. She told the court how she had extracted Pete's DNA from his asthma inhaler. When Pete disappeared I had hoped that he was still alive and I had worried that he was without his inhaler. I was worried he might have an asthma attack and not be able to do anything about it. Sitting in the courtroom listening to Carmen Eckhoff talk about Pete's inhaler brought back this memory. I whispered to Sharon that I was just going to get a drink of water and went and sat alone in the unused jury room at the end of the hall.

The court must have taken a break because the next thing I knew Sharon, Nannette and the Falconio family entered the room. I stood up and wiped away my tears. Sharon told me quietly to tell her if I was upset and not to pretend to be getting a drink of water. I nodded.

Later that day a ballistics expert gave evidence. His descriptions were graphic. Joan got up and left the courtroom. I stayed to listen. If I could stand it I wanted to hear all the evidence that would be presented in the trial. Before this I hadn't been able to know any of the evidence in case it contaminated my own recollections. I knew I'd never get another opportunity to have the facts presented so fully.

When the expert began to describe a gunshot entry to the head I couldn't handle it. I had to leave. I walked past Megan in the hallway on my way to the bathroom. Sharon followed me. The bathroom was the only place I could think of where I could have some privacy. Before that moment I had never thought about Pete and the gunshot wound, or where Murdoch had aimed his bullet. I had refused to even go there. When the expert had concluded that Pete had most likely been shot in the head I had to get out of the courtroom. I didn't want that image in my mind.

But by then, of course, it was too late. Murdoch's cold-blooded execution of Pete is something I will have to live with for the rest of my life.

I waited until the ballistics expert had finished before re-entering the courtroom. Carmen Eckhoff was recalled to the witness stand to discuss the DNA match to Murdoch.

MR ELLIOTT: Was there a match between the Identifiler
results from 2004 and the results from the shirt taken
in January 2003?

MS ECKHOFF: Yes, there was.

MR ELLIOTT: At all loci?

MS ECKHOFF: Yes.

MR ELLIOTT: And when you calculated the matched statistic,
what did it turn out to be?

MS ECKHOFF: 1.5 times 10 to 17th. Which hopefully I've
transcribed correctly.

MR ELLIOTT: You've got there a matched statistic greater
than, and then there's the number, 150 followed by 15
zeros to 1?

MS ECKHOFF: Yes, there's about 150 quadrillion.

I was spellbound. What she was saying was that the DNA found
on my T-shirt was 150 quadrillion to one (that's 150 with 15
noughts after it) more likely to be from Bradley Murdoch than
from any other person selected at random. How was the defence
going to deal with this? The only explanation Murdoch ever came
up with was that we had both been at Red Rooster at different
times on the same day.

I concentrated hard on Algie's cross-examination, and I didn't
think he made any dent in the DNA evidence, but he did go over
one thing that upset me greatly. A cigarette butt had been found
at the crime scene and the police had collected it for DNA testing,
hoping it was from the attacker. It turned out it was from a police
officer who had been one of the first at the scene. I couldn't believe
this carelessness – to let something like this contaminate the crime
scene and, again, divert precious time and resources from the
investigation. But I suppose after learning that it took three months
to find some of the other evidence I shouldn't have been surprised.

After court finished, I walked over to the DPP with Sharon and we had a discussion with Anthony Elliott about the day's evidence. Anthony became very engrossed in our conversation and began talking in great detail about the possibility that my denim jacket, which was missing from the Kombi, had been used by Murdoch to wrap around Pete's head after he had shot Pete.

In the past I had been upset by Anthony's insensitive remarks, but after seeing him in action over the weeks of the trial, I realised that it was just his way and that he meant well. However, it was still distressing to hear him talk about Pete like that and I made an excuse and left.

That night I was in need of a drink and some light relief. My head was full of DNA comparisons, ballistics and guns. Sharon and I sat outside on the balcony, listening to music and sharing a drink. We had our own party for two. I desperately needed to break free from the upsetting details of the trial, away from the public, police and media attention. I was lucky enough to be with someone who would never judge me or think I was acting inappropriately. Sharon caught me looking over the balcony at the pool and asked me if I'd been in. I hadn't.

We both looked down as the turquoise water shimmered up at us through the dark night. Sharon decided that it was about time that I used the pool so we both went and changed.

The water was warm but refreshing. I felt invigorated. It was quite late so it wasn't a surprise to have the pool to ourselves. I swam a few lengths and then Sharon and I had an underwater handstand competition. It was silly and childish but a lot of fun. I felt a thousand miles away from the sterile airconditioned courtroom.

There was a spa at the end of the pool and after we'd made ourselves dizzy from too many handstands we got in. Sharon and I lay there with our heads tilted back against the sides and stared up at the stars. The water bubbled over us and the night was calm and peaceful.

After a while Sharon got out of the spa. I was disappointed as I wanted to stay there longer but I didn't want to stay outside alone in the dark. Sharon told me she was just going back up to the apartment to fix us both a drink. I relaxed and sank back under the bubbles.

A few days later I was swimming laps in the pool one morning before going to court and I noticed a CCTV camera. I laughed to myself, thinking back to our handstand competition, and couldn't stop myself from wondering what the media would have made of that.

* * *

When I turned up at the Supreme Court with Sharon I was pleasantly surprised. There hadn't been very many photographers waiting on the steps. Lorelei told me that a lot of the media had left Darwin but that they would be returning for the final week of the trial. Having said that, it was more like the circus just downsized a little because there was still a strong media presence.

During the lunch break I went to the Director of Public Prosecutions building with Sharon and Paul. I wanted to introduce Sharon to Tony Stafford and to give her the opportunity to thank him. Tony had arranged all of our flights. I can imagine that this was very time-consuming for him, because no one knew what date the trial would end, and throughout the trial our flight details needed to be altered often as the trial went on and on.

Paul needed to speak to Tony too. He had decided to fly back home and return again towards the end of the trial. It had been a difficult decision for him to make, as he was reluctant to leave his parents, but he had a business back in the UK to run. When Paul had travelled out to Australia in July 2001 and stayed with me for three months, he returned to find his business had suffered. He'd been striving ever since to build it back up to what it was. I know Paul was there also for his own loss but I will always appreciate the support he provided me, particularly in the days after the crime.

* * *

After court was finished for the day I walked over to the DPP building to use Nannette's computer so I could send emails to Phil and Diane. There was an email waiting on my account from Phil, he'd written to me on his first day back at work. I still had that nagging feeling of disappointment that I hadn't said an adequate goodbye to him so it was great to hear from him. As I reached the end of his email my disappointment evaporated. He wrote:

> Jo,
>
> I had a plan that I would make a great speech to you as I left the other day, saying how proud of you I am, how well you have done and how well you are doing. I think you have stood up so well to everything that has been thrown at you; you have bent and moved with requirements of everyone around you. You carry yourself with dignity and self-respect, which are not compromised by the many distractions placed in your way.
>
> You are very near now to realising the end product of a long and painful journey. Stay strong. Be yourself...

There have been very few people that I have met throughout my life who have earned my respect and admiration – Phil is one of them. That is why his words meant so much to me. I've endured hurtful innuendos and slanderous comments in the past in the media and by members of the public whose only knowledge of me had been gained through the media, but none of those people knew me. To receive positive comments from a person I admire outweighs those thousands of negative comments. Towards the end of the trial, one other person's words would have a similarly powerful effect on me.

* * *

On Thursday the 10th of November Murdoch's friend and business partner, James Hepi, was sworn in as a witness. Hepi told the court that in 2001 he and Murdoch were involved in transporting cannabis between Broome, in Western Australia, and Sedan, in South Australia. He testified that they would take it in turns to make the 3000-kilometre trip and that both men relied on amphetamines to stay awake. Hepi had caught up with Murdoch after his latest drug run in mid-July, shortly after Pete and I were attacked.

Rex Wild handled the examination.

> REX WILD: Now, when you saw him, did you notice anything about his appearance?
>
> JAMES HEPI: Yes. His face had – his mo was shorter. His hair had been cut.
>
> REX WILD: And was there any – what was his behaviour like?
>
> JAMES HEPI: Scattered. He'd been on the gear [amphetamines] for four or five days, racing around the country, he was fairly scattered.

Hepi went on to testify that during one conversation with Murdoch in 2001, Murdoch had asked him what he would do in the middle of the desert with a body.

> REX WILD: Did you have a conversation with Mr Murdoch about spoon drains?
>
> JAMES HEPI: Yes, we did.
>
> REX WILD: What was that about?

JAMES HEPI: Brad claimed it was a fairly good place to put
a body. The digging was easy in a spoon drain.

REX WILD: Why, why is it easy?

JAMES HEPI: Because they regularly get turned over by
machinery, the ground is turned, it's soft.

REX WILD: And how did this conversation come up?

JAMES HEPI: It came up in a conversation as, 'What would
you do in the middle of the desert?' You know, 'Where
would you put a body?' I said, 'Well, I don't need to, I run
drugs not kill people,' So yeah, and he told me where he
would put a body.

I didn't look at Murdoch while James Hepi was on the stand
but it was obvious to everyone there was no love lost between the
two. Hepi had testified about the spoon drains and that he had
seen Murdoch making handcuffs out of cable ties. Then Rex Wild
moved on to talking about how the partnership had fallen apart.
As Hepi spoke, Murdoch muttered, 'You're a fucking liar.'

James Hepi turned towards Murdoch and said, 'Fuck you.'

Under cross-examination, Grant Algie suggested that James
Hepi had made up his testimony to get a reward, or to get back
at Murdoch. He suggested that Hepi was giving evidence only
because he believed Murdoch had given the police information
that led to his own arrest in May 2002.

GRANT ALGIE: Would it be wrong to suggest to you, Mr Hepi,
that you are lying, fabricating and exaggerating in your
evidence in implicating Mr Murdoch?

JAMES HEPI: Yes, it would be wrong.

GRANT ALGIE: And it would be wrong to suggest that you
might be doing that in order to save your skin?

JAMES HEPI: My skin's already saved, mate, I'm sitting here.
He's sitting there [in the dock].

I sat and listened as James Hepi talked about people and acts that seemed to me from another planet. His world of criminality, drug-running and guns had brutally collided with mine. I couldn't help thinking, If only... if only Pete and I had left earlier, or later. If only Murdoch had gone a different way, or got a flat tyre so he missed us on the Stuart Highway. But to do that can drive you crazy. I felt so sad that fate had meant Pete and I were travelling that stretch of road at the same time as Murdoch.

* * *

Having Martin, then Sharon, then Diane arrive to support me meant a great deal. On the Friday night before Sharon left, a crowd of us went out, including Nick and Shaun. After a few drinks in Kitty O'Shea's bar we went across the road to the Pub Bar. We were sitting around a table chatting when a young man walked past on his way back from the DJ's box. He caught my eye and said simply, 'The next song is for you,' and walked away. Everyone around the table stared at each other wondering what song the man had chosen for me. Sharon and I laughed when the theme tune to 'Greatest American Hero' started blaring out. It was perfect. It was a feel-good, uplifting song. Since then it never fails to make me happy whenever I hear it.

I was hoping that I would feel that way at the end of the trial. I was touched by that young man's gesture and appreciated his support. He had shown me in a very quiet and very moving way that he was behind me. I received many such gestures while I was in Darwin and they meant a great deal to me at the time and still do.

* * *

After saying goodbye to Sharon I had two days until Diane arrived. Rosey drove me to the airport to meet her.

At 3.30 am Rosey and I were standing in Arrivals waiting for Diane to appear. As I waited I noticed one of the security guards who sat in the dock sometimes guarding Murdoch. He had once given me a supportive wink while I was being cross-examined by Algie. I said hello to him and he told me that he was waiting for his mum to arrive from Ireland.

I saw Diane walk through the doors and stood back out of sight and watched as she scanned the area looking for me. I didn't mind giving her a few moments of panic because the day before she had sent me a text message saying that she had missed her flight. It was a joke but completely believable because if any of my friends were to miss a flight it would be Diane.

I couldn't leave her hanging and so I ran out and hugged her tightly before I introduced her to Rosey. She was surprisingly full of energy after her long flight and she talked non-stop in the car back to the Marrakai. I took Diane up to the apartment and did the tour before handing her a cold beer from the fridge. This is our customary way of welcoming each other, and it didn't matter that it was so early in the morning because Diane was still on European time. We sat together on the balcony and watched the sunrise as I gave Diane a run-down of what had been happening. Once the sky had lightened I left Diane to unpack and went to the pool to do some laps before we both got ready for court.

* * *

As I walked across the upstairs hall outside courtroom six later that morning I could see Libby Andrew, dressed in her beige sergeant's uniform, among a group of people standing in the centre of the hallway. I suddenly felt very nervous. I hadn't seen Libby in four years though we had kept some contact by email. I have so much respect and admiration for her. I slowed my pace as I walked towards her and, as I got closer to the group, Libby turned around and saw me. Her face lit up with a warm smile and my nervousness vanished. She looked pleased to see me and I was glad. It was a pleasure to introduce Libby to Diane, as they had both heard a lot about each other and had spoken by phone in July 2001.

During the lunch break, Libby, Diane and I went and sat in a cafe for lunch. It felt so good to be sitting around a table with two of my favourite people. That evening Diane was exhausted from her journey so she crashed out and I went to dinner with Libby. Libby told me all about her work in the bush communities and gave me two files containing three years worth of monthly newsletters. We talked non-stop and caught up on each other's lives. I went to bed feeling exhausted but content.

The next morning Diane came into my bedroom at 7.00 am to bring me a mug of tea. I felt guilty and thought that I should have been doing this for her. She'd only arrived the day before and had been on the go ever since, going straight to court and meeting lots of new people. Sitting up to drink my tea I thanked her. Diane sat on my bed and proceeded to describe to me the dream she had had. This became a regular occurrence because both Diane and I had the strangest dreams throughout the trial. The same thing had happened to Sharon, it seemed that all of our dreams were influenced in some way by the trial.

That day Libby finished giving evidence. She had to leave Darwin straightaway to return to work at Ali Curong. I arranged to have a drink with her during the lunch break before she caught her flight. Libby told me that she really wanted to be with me on verdict day, but as no one could predict when that would be it seemed unlikely she could be. As we walked out of court, Libby and I couldn't resist. We had a photograph taken of us standing at the top of the courthouse steps. We both pretended that it was verdict day and that Murdoch had been found guilty, just in case

Libby couldn't be there on the day. We both wanted justice for Pete so badly. That photo is one of my favourites.

We sat together and talked in the lounge bar inside the Crown Plaza Hotel until she had to leave to get her flight to Alice Springs. Libby walked with me back to court and it started to rain so we had to run. I welcomed the rain; the humidity in Darwin was stifling. I said goodbye and made my way towards the lift. I wouldn't allow myself to become emotional and composed myself by telling myself that I would see Libby again. It still hurt. I hate saying goodbye.

I knew I had to toughen up. I had to go back into the courtroom and listen to taped prison telephone conversations between Bradley Murdoch and his mother and father; between Murdoch and his girlfriend, Jan Pittman; and a conversation he had with another friend. I had to stay strong and see this through.

* * *

Joan and Luciano were amazing. Each day they sat in that courtroom and listened as the prosecution put together the evidence that Bradley Murdoch had murdered their son. Some of the evidence was horribly disturbing and other evidence would have been laughable if it wasn't so serious. When the owner of a service station in Bourke testified that he had seen Peter on the 22nd of July and claimed Peter had bought a bottle of Coke and a Mars bar from him I could have wept. If only this was true. But this was not Peter. Robert Brown and his partner, Melissa Ann Kendall, both said Peter had come into their service station on that day. They claimed they recognised him but that he had dyed his hair blond. I couldn't believe how casual Mr Brown was. As he finished giving his evidence he had the audacity to look straight at me and say, 'How ya going?' Things like that were hard to confront.

One day later in the trial Grant Algie called Professor Maciej Henneberg as a witness for the defence. Professor Henneberg was the head of the Department of Anatomical Science at Adelaide University and was there to counter earlier evidence by anatomist Meiya Sutisno who had positively identified the man in the truck-stop CCTV footage as Bradley Murdoch. Professor Henneberg started to talk about left- and right-handedness and stated that most people are right-handed. Luciano was restless throughout the professor's testimony but was paying enough attention to tease Joan when Professor Henneberg talked about the high incidence of left-handedness in Eskimos. Three out of Joan and Luciano's four children are left-handed and Luciano had a twinkle in his eye when he leaned over and asked Joan if she had had an ongoing affair with an Eskimo that he should know about. I had to bite my lip to stop from laughing out loud.

I know some people would think it impossible to find humour in anything at a time like that. But we did. We had to; it was the only way we could get through it.

As much as some sections of the media would have liked it to be otherwise, the Falconio family and I are very close and we did our best to look after each other during the trial. We did our best to bring normality to our lives. This included doing the things normal people do, like having friends and family around for dinner. One night Diane and I invited Joan, Luciano and Nick around to the apartment for dinner. Despite the Darwin heat I planned to make a beef stew. It is one of my prized dishes.

I got up early on the Sunday morning to go to the local supermarket to buy everything I needed. Doing things like this contributed to that sense of normality and I enjoy cooking for people I care for. It is my way of looking after them. As I was walking around the refrigerated section trying to find the meat I wanted, a man approached me. I felt sure he was going to ask me about the trial, so before he had a chance to speak I asked him if he knew where the beef was. Rather than pointing in the direction, he offered to show me. I couldn't not follow him and as we walked he introduced himself and asked me what I was cooking. I felt a little weird replying 'Beef stew' because even though it was early in the morning it felt like it was 1000 degrees outside. Definitely not beef stew weather. He didn't look at me strangely, which was good, and then he told me he was planning to cook a Lancashire hotpot. I laughed.

Once we found the beef I thanked him. He wished me well and said goodbye. I appreciated his good wishes but I will never get used to people knowing so much about me. I know that might sound strange because I am writing this book, but it is my hope that people will know *me* after they have read this and not a media-created myth.

I finished my shopping and went back to the apartment and then Diane and I spent most of the day getting ready for our dinner party. It turned out we didn't have enough pans so had to borrow some. By the time we were organised and the ingredients were cooked it was almost time for the Falconios to arrive. The stew smelled wonderful. As we were waiting I was getting hungrier and hungrier and so was Diane. We had completely forgotten to eat lunch so we decided to have a very small bowl before Joan, Luciano and Nick arrived. I know it was rude but we were starving. We thought we could be finished and cleaned up ready for seconds before we had to go down and open the security door. Halfway through the bowl we heard three loud knocks on the door. We were sprung, someone had already let them into the building. I opened the door and as soon as I saw Luciano and Joan I had to own up straightaway. Joan pretended to be cross but wasn't really. We had a lovely evening and laughed together the entire time.

* * *

One day as I walked out of the courtroom a man approached me. I hadn't seen him before but Nico later told me that he was an expert witness from South Australia who had given evidence in relation to Toyota vehicles. I had missed his evidence because I had been saying goodbye to Libby at the time. Nico, who has a keen interest in cars and motorbikes, would have filled me in on anything important.

The man asked me for my autograph. I didn't think this was an appropriate thing to do so I replied that I was a victim and a witness, not a celebrity, and I declined to sign anything for him. I smiled and shook his hand instead. I turned and walked away, hoping that the man didn't think that I had been rude to him.

Nico caught up with me. He had seen what had happened and told me that he was impressed with how I had dealt with the situation. I was pleased. I remembered how badly I had reacted the last time someone had asked me for my autograph. I had been standing behind the counter serving a customer at Dymocks in Sydney. It was six weeks after the crime. The customer asked for my autograph. It was a complete shock and I turned around and locked myself in Gary's office for ten minutes until the customer had left and I could compose myself. I've come a long way since then.

* * *

Even though I had handled myself well I hated this recognition. The apartment was really my only sanctuary; the only place I could get away from prying eyes and ears. Each day of the trial was exhausting and the attention would start as soon as I approached the courthouse wondering how many cameras would be there that day. Sitting with Joan and Luciano we focused on the evidence and though sometimes I was baffled I never let my concentration waver. The lunchtime break was always welcome but the dilemma of what to do or, rather, where to go was a strain.

If you have not been to Darwin, I can assure you that it is almost impossible while wandering around in the stifling heat not to bump into the same people again and again. The defence or, frighteningly, sometimes the defence's witnesses were all out of court looking for something to eat during each lunch break. On a bad day Diane and I couldn't eat our lunch. One really bad day we took refuge at the DPP. Otherwise we just wandered around together, always watching out and wondering who would pop around the corner. Once I was walking home after court and I passed Murdoch's girlfriend as she sat outside the Deck Bar having a drink with the owners of the Fitzroy Crossing Roadhouse. They would give evidence that Murdoch had been at the roadhouse at a certain time and therefore couldn't have been on the Stuart Highway. I kept my head high and kept walking. I didn't look back.

Each day I would sit in the Supreme Courthouse and listen to more evidence. Sometimes that evidence was compelling, sometimes it was dramatic, and sometimes it was just plain sad. Then, when court finished, I would walk 'home' with Diane.

Diane and I were never stuck for something to talk about; in fact we talked non-stop and now I wonder what the hell about? One day whilst swimming in the pool Diane told me about the rise of sex slavery in Europe and about a film that had been recommended to her by Anna Lind, the late Swedish Foreign Minister. It was called *Lilja 4eva*. I told Diane about SBS, the Australian TV channel that shows foreign films, and then we moved on to talk about something else.

That night as we sat and stared at the television I started flicking through the channels. All of a sudden Diane screamed 'Lilja 4eva'. The film she had told me about was showing on SBS right then. It was spooky. Diane thought it might be too disturbing to watch but I wanted to see it, so we did. It's a truly sad and realistically gruesome film. It reminded me of just how fortunate I am and that other people have experienced and are experiencing far worse than me.

* * *

On Monday the 28th of November I was outside the courtroom shortly before I was due to give evidence for a second time. I was chatting and joking nervously with Diane. Detective Senior Constable Paula Dooley-McDonnell was sitting in the seats opposite us, next to crime-scene examiner Tim Sandry. They were both waiting to give evidence. Paula Dooley-McDonnell never acknowledged me or Diane and she never made any eye contact. She may not have realised but we could see her facial expressions and saw her raise her eyebrows or grimace as she listened to Diane and me talking. She continuously looked sideways towards Tim Sandry as she reacted to our voices. I tried not to be unsettled or upset by her behaviour but it was hard. I didn't expect her to like me, but I did expect her to respect that I was a victim and a witness at the trial of my boyfriend's murderer. Perhaps she was upset about the way I had reacted to her when I was inspecting the Kombi in 2001?

The situation became quite embarrassing and Diane went into hyper-quick make-a-joke mode to get me to laugh about something else rather than get upset. Tim Sandry played no part in this and actually took the time to compliment me on my evidence. I was enormously relieved when my name was called out by the court assistant and I could get up and walk away.

18

Listening

The trial had been going for nine weeks and the prosecution had rested its case. Fifty-five witnesses had been called. Grant Algie was focused on trying to discredit any evidence – especially mine – that pointed to Murdoch being guilty. It was disheartening to sit in the courtroom and listen to the defence knowing that they were working for a guilty man.

On the opposite side of the road from the Marrakai apartments was a small church called St Mary's. You could see it from every window in the apartment. I passed that church every day; I heard its bells chime every Sunday morning. I can't explain why this gave me comfort, but it did. Even though I'd describe myself as being spiritual as opposed to religious, I gain peace and comfort when I'm in a church.

One day as we walked back from court to the Marrakai, Diane and I respectfully stopped talking as we approached the open doors of the church. We stood in the doorway and I looked across the empty church. Its solitariness was welcoming.

Without discussing it, we separated and walked down opposite aisles. Diane and I have attended our local church in Huddersfield together many times over the years, usually when we are both back home for Christmas.

As I walked to the front of the church, rays of sunlight fell through the stained-glass windows and the peacefulness surrounded me. I sat down on a wooden seat in the front row and let the day's events drain away from my body and cleared my mind of the constant cloud of murder and brutality that I endured every single day while I sat in court or went about my business in Darwin. There were rare moments outside of the apartment when I wasn't reminded of the trial or being stared at. If it hadn't been for the warm air that circulated through the church I could have forgotten I was in Darwin. I could have been anywhere. It felt good for my soul to stop for ten minutes and to think of nothing, or at least not about the trial.

I got up from my seat and walked over to Diane. She was lighting candles. I lit two. Smiling we walked out of church and across the road to the Marrakai.

When we got back to the apartment Diane handed me a refreshing beer. We sat and reflected on our day. It was only Monday but it felt like the end of the week. That day had seemed like five days rolled into one. I was emotionally drained and had no energy or enthusiasm. Diane could see I was struggling and told me I needed to start taking care of myself more or I would burn out. She pointed out there would be more tough times ahead. She suggested that I try to relax that evening and perhaps I shouldn't rush to court in the morning. Algie had indicated that afternoon that he would have legal arguments in the morning and we both knew they always took a while.

Diane ran me a bath and added olive oil, milk and drops of lavender oil to the water. I was sceptical that it would do any good but how could I refuse such a kind gesture? I was pleasantly surprised at how nice it was.

The next morning, as Diane had suggested, I didn't rush in to court. I was still in my pyjamas as I prepared us both a nice breakfast. Whenever I felt guilty Diane told me not to and said not to think of it as a Tuesday but to treat it like a Saturday morning. My phone kept ringing constantly but I chose to ignore it. I was supposed to be taking time out for myself. Over breakfast I read a letter I had received from the Ombudsman to Diane. We sat leisurely at the table reading and drinking mugs of tea and my phone continued to ring. I decided that I should at least listen to my messages, just in case it was something important.

I put the phone to my ear and listened to the first message. I heard Lorelei's voice, which was unusually low and unsteady. In a serious tone she said, 'I don't know whether you will want to know this, but Murdoch has just taken the stand.' I didn't listen to the rest of the message or any of the others. I threw the phone across the table and simply said, 'Murdoch's taken the stand.' I told Diane I would be leaving in fifteen minutes if she wanted to come with me. I screamed at myself throughout my quick shower. I was furious at not being there.

In less than fifteen minutes I had showered, dressed and ordered a taxi. Diane couldn't help herself and in a cheeky voice told me that she was impressed. She reminded me of all the times in the past she'd been waiting for me to get ready and concluded by saying that now she knew how fast I could get ready when I needed to she wouldn't be so patient in future. I am lucky to have such good friends who can make me see light and humour in the darkest of circumstances.

Diane and I waited outside the apartment block for the taxi to arrive. When it pulled up we jumped in and I asked to be taken to the Supreme Court. The journey seemed to take forever. When the taxi pulled up outside the courthouse steps, a couple of cameramen were standing there and they looked surprised to see me. Almost before they had time to reach down for their cameras I was rushing up the steps.

I walked swiftly through the foyer and into the lift. Adrenaline was racing through my body. I stepped out of the lift and saw a congregation of people outside the door of courtroom six. I tried to pass through them but no one moved. They were transfixed, looking through the small glass window in the door. I pushed my way through saying 'Excuse me' as I went. When I got to the door a guard blocked my entrance. He had his back to me and was also looking through the window. The people behind me had stopped murmuring and it suddenly fell silent. I tapped his shoulder, willing him to move out of my way. The guard turned around to see me and immediately stepped to one side, allowing me to pass.

I took a deep breath before I swung open the door that led directly into the courtroom. The sound of the door opening was loud because the room was so silent and everyone turned to look at me. I stared straight at Murdoch. I wanted him to look at me. Face me. With my eyes I challenged him to acknowledge me as his victim and witness of his crime. I knew he would not. He is a cowardly liar.

Standing at the bench, Algie was questioning Murdoch.

I slowly walked over towards my usual seat. Taking very small steps, I dragged my hand across the wooden bench that parted the public and counsel. I couldn't remove my eyes from Murdoch. I hoped that there wouldn't be a free seat for me to sit in and I would be able to stand. I reached my seat, it was free. I reluctantly sat down next to Superintendent Gwynne. She leant over to whisper something to me and in a low voice I asked her not to speak to me right now. I wanted to hear every word this man had to say.

As Algie questioned Murdoch he admitted that he transported cannabis from South Australia to Broome and talked about the routes that he and James Hepi would take. He told the court that the Tanami Track was his preferred route. He also admitted to owning two guns, but though I knew he had a silver revolver, he denied it.

GRANT ALGIE: What sort of gun or guns did you have?

BRADLEY MURDOCH: I had two guns. They had [sic] a 357
— it's a cold brand, large barrel very dark grey. They're called a 'Dirty Harry' gun, it is, it's got a 10" barrel on it, big handle. The other gun that I had was a black 38 Beretta, roughly around palm size, which was a 38 calibre.

GRANT ALGIE: And that's a Beretta?

BRADLEY MURDOCH: A Beretta.

GRANT ALGIE: What's that look like?

BRADLEY MURDOCH: It's just a flat black gun, so handgrip, barrel about so, or it hasn't got a barrel it's got an actual slider, the magazine goes up inside your – where your handpiece is.

GRANT ALGIE: The magazine with the bullets goes up inside the handpiece?

BRADLEY MURDOCH: Yes.

GRANT ALGIE: So is that what you would call a pistol as opposed to a revolver?

BRADLEY MURDOCH: Well, as far as I know a pistol is a revolver. A revolver is a revolving chambered gun and it's a pistol.

GRANT ALGIE: Did the Beretta have the revolving?

BRADLEY MURDOCH: No.

GRANT ALGIE: And what colour was the Beretta, you might have said?

BRADLEY MURDOCH: Black.

GRANT ALGIE: Did you own a silver revolver?

BRADLEY MURDOCH: No, I did not.

I watched Murdoch blink as he sat there and lied. He lifted up the Styrofoam cup in front of him, taking small sips of water before answering a question. Earlier in the trial Julie-Anne McPhail, a prosecution witness, had testified that she had met Murdoch at a service station while travelling from Perth to Adelaide in late June 2001. They had met up a number of times during the journey and when they stopped they would have a line of speed, smoke cannabis and drink beer together. At one point Murdoch was stopped at the side of the road and Julie-Anne pulled up behind him.

REX WILD: Did you have a talk with him?

JULIE-ANNE McPHAIL: Yes.

REX WILD: And can you remember what the discussion that you had with him was?

JULIE-ANNE McPHAIL: Yes, I went around to the passenger side of the car and he had the door open and he pulled out a small gun and offered it for sale.

REX WILD: What sort of gun was it?

JULIE-ANNE McPHAIL: Just a palm size revolver.

REX WILD: What colour was it?

JULIE-ANNE McPHAIL: Silver.

While on the stand Julie-Anne McPhail had stated that she had contacted the police. Joan and I whispered to each other at this point. We couldn't help wondering when she had contacted the police. When Julie-Anne had finished on the witness stand Joan and Nicholas followed her out of the courtroom to find out. She was crying as they approached her because Grant Algie had given her such a hard time. When Joan asked her when she had first contacted the police she couldn't believe what she was told. Julie-Anne had recognised Murdoch from the COMFIT image released in the days after the attack. She had called the Western Australia police and also Crime Stoppers on a couple of occasions but she was always fobbed off. The last time she called, long before Murdoch's arrest, Julie-Anne had been told that they had somebody. Was that me?

* * *

I sat in that courtroom and looked at Murdoch. I had so much fury and hatred inside me that my body burned with white heat. It's difficult for me to put into words just how I felt. I was sitting just metres away, watching and listening to the man who had murdered Pete, and would have murdered me if I hadn't escaped. Every word he uttered was a lie. He knew full well what he had done.

At 4.30 pm court was adjourned until the next day. I filed out of court with everyone else. People came over to talk to me. I asked them to please leave me alone. I explained that I wasn't being rude but that I just didn't want to speak to anyone. They were respectful. I didn't trust myself to speak. I thought I might explode, offend someone or say something I may later regret. I just wanted to go back to the Marrakai, where I could scream and swear in private.

I hurriedly walked down the stairs from the first floor. Diane trailed behind me, trying to keep up. I needed to get out of the building. I passed a lady on the stairs and she stopped me. I'd never seen this woman before but she spoke to me as if she knew me. She said in a bright, cheery voice that I was wearing a lovely suit. Through gritted teeth I tried to politely smile back at her and carried on walking down the stairs. I'd just had to endure Murdoch's lies and this woman was telling me what a nice suit I was wearing. I had rage in my heart and talking about what I was wearing was irrelevant and trivial. I wished that people would understand that. Who cares what I'm wearing, it really isn't that important.

* * *

When Diane flew back to Berlin, my friend Ali flew from Sydney to support me. I don't know what I would have done without my friends. They made sure I didn't lose myself in the everyday trauma of the trial. By this late stage of the trial there were even more media as I entered the court each morning. One day I was sitting in the hallway with Ali and the Falconio family as we waited for the courtroom to open. I watched as Paul walked across the hallway towards us. I was so pleased that he was back and when he reached us he gave me a big hug. I care a lot for Paul and though we never refer to the time we shared in Alice Springs I am so glad that he was with me. Maybe we don't talk about it because we were both there and don't need to. Maybe I don't mention it because I know what a painful time in my life it was and I know Paul must feel the same.

* * *

On the 5th of December 2005 Grant Algie began summing up his defence.

> GRANT ALGIE: What about the manacles or the handcuffs
> themselves, is there something just a little bit strange
> about that? If you've got cable ties and you want to handcuff
> somebody or manacle, don't you just grab the cable tie
> and put both hands in it, and go zip, and there you've got
> them, just like that, no problem? What is the point, members
> of the jury, on any rational assessment of these somewhat

elaborate handcuffs and perhaps more to the point, why build them with three loops in the middle of them, what's the point of that? And again I invite you to reflect on this, and other issues and ask yourselves, 'Is that odd? Am I comfortable with that?' or is there something strange about that? Because you might think it's the presence of the three loops and the distance that they provide that allows the relative ease of movement from the hands behind the back to the hands at the front. But then again, if you've got a bad guy building handcuffs, why, what is the point of incorporating that feature? It may well be that feature that allows the lip balm to be got out of the pocket, whereas if you just cable tied your two wrists together it would be unlikely, you might think, you could do that, certainly if your hands were behind your back. It's just strange, members of the jury.

Could you drive a car with three loops between your handcuffs? Because that might be something you might need to consider in the course of your reflection on Barrow Creek.

Perhaps a better example, members of the jury, again arising from this case, is the extraordinary tale of the lip balm lid, the lip balm and the black tape. Now you've got the photographs that were taken in July 2001 showing the lip balm in place. You can see them, you can study them, and I suggest to you that when you look at them carefully and Mr Elliott's produced blow-up ones now as well so you can see them even better, you can see that all that is present in the area depicted in those photographs under the tree is 1 x lip balm lid, that's it.

Now again it's a matter for you, but I suggest it is wincingly obvious that when Officers Sandry and Spilsbury were shown that area with the lip balm lid, they would've searched it. It is almost embarrassing to suggest that two crime-scene officers, in those circumstance, having a lip balm lid identified to them, would not have searched around there. Of course they did, but all they found was a lip balm lid, and you can see by looking at the exhibits that all that is there is a lip balm lid. So fair enough, they seize the lip balm lid, that's all good.

Three months later a group of officers go back there – and this is October, I think – yes. Three months later they go back there and there it is, right in the same place, we've got the lip balm now and two bits of black tape, and you can see it because they photographed it all, and you can compare the area of the two photographs, one in July, one in October. And you can see by reference to the little nodules on the roots and things that it is the same area, but it wasn't there in July and it is there in October. Well, that's an amazing thing you might think, what are we dealing with there?

Well, members of the jury, there's a couple of possibilities you might think, probably the most obvious one is that somebody, one of the police officers who went out there in October or perhaps a police officer who went out there before October, has put them there, it's as simple as that. But you know, no harm done, I mean what difference does it make, it's just sort of confirming the area, it's just a bit of a lip balm, and a bit of black tape, it's not you know, it's not the crime of the century, it's just making everything fit in the picture, and after all that's what we like, a nice neat picture if we're investigating these things.

It's no big deal – I mean whether somebody actually went and bought the lip balm and threw the lid away and cut a couple bits of tape and put them there like that, that's one possibility, or whether the lip balm lid and the tape were actually found out there, but a few metres away, but that didn't quite fit the picture, so somebody has picked them up and put them where they'd rather have them be, probably is not necessary to resolve. What is important, you might think, is somebody has played around with the evidence to make it look like the lid and the tape was there when it wasn't. No harm done.

Or is it to be as Mr Twiggs said, was suggested in re-examination, that some kangaroo came along and took away the lip balm lid for a few months and then brought it back or the wind blew it, a little zephyr of wind moved it away, another zephyr came along later and put it back. Or perhaps it was a dingo, who knows, but members of the jury, I commend it to you. I commend it to you as yet another example of police manipulating evidence to perhaps help the case, make it a little better in circumstances where there's really no harm done. And in circumstances where you might think the attitude of the police has been Bradley Murdoch did it, it's his DNA on the shirt, therefore it must be him, there'd be no harm done to plant a little bit of DNA on the handcuffs. It just completes the circle to make sure we have a better chance of getting a conviction. It's a possibility, isn't it, it would be no better or worse than verballing a suspect, no harm done, members of the jury.

Is there any evidence that this has in fact happened, well, it may not surprise you if I suggest you're never going to get it from the police. You could systematically call every police officer in the Northern Territory and ask them if they had anything to do with planting DNA on the handcuffs and every one of them will tell you, you may be reasonably confident I think – every one of them will tell you that they did not. Including the one or the ones that did.

Algie also suggested to the jury that the evidence of Robert Brown and Melissa Kendall be given enormous weight and that the jury should conclude that Peter had not been murdered on the Stuart Highway.

> GRANT ALGIE: These are the sorts of things you'll need to consider, members of the jury, I mean from your own experience, knowledge of the way the world works. You probably know that from time to time some people do disappear themselves for reasons perhaps best known to them. Sometimes they turn up later, sometimes they don't. But the difficulty for you, members of the jury, is as I said before, you will be asked to convict my client of murder and there is no body.
>
> Now, true it is, and it will probably be said to you that there are cases where there is no body found and yet a murder has occurred. Well, that is undoubtedly so. But you might think there are normally cases where there is an explanation, at the very least, for what has happened.

I couldn't believe what I was hearing. There was an explanation for what happened to Pete. That cold-hearted bastard Bradley Murdoch had murdered him. Algie was asking the jury to disregard everything I had told them, to disregard the evidence of people like Pamela Brown and Jasper Haines, to disregard Julie-Anne McPhail. To ignore all the forensic evidence that supported the truth of what I had told the court under oath. To throw out the fact that there was a DNA match to Murdoch that couldn't be explained by saying we had both been to the same Red Rooster.

To ignore the fact that CCTV footage showing Murdoch at a Shell service station supported my description of our attacker. Algie had the audacity to imply during the trial that the person on that footage couldn't be Murdoch because he only bought petrol at BP service stations.

Basically Grant Algie was advising the jury that Bradley John Murdoch, a drug and gun runner who had proved to be violent, was now telling the truth and that everything I had said was made up!

* * *

Rex Wild followed Algie the next day for his own summing up.

REX WILD: Now I've heard it said at different times that this is the Falconio mystery. In our submission, it's no mystery. Peter Falconio died on 14 July 2001, his body was hidden. Joanne Lees was threatened at the time, she was attacked, she was handcuffed, you've seen the style of handcuffs used, they're broken down over there in P176, exhibit P176 which you'll have with you. Meticulously put together you might think, somebody with a great deal of time and patience and attention to detail has assembled these handcuffs. A certain style about the man who did that...

...Now this is the way this young woman was feeling throughout this episode and when we come to examine it closely and minutely what she says about the precise colour of the vehicle and the colour of the bullbar and the other configurations of it, you might make some allowance for the situation in which she found herself. She was not there taking notes, she had the most terrifying experience of her life or of any person in this room could ever have. So when you go into the jury room later and talk about her evidence and talk about what my learned friend says

about the discrepancies, you make proper allowances for
the situation in which she found herself.

... Just as a little side issue. He's had a moustache, I
suggest to you, throughout the relevant period. The
moustache he had throughout the relationship with Bev
Allan, she told you, and that's between the end of 2000
and July 2001. The significance of that, the Crown says,
is that he suddenly shaves it off on 16 July 2001 and
that in the context of this case is a significant matter,
even though he says to you, 'Well, I shaved it off and I
grew it again...'

Rex Wild reminded the jury that Murdoch had admitted to
being on the Stuart Highway at the same time as Pete and me.

REX WILD: He's certainly in the vicinity, on the Crown case,
he's the man but he's up the Stuart Highway with a dog
and other people that might've been on the Stuart Highway
on 14 July didn't all have moustaches, didn't all have
guns in their vehicle, they didn't all drive four-wheel
drives. They didn't all have what you might think is a
slightly stooped shoulder effect, so there's a lot of
coincidences there for you to consider. And the Crown's
submission to you is they're not coincidences, they are
part of the circumstantial case. The circumstances that
you can use in relation to Bradley Murdoch in finding that
he was the man.

Rex Wild asked the jury to reject the testimony of Robert
Brown and Melissa Kendall.

REX WILD: Ms Kendall said that the man would come up to
Mr Brown's chin. Mr Brown said up to his nose. Well,
that's not much difference, it's only a few inches. That's

the sort of difference you might get with different views of things.

Ms Kendall said he had a shaved head with dark stubble growing through. Mr Brown said he had blonde [sic] or sandy hair, which is about the same length as his own, which was, as you remember, reasonably lengthy hair. Both said they had a stocky build, the man had a stocky build, and you can have a look at the pictures of Peter Falconio that you've got and see whether you agree with that.

Ms Kendall said the man had a fair complexion, Mr Brown said it was white. That's very extreme in fairness. Ms Kendall didn't notice any accent, Mr Brown said the man had a slight accent. Ms Kendall said it all happened in the afternoon, it was still light. Mr Brown said it was just on dark at around 6.00 pm. Ms Kendall said she served the man. Mr Brown said he served the man. Ms Kendall said that once both men had left, she went and told Mr Brown who was in the kitchen washing the bain-marie. Mr Brown said that when he came out, Peter Falconio was still in the shop. And he called him Pete, you remember, very familiar, but that was his style.

While Rex Wild talked about the facts that implicated Bradley Murdoch directly I sat transfixed:

REX WILD: Now, all of that is evidence of premeditation. The importance of that is that the man who shot Peter Falconio must have intended to do so and intended to either kill him or do grievous harm to him. His Honour will explain that to you.

But, if you put those circumstances together, then it's the Crown submission although you didn't see it happen and Joanne Lees didn't see it happen, you can use the circumstances which you find to be proved before you to find Bradley Murdoch guilty of murder. And that's the way that you should carry out your exercise.

Now, ladies and gentlemen, what type of person would manufacture those handcuffs? Try to hide the blood, would clean up the scene, would try to prevent blood going into his car, perhaps using Joanne Lees' jacket? Would hide the car, would dispose of the body in such a way as it wouldn't be found for a long, long time, if ever?

I suggest to you it would be a meticulous, perhaps obsessive person who would do those things, someone just like Bradley John Murdoch. You should be so satisfied that he was the man.

I knew that the Crown case was strong.

I knew for sure that Bradley Murdoch was guilty.

Once Rex Wild finished his summing up all I could do was pray that the jury believed beyond all reasonable doubt what this man had done.

* * *

On Wednesday the 7th of December, Chief Justice Brian Martin started to deliver his final instructions to the jury. He was thorough and careful in instructing the jury and emphasised that they alone had to judge the facts. He spent time discussing memory and how many factors can affect recollection.

CHIEF JUSTICE BRIAN MARTIN: Sitting in this court over the last few weeks some of you will have noticed things happening in the court or expressions on the faces of people in the court that others will not have noticed or remembered.

May I give you a couple of simple examples in this case from the uncontroversial evidence of the truck driver, Rod Adams, who was asleep in the truck when Ms Lees jumped out onto the highway. Mr Adams told you that after they helped Ms Lees into the truck there was conversation. And then he gave this evidence:

'There was a small conversation but she kept asking about her boyfriend and I just looked at Vince and he looked at me and went, "What boyfriend?" and she said, "Peter". I'm still taken by it. A lot of things get said, a lot of things don't get said, you remember certain things, you remember nothing.'

You might think that is a good example of an honest and generally reliable witness telling you how difficult it is to remember details and how we remember some things but not others. The same witness later said he knew he wiped Ms Lees' knees, but he could not remember whether he wiped the injuries on the elbows. When he was asked whether Vince Millar pulled the prime mover forward before doing a U-turn, Mr Adams said:

'This night, everything happened so fast, so quick, that is something that is not taken into consideration by myself or any other professional driver out there.'

Another example: Mr Millar said they went looking – sorry, that when they went looking, he got out of his truck to look at the pile of dirt on the road. Mr Adams said they stayed in the truck. These are just small examples of how honest witnesses remember events differently and remember some things, but not others.

The judge also focused the jury's attention on the trauma he believed I had faced:

CHIEF JUSTICE BRIAN MARTIN: The other factor arising from the events out on the Stuart Highway that night that you might think is of particular significance in this case is the sheer trauma of those events. Leaving aside questions of detail and leaving aside the issue of identification of the man in the 4-wheel drive, if you accept the evidence of Ms Lees about the essential events of being pulled over and attacked, you might have little difficulty in concluding that Ms Lees underwent a terrifying ordeal. A pitch black night in the middle of the Australian outback confronted by a man with a gun who she feared had just shot her boyfriend. Tied up tight. Afraid for her own life and of being raped. Escaping into the scrub. Hiding under a bush for hours.

Speaking generally about the evidence of Ms Lees and not about any aspect for the moment, if you accept that she was attacked in this way, you will need to consider whether the trauma of the experience has or might have affected the reliability of her observations and recall. Traumatic events can impress themselves upon a mind quite vividly, but there is also the potential for the trauma and distress to lead to inaccurate or incomplete observation or recall. You will need to consider carefully the impact of trauma and distress upon Ms Lees' ability to take in and later recall details of the events that were occurring and of her surroundings.

I was struck by the power of the judge's words. The judge had gained my respect throughout the trial. He had given each witness the same respect and had treated everyone fairly. He clearly had a sharp mind, spoke wisely and listened carefully. He was the first person that had ever acknowledged the sheer trauma I was experiencing during the crime and the effect that it would have on my recall. This was a significant moment for me. I felt myself becoming increasingly emotional, and I struggled to suppress my tears. I wanted to leave the court as I felt that I couldn't hold back my emotions and didn't want to break down in public. Coincidently the judge adjourned the court to allow the jury a break. I waited in line with the public and media to exit the court. As soon as I got through the doors I ran across the hall towards the little witness room that I had been allowed to use from time to time for some privacy. The room was locked. Tears began to roll down my cheeks, I felt frustrated that I had nowhere to hide. I turned around to see Ali who instinctively gave me a hug. I could hear the voices of other people approaching. I grabbed Ali's arm and we ducked into a small interview room. The light inside was switched off and the room was in complete darkness. Ali was about to switch on the light but I asked her not to. I kept the door slightly ajar; I heard the voices fade away.

Sitting in the dark I apologised to Ali for being in such an emotional state, it had come so unexpectedly and I was shocked at how emotional I felt. I began to explain how the judge's words had overshadowed the hurtful comments I had received in the past, the insensitive interviews and the relentless questioning from the defence and the innuendos Algie had made during his summing up. Ali told me she understood and I needn't explain. She encouraged me to let my feelings out and handed me a tissue through the dark. I wiped my eyes and then switched on the lights. I asked Ali if I looked as if I had been crying, she inspected my face and said 'No'. We left the room and walked back to court to listen to the rest of the judge's summing up for the day.

That night, when I arrived back at the apartment, I was completely drained and fell asleep for two hours. When I woke up I hurriedly got showered and dressed for dinner. Ali and I were having dinner with Megan Hunt from the Foreign Office.

During my stay in Darwin I had eaten in a little Italian restaurant called Giuseppe's several times. It's well known among my friends that pasta is my comfort food. I had invited Megan Hunt to eat with us there. The waitress was always very friendly and passed on messages of support to me that had been left by other diners. That night over dinner I helped to organise Ali's sister's hen party. Ali's sister Kathy was getting married the following week. Ali was in charge of organising the hen party but hadn't had time to as she had come to Darwin to support me. It was a welcome distraction and we came up with lots of ideas. The waiter got involved too and brought us out lots of cocktail books for us to get some ideas from.

At the end of the evening the waitress asked me to call in and see her on Friday, she wanted me to have one of their special pepper mills and was going to buy one for me, I told her that it really was not necessary but she insisted. I appreciate the kindness and support from the people that I had met in Darwin. One very unexpected outcome of my time in Darwin was that I fell in love with the place and grew fond of the people. I know I have made some friends for life.

* * *

The judge continued with his instruction on Friday morning. There were eighty-five witnesses and over three hundred exhibits that the jury had to consider.

At lunchtime after court had finished for the afternoon I stopped by Giuseppe's to collect my pepper mill and to say goodbye to the waitress. As I left the restaurant a table of people were looking up at me waving and smiling. It was Rex, Nannette and some others from the DPP, they were on their work Christmas lunch. It reminded me that I had missed my work Christmas party. I usually organised it but not this time. I planned to give Christmas a miss altogether this year.

As I walked back to the Marrakai I called in to St Mary's church and said a prayer. I lit two candles. As I started to leave I had a strange feeling. I felt like I had forgotten something, I couldn't think what. As I walked through the door I realised what I was missing, my friend Diane.

Ali was leaving to fly back to Sydney that night. She had to be back for her sister's party and wedding. It was looking more and more likely that I wouldn't be able to attend. It was a shame but I had to be in Darwin. I was actually content to be alone. It somehow felt fitting that I should end this journey alone, just as I had been alone on the Stuart Highway when it began.

Ali gave me two presents before she left. The first was a bottle of her favourite wine. The second was the Bernard Fanning CD. The CD title was 'Tea and Sympathy'. Ali and I couldn't help but think of Nannette, who had constantly been offering me cups of tea and sympathy throughout the trial. Ali played the CD and told me that one song summed up what she had heard everyone saying to me while she had been in Darwin. That song is called 'Wish you well'.

* * *

On Saturday the 10th of December I woke early and went for a swim. Because of the build-up to the Darwin wet season, the humidity was high and the days were scorching. The pool was the only place outside where I could be comfortable.

After my swim I walked back up to my apartment and took a shower. I was still being inundated by media requests and had been told by Lorelei that it would probably get worse before it got better, particularly with the end of the trial approaching. She had suggested I contact a media adviser to get instruction on handling all the attention. Though I was reluctant to have anything to do with the media, I valued Lorelei's advice and could see the wisdom in her suggestion. She had given me a name, Brian Tyson from a communications company in Sydney, and his number. While towelling my hair dry I decided I would make the call.

As soon as I told Brian who I was, he offered to give me strategic advice and told me that he would speak frankly to me about the media and how I should handle the attention at the conclusion of the trial. This was what I needed and I appreciated that. I began to warm to him. I knew that I would have to put my feelings about the media aside. That I may need to do things that I wasn't comfortable doing if I wanted to satisfy the public's curiosity. In doing so I hoped the media would leave me alone and I could be free to get on with my life. Brian suggested that we could meet for a couple of hours before court on Tuesday. As I put down the phone I felt like I was taking control of my life and it made me feel good.

Lorelei came to pick me up from my apartment and we drove over to her sister Dallas's house. We had arranged the night before that I would spend the day with Lorelei and her family. In a short amount of time I had grown very fond of Lorelei. I consider it the greatest honour to be welcomed into another person's home and family. We were greeted on arrival by two very excited and very cute dogs, Bintang and Buddy. Lorelei and I decided that we would give them both a wash. This was a source of great entertainment, because after managing to shampoo the dogs they ran off, chasing each other, covered in foam and Lorelei and I had to chase after them with the hose.

Afterwards we went to cool off in the pool. Dallas works for Qantas and is usually working shifts, but she had five days off from work. Sitting in the pool Dallas asked me if I would like her to be with me on the day of the verdict. We all imagined that it would be a day of anxious waiting. I was deeply touched by Dallas's offer. Other than the Falconio family, everyone else would be there because it was their job in one way or another. Dallas would be there to offer support to a friend. We drank a glass of wine in the pool and then ate dinner outside as more and more members of Lorelei's family arrived. It was wonderful to spend time with all of them and the normality of a family gathering was just what I needed before the final days of the trial.

* * *

Almost the first thing the court heard on Monday was Algie's objections to some of the judge's summing up. I listened in disbelief as Grant Algie disputed the judge's directions to the jury about trauma. I should have predicted that he would object to this, the judge's words had had such a powerful effect on me I could only think the jury would have felt the same. As I listened to Algie I thought he was foolish. The judge told Algie that he would not be altering his directions to the jury.

During one of the court adjournments that day Shaun telephoned me to ask if he and Rosey could stop by that evening to say goodbye. I had been focusing so much on the judge's summing up and the imminent verdict day that I hadn't stopped to think that soon I would be able to leave Darwin. It was only just dawning on me that I would have to say goodbye to people I had grown fond of.

In the afternoon the judge told the jury that he would be sending them out the next afternoon to consider their verdict. This news wasn't unexpected but to finally hear the judge confirm it stunned me and I think everyone else who was sitting in the courtroom. The entire trial, and for me and the Falconios, the last four and a half years, had been leading up to this moment.

It had been such a long process and I found it hard to believe that it was finally here.

Nine weeks of gruelling evidence, witnesses, cross-examinations, forensics experts and others, and now the jury would be considering all the evidence and passing judgment.

* * *

In the evening Rosey, Shaun and I went to the Lizard Bar for a few farewell drinks. It was hot and we sat outside around a table and reminisced about our shared experiences over the last nine weeks. I told them that I hadn't heard from Phil for a couple of weeks and said I was worried. As soon as I had spoken I thought how selfish I was being. Phil had given me a lot of his time and I concluded that he was most likely helping out someone else who was in more need of his support than me or, hopefully, spending time with his family. A small part of me did feel disappointed that Phil hadn't been in contact. He'd been a constant support in my life for the last eighteen months and I just wanted to talk to him.

Rosey and Shaun walked with me to my apartment building. Standing at the bottom of the driveway they both wished me all the best for the rest of the trial. Shaun told me to look after myself and I replied that I would try my very best.

I turned and walked up the drive towards the Marrakai. I didn't know what the future held for me, but I felt determined that I would do everything within my power to take care of myself.

But that would come later. We still had the verdict to come. For the Falconios and me, the wait was almost over. Four and a half years after Pete's life was brutally taken away and our lives were turned upside down, we were about to receive an outcome. An outcome that we prayed would bring justice for Pete.

19

Verdict Day

I couldn't sleep throughout the night. I tried desperately, but my mind was filled with 'what if'. I knew what Bradley John Murdoch had done. I had been there. I was convinced that he would be found unanimously guilty by the jury but what if he wasn't? I tormented myself. I tried to get some sleep. I knew that I had a big day ahead of me. I could hear my phone ringing in the living area, the melody echoing around the apartment. It was the early hours of the 13th of December 2005 and I didn't feel like speaking to anyone, so I let it ring. The apartment felt so big and empty. I'd been used to sharing it with my friends. I was conscious of being alone and I lay there, aware of every sound. I listened to the humming of the airconditioning and tried again to clear my mind and go to sleep. A frightening thought of a not-guilty verdict entered my head and I had a vision of Murdoch walking down the Supreme Courthouse steps, basking in the media spotlight, shouting obscenities at me and the Falconio family as we walked past.

I shuddered and sat upright. I didn't want to go to sleep if I was going to have nightmares and images like that. I got up and walked into the living area. I put on a CD, curled up on the sofa and lay in the dark looking out of the glass patio doors in front of me. Occasionally my phone would ring, disturbing the calm. I watched as darkness slowly turned into light and I could see the grey clouds across the sky. I watched, hypnotised, as rain poured down. I'm not a superstitious person but I couldn't help wondering if the grim weather was to be a reflection of my day. It had been glorious sunshine for almost the entire nine weeks of the trial.

On the way to the bedroom to get ready I picked up my phone and began to listen to my messages. The first message was the voice of a woman crying. I couldn't make out her words. Then the message ended. I was concerned and immediately felt guilty for ignoring my phone calls. I listened to the next message. It was the voice of the same woman but this time she sounded more composed. She introduced herself as Nicki, Phil Banton's wife. Now I really was concerned. Nicki explained in her message that Phil had been diagnosed with cancer and was in hospital. She said that she and Phil would be thinking about me today.

I felt every ounce of energy leave my body and I forced myself to get ready. I stood in the shower and cried and cried. I cried because Phil is a great and decent man, whom I care deeply for. He had helped me more than he would ever know. I cried because I wanted to put my arms around his wife and give her comfort, to somehow try to repay the support that Phil had given to me. I cried because the world is not always fair and I was thinking that this might not be the only devastating news I would get that day. I felt sorry for myself and started to think of how unfairly life had treated me.

But I couldn't wallow in my unhappiness or jump on a plane to comfort Phil's wife; I had to get to court. I used the make-up concealer that Sharon had bought for me. It works miracles under your eyes, concealing the tell-tale signs of a sleepless night or that you have been crying. I felt it necessary to at least try to make myself look presentable and as if I hadn't been crying, because I knew I would receive a lot of attention from the media. I didn't want them to know the turmoil I was in.

At 8.00 am, as previously arranged, Lorelei and her husband, Neville, came to pick me up. Brian Tyson was with them, sitting in the back seat. I tried not to let anyone know I was upset. Brian and I greeted each other formally and then we sat in silence as Neville drove us to the DPP. Once there Brian and I were given the use of a small vacant office.

Brian sat behind the desk and opened up his laptop. I pulled up a chair and sat across from him. Conscious of our limited time together before I had to go to court, Brian and I got down to business straightaway. There was no time for me to be shy. I had to push thoughts about Phil away and concentrate. It was good to have someone to talk to and get advice from about the media, and I showed him what I planned to say in the statement I was going to read out at the end of the trial.

At 9.45 am I was driven to court by Kelly, who works for the DPP, with Sergeant Megan Rowe. Kelly commented on the wet weather and mentioned that rain on your wedding day is considered lucky. This stuck in my mind. It was a very strange thing to say, especially because while I was preparing for this significant day, one of my friends had been preparing for a significant day too: her wedding day. Two significant days, so vastly different.

As our car pulled up outside the courthouse steps Megan warned me to walk carefully as the rain had made them slippery. There were as many journalists waiting there as there had been on the first day of the trial. I got out of the car and carefully began walking up the courthouse steps. My shoe, God knows how, became stuck on a step for a few seconds. I freed it by moving my foot and continued up the stairs. A fear stirred inside me. I thought that nothing was going to go right today.

Megan reassured me by saying that Rex Wild had slipped and almost fallen over on the wet steps earlier. I convinced myself in the lift on the way up to the first floor that these were in fact positive omens. If everything bad comes in threes, I'd already received my three, all before 10.00 am.

As I walked from the lift over to the seating area where I usually waited, I saw Rosey from the TRS dressed in his uniform. I was confused as I had said goodbye to him the night before. He informed me that the TRS were back acting as security again for the day. I was pleased to see a friendly face. I left Rosey to continue doing his job.

I made my way to the seating area and sat down alone. There were lots of people around but I wasn't really registering their presence. I kept thinking about Phil. I knew that he wouldn't want me to, and that made me think of him even more. When Nick arrived he could tell that there was something wrong but I didn't want to tell him. Nick persuaded me to go and have a chat with him in private. I explained to Nick how I was feeling and that the news from Phil's wife had put everything into perspective, that I didn't care anymore because a guilty verdict wouldn't bring Pete back. Nick was calm and sensitive but firmly reminded me that I did care. He agreed that it wouldn't bring Pete back, but we could achieve justice for him.

Nick and I walked back to the seating area. I sat back down again in the chair alone. Luciano and Joan had arrived. Luciano sat next to me and instinctively put his arm around me and gave me a cuddle. He softly asked me what was wrong. I eventually whispered to him that my friend was ill. He continued to cuddle me and I did feel a bit better.

At 10.00 am courtroom six opened and the judge continued his summing up. At 12.44 pm he finished and the last words the judge said to the six men and six women who made up the jury were: 'The verdicts, whether they be guilty or not guilty, must be unanimous. Would you please retire to consider your verdicts.'

* * *

Once the jury had left the courtroom, the Falconio family, Megan Hunt from the Foreign Office and I met with Brian Tyson at the DPP. Paul had agreed to support me and the whole family wanted to hear Brian's advice. We all crammed into the same small office that Brian and I had borrowed that morning. It was such a tight squeeze that if anyone wanted to enter or exit the room Paul and Nick had to stand up and move their chairs. I introduced Brian to everyone and explained that he had flown to Darwin to give me guidance on how best to deal with the immediate media attention. Even though I'd only met Brian that morning I liked him already, his manner was calm and professional. We spent the time talking about what the media would expect and Joan, Luciano, Nick and Paul listened to everything Brian said and accepted all his suggestions. At the end of the meeting Paul and Nick discussed with Brian what they would like to say while Joan focused on looking after me and asked me what I would like to do for dinner.

The meeting took up the entire lunchbreak and, though I wasn't feeling hungry, when Megan Hunt asked if I wanted anything from the shops I requested some fruit and Lucozade. My Mum had always given me Lucozade to drink whenever I was ill and I thought it would help me now. I needed that comfort and connection to my Mum.

It was time to head back to court and wait for the verdict. I set up camp at the far end of the hall. There were two sets of lounges and tables, a few metres apart. We occupied them all.

Sitting at my table were the Falconio family, Dallas, Lorelei, Megan Hunt, Nannette Hunter and Brian Tyson. The TRS were sitting around the other table between us and the media and Murdoch's group. Everyone was feeling anxious and dealt with it in their own way. No one stayed still and I watched Nick and Paul pace the huge hallway. My hands felt clammy and the knot in my stomach grew.

People were scattered throughout the upstairs hallway, waiting; journalists and members of the public, some of whom had sat in the public gallery many times throughout the trial. Some journalists sat on the steps that led to the bathrooms and the media room, playing Scrabble. I walked past them from time to time on the way to wash my hands to rinse away the clamminess.

The informal divisions in the hall area still remained in place. Invisible barriers separated myself, the Falconio family and our team of support from the journalists who remained in their area. The general public and Jan Pittman kept to their side.

I sat quietly at the table and listened to the small-talk taking place around me without really concentrating. I was so disconnected it was like flicking through radio stations. Someone spoke of all their Christmas shopping still left to do, someone about their forthcoming holiday, others about family members. I felt disorientated and tried to snap out of it by joining in the conversation.

Lorelei's sister Tanya had told me and her family a joke a few days before, which her cousin's four-year-old daughter had told her. The joke was funny but it was her impersonation of the four year old, who spoke with an endearing child's tone, and her actions that had me in stitches. I asked Lorelei to repeat the joke to me. To this day, whenever I feel down I just think of this and an instant smile spreads across my face.

Lorelei retold the joke and it was so ridiculous I had to laugh despite myself.

The hours passed slowly. Dallas produced a pack of cards for us to play with. I hadn't played cards in years and could barely remember how to play anything. I assumed that as it was Dallas's idea to bring a pack of cards, she must enjoy playing and could teach me a few games. I soon found out to my amusement that Dallas hates playing cards and didn't know how to play a single game. She just thought that I might have liked to play to pass away the time. I was touched by her thoughtfulness and we decided to give it a go. I could remember vaguely how to play Gin Rummy. We played a couple of games but couldn't focus and the games felt long and drawn out. We abandoned the cards for the time being.

At around 6.00 pm a message spread across the upstairs hall that the jury had a question of the judge. Everyone began filing back into courtroom six. I felt so sick and anxious that I couldn't decide whether or not to go in. But I had to. I had to hear their query for myself.

I entered the crowded courtroom, where all the seats were taken and many people congregated near the doorway. I took a seat that had been reserved for me. The atmosphere in the courtroom felt different, so much so that I barely recognised it as the same place. The air was thick with tension.

The judge spoke directly to the jury.

HIS HONOUR: Ladies and gentlemen, you have asked for clarification of a guilty verdict for murder without a body. The first thing I need to say to you is that the absence of a body is not a bar to a guilty verdict of murder. The critical question for you to consider on this issue is whether on the whole of the evidence, not withstanding that you do not have a body, you are nevertheless satisfied that Peter Falconio was killed that night.

That is the first question. Are you satisfied from all of the evidence that Peter Falconio was killed that night? If you are not satisfied that Peter Falconio was killed that night then obviously the Crown has failed to prove a case of murder and you would acquit the accused.

If, however, from the whole of the evidence you are satisfied that Peter Falconio was killed that night, the next question is whether you are satisfied that he was killed by the accused.

If you are not satisfied he was killed by the accused then of course the accused is to be acquitted.

If you are satisfied that Peter Falconio was killed by the accused then you must consider whether the Crown has proved the four elements of the offence that are set out in the aide-memoire for you.

And as I said to you in my remarks, the issue that has been fought in this trial, or the two issues, are whether you can be satisfied that Peter Falconio was killed and if you are satisfied that he was killed, whether you are satisfied whether the Crown has proved that it was the accused who killed him.

If you are satisfied that the accused killed Peter Falconio, the elements of the offence set out in the aide-memoire you might think, would not cause you any difficulty. But they must be proven. So if you were satisfied that the accused killed Peter Falconio then you ask the questions, has the Crown proved those four ingredients that are set out in the aide-memoire? Does that answer your question?

Thank you, if you require any further assistance just let me know. Would you now retire again.

Everyone filed out of the courtroom, many whispering to each other their interpretation of the jury's question. I felt hopeful. I viewed the jury's question as a positive indication as to what direction they were taking. I sat back at the table and listened to some more small-talk. When I couldn't stand to listen to any more I went and walked beside Nick who was pacing up and down the floor.

At 7.00 pm a message was sent around the hall to say that the jury were retiring for dinner and a verdict would not be given during the next hour. The floor soon began to clear. The Falconio family were going back to their apartment at the Seville for dinner and invited me to go with them. I didn't want to leave the building. I knew that nothing was going to happen in the next hour but I wanted to stay there. Luciano tried to persuade me to go with them but I remained firm and stayed behind. I surprised myself when I did this as usually I can't say no to Luciano.

Shaun Gill from the TRS stayed with me as he was working as my security. Megan Hunt and Nannette Hunter also chose to stay and keep me company. The huge hall was empty and peaceful and I appreciated the wide-open space and the privacy. I walked the length of the floor, which passed by the jury room. Behind that door were twelve people who would decide whether justice would be served.

I continued to feel anxious and my anxiety increased as the hours dragged on. I'd felt hopeful immediately after the jury's question but that hope began to diminish as time passed by. I sat through the dinner hour reading through my media statement, talking to Shaun, Megan and Nannette, and occasionally getting up to pace the floor.

By 8.00 pm everyone had returned and the waiting continued. Everyone would startle at the sound of a door opening or a person running across the floor. On one occasion Anthony Elliott broke out in a run just to tease everybody for his own personal amusement. I'm sure he meant well but no one thought it was terribly funny.

Rex Wild came over to sit beside me briefly. I asked him if he would like to see the final draft of my victim impact statement. He said that he would and when he finished reading it was visibly moved. He told me it was very powerful and asked me if I was going to read it out. I knew I couldn't. It would be too difficult. I wouldn't be able to get through to the end. It would be too emotional. He said that he would also find it difficult to read, but agreed to do it.

The minutes ticked by slowly. Every so often the jurors would be led out by a sheriff's officer for the short walk from their jury room to their own private balcony, I presumed to have a cigarette.

When I looked outside through the floor-to-ceiling glass windows at either end of the hallway I could see it was dark. It was a reminder of how long we had been waiting. In all the times that I had imagined this day, I'd never imagined it running late into the night. I just hoped that the jury would be able to give a verdict that day. I couldn't bear the thought of another sleepless night of anxiety and another day like today. Someone had commented earlier that a jury can take days to decide their verdict but I hadn't really considered how this would affect everyone waiting.

The later it got, the more concerned I became. I tormented myself. I felt that after hearing all the evidence over the weeks the jury surely would have made their minds up by now. I felt that their long deliberations were an indication that they somehow were in disagreement with one another. I had to stop myself from these negative thoughts so I initiated another game of Gin Rummy with Dallas. I was willing to do anything to pass the time and prevent myself from having to make or listen to any more small-talk. Brian Tyson joined in. Despite my lack of concentration I was winning every game. I joked that we should leave and go to the casino.

At 8.45 pm word spread that the judge was going to enquire how the jury were getting on, and to find out whether arrangements needed to be made for overnight accommodation for them. I felt despondent. It looked like we weren't going to get a verdict that day after all. The entire floor entered the courtroom. I sat in the second row between Paul and Megan Hunt, behind Joan, Luciano and Nick. There was a discussion between counsel and the Chief Justice as to a unanimous verdict and a majority verdict. In the Northern Territory, in the event of a hung jury, the law enables a conviction through a majority verdict. The Chief Justice explained his view that a majority verdict should not be considered inferior to a unanimous verdict, but I wanted a unanimous verdict. I always had.

Grant Algie talked of the length of time that the jury had been deliberating for, that consideration should now be given to their state of mind and fatigue. Algie commented on a hotel for the jury to retire to for the evening and suggested we resume in the morning. I hoped to God that this would not be the case but it was looking increasingly likely.

The Chief Justice asked for the jury to be brought in.

The court assistant stepped over to the door that was only a few metres away on my right. The assistant opened the interconnecting door and gave three hard knocks on the jury room door as is the tradition. There was no response. There was a long pause before the door opened. I had thought that it would have been impossible for the tension in the room to heighten but it hit the roof in the few minutes that it took for the jury to respond by opening the door. I felt everyone become on edge. I heard people whispering, 'This is it', 'Verdict.' The Chief Justice appeared unaware.

The first juror walked through the door clutching a piece of paper. He was a middle-aged man who had been at the end of the front row in the jury box nearest to me throughout the trial. He'd always appeared conscientious, taking notes and examining exhibits carefully. I had speculated to myself that he may perhaps be the foreperson. He seated himself in the foreperson's chair. The other jury members sat in their usual seats.

My whole body became stiff and I could barely breathe. Tears stung my eyes. Every second felt like an hour. Every movement appeared to be in slow-motion and I just wanted to fast-forward.

The Chief Justice seemed oblivious to what I could see, feel, sense, and oblivious to what everyone else had concluded.

> HIS HONOUR: Ladies and gentlemen, I have interrupted your deliberations because you've been at it for a long time now, something in the order of eight hours in your deliberations and of course you've been here at work, so to speak, since 10 o'clock this morning, it's a very long day. If you wish at this time we can . . . sorry.

The Chief Justice had been interrupted by the sheriff's officer who whispered something to him. The judge then turned again to the jury.

> HIS HONOUR: Mr Foreman, do I take it you're the foreman, sir?
>
> THE FOREMAN: Yes, I am.
>
> HIS HONOUR: All right. Do I understand from what I've just been told by the Sheriff's Officer that although I've called you in to say do you want more time tonight or do you want to call a halt, that you have in fact reached your verdicts?
>
> THE FOREMAN: Yes, we have.

> HIS HONOUR: Is that on all three counts?
>
> THE FOREMAN: Yes, it is.
>
> HIS HONOUR: Thank you.
>
> Now would you please listen very carefully to the questions that my associate will ask you. She will ask you first on each count whether you are unanimously agreed upon your verdicts.
>
> Do I take it that you have unanimous verdicts on all counts?
>
> THE FOREMAN: Yes, we do.
>
> HIS HONOUR: All right, thank you. Would you just answer the questions that my associate puts to you?

Paul put his arm around me and I buried my face in his chest. Megan Hunt reached out for my free hand and held it tightly. I held my breath and closed my eyes. I'd been waiting for this moment for almost five years. Paul gripped me tighter.

> THE ASSOCIATE: Foreperson, please stand.
>
> Ladies and gentlemen of the jury, are you unanimously agreed upon your verdict?
>
> THE FOREMAN: Yes, we are.
>
> THE ASSOCIATE: In relation to count 1, that on 14 July 2001 near Barrow Creek in the Northern Territory of Australia, the accused murdered Peter Marco Falconio.
>
> Do you find the accused: guilty or not guilty?
>
> THE FOREMAN: Guilty.

I heard the word 'guilty' and instantly the tension released from my body. I still held my breath, keeping my eyes closed, my face buried in Paul's chest. Megan continued to squeeze my hand. I could feel the eyes of the media and public on me. I wanted to shut out the world for a few moments to absorb what I had just heard, what had just happened, to deal with my immediate emotions in privacy.

The journalists hadn't expected a verdict to be given when they had taken their seats in the courtroom. They were sitting near the door and didn't have a good view of me. Brian later told me that the journalists were straining themselves to look at me. One journalist had a better viewing position than the others and other journalists asked him if I was showing any emotion. He dutifully relayed to the others my reaction.

The words that followed were a blur. The only words I registered were my full name spoken by the associate. These words kept pounding out and the response given back by the foreperson 'guilty' repeatedly being reinforced. I hadn't realised that there were so many counts. To me each one was important. Of course the murder charge was the ultimate, but he had committed serious crimes against me, those charges, I believe, are often forgotten by others, but I can't forget and to hear the repeated word 'guilty' gave me some satisfaction that I had gained justice for myself too.

THE ASSOCIATE: Is that the verdict of you all?

THE FOREMAN: Yes, it is.

THE ASSOCIATE: In relation to count 2, that on 14 July 2001 near Barrow Creek in the Northern Territory of Australia, the accused deprived Joanne Rachael Lees of her personal liberty.

Do you find the accused: guilty or not guilty?

THE FOREMAN: Guilty.

THE ASSOCIATE: Is that the verdict of you all?

THE FOREMAN: Yes, it is.

THE ASSOCIATE: In relation to count 3, that on 14 July 2001 near Barrow Creek in the Northern Territory of Australia, the accused unlawfully assaulted Joanne Rachael Lees.

> Do you find the accused: guilty or not guilty?
>
> THE FOREMAN: Guilty.
>
> THE ASSOCIATE: Is that the verdict of you all?
>
> THE FOREMAN: Yes, it is.
>
> THE ASSOCIATE: In relation to the circumstances of aggravation, namely that Joanne Rachael Lees suffered bodily harm.
>
> Do you find the accused: guilty or not guilty?
>
> THE FOREMAN: Guilty.
>
> THE ASSOCIATE: Is that the verdict of you all?
>
> THE FOREMAN: Yes, it is.
>
> THE ASSOCIATE: In relation to the circumstance of aggravation, namely that Joanne Rachael Lees is a female and Bradley John Murdoch is a male.
>
> Do you find the accused: guilty or not guilty?
>
> THE FOREMAN: Guilty.
>
> THE ASSOCIATE: Is that the verdict of you all?
>
> THE FOREMAN: Yes, it is.
>
> THE ASSOCIATE: In relation to the circumstance of aggravation, namely that Joanne Rachael Lees was threatened with an offensive weapon namely a gun.
>
> Do you find the accused: guilty or not guilty?
>
> THE FOREMAN: Guilty.
>
> THE ASSOCIATE: Is that the verdict of you all?
>
> THE FOREMAN: Yes, it is.
>
> HIS HONOUR: Thank you, Mr Foreman, would you just sit down.

I composed myself and sat upright. I broke my hand free from Megan's grasp. Sitting in the row in front of me, Joan, Luciano and Nick turned around to face me and each squeezed my hand. I became conscious of journalists leaving the courtroom to report the verdict to their editors. I was overcome with the need to contact my friends and family, to break the news to them personally. I turned to Paul and told him that I was just going to make a phone call. Paul softly replied that I should stay, that I would want to hear what was said next. He was, of course, right and I am so glad that he encouraged me to stay.

HIS HONOUR: For what it's worth, can I say with respect to your verdicts that I entirely agree with your verdicts.

In the future, and I'm repeating what I said during my summing up, do not look back with second thoughts of any sort. You will never in the future be able to recreate the circumstances and the knowledge that you've had in that jury room. Details will fade, you might not think so today, but they will, memories change.

There will be reports in the media of one form or another, and I understand that there are a number of people running around preparing books. I understand that one of the books is supposed to be published within the next forty-eight hours. Well, one can only wonder about the in-depth analysis of the evidence and everything that's occurred in this court if something is to be published that quickly.

You are the ones, as I said, who know precisely what went on and others do not. You are the ones who are in the position of having to make the judgment others are not, they are approaching it from completely different perspectives.

The judge then adjourned the court.

Everyone stood up to leave. I watched as the people I had seen regularly sitting in the courtroom congratulated the Falconio family. They then turned and tentatively congratulated me from a respectful distance, perhaps they were unsure of how I was feeling emotionally. I hadn't ever spoken to them before. I had no idea who they all were but they were here and had shared this moment too.

Jane Munday, the court-appointed media liaison officer, offered me her congratulations. I had never had much contact with her, all my dealings had been with Lorelei. I gave her a big hug. I looked at Nannette and she had tears in her eyes.

It had been arranged for us to wait in a jury room, the one I'd used to wait in during the committal hearing. I'd spent many anxious times waiting in that room during all the delays throughout the committal hearing. I thought that the room felt completely different now. On reflection I now realise that it was me who felt completely different.

Lots of people gathered in the room, the Falconio family, Megan Hunt from the Foreign Office, Nannette Hunter, Lorelei, Jane Munday, Shaun from the TRS and Brian Tyson. There may well have been others. The room felt busy, people periodically coming in and out. I was conscious of organising taking place around me and I felt disorientated, all of a sudden everything was happening so fast.

Nick asked me for a hug. I felt a pang of guilt that I hadn't hugged him already and that he'd needed to ask.

I sat down at the round table and sent a pre-written text message to several friends. The message simply read 'GUILTY!'

Once I had done that, I leant forward and rested my head against the table, closing my eyes, allowing myself a moment to reflect upon what had just happened.

Shaun interrupted my thoughts, declaring that his job wasn't finished until he had taken us all safely away from the building. Feeling like I had just been woken up from a dream I raised my head. My job wasn't finished either. I had to stand at the top of the Supreme Courthouse steps and read out my media statement in front of the many journalists and their cameras. I suddenly felt very tired.

Jane and Lorelei left the room to organise the media outside, and Shaun left with them to ensure that the media would be standing a respectable distance away, and that we would have a clear pathway to leave after we had delivered our statement. Paul and Nick didn't appear daunted in the slightest about issuing a statement; they both wandered in and out of the room, restless with pent-up energy.

Joan, Luciano, Megan Hunt and Brian Tyson stayed with me. They encouraged me to stand in front of them and practise reading out my media statement. I tried but it felt unnatural, and feeling frustrated I stopped. I queried Brian as to whether I could shorten my statement, but I knew what his answer would be. I also knew that I wanted to say every word that was on the page that I held in my hand, it just felt overwhelming. I read it aloud one final time to Joan and Luciano. When I had finished Joan said simply, 'Beautiful'. That was the only encouragement I needed to hear. I drew a big smile across the bottom of the page and knew that I would be smiling when I'd finished reading it.

It wasn't long before everyone returned and filled the room. I was informed that the media had positioned themselves and were ready for us. I asked Jane Munday to take some photos for me using my camera, which she agreed to do. I then asked Megan Hunt if she would film us on my camcorder. Megan was more than happy to do this. It was time.

I walked out of the jury room into the vast empty hall. It looked like the aftermath of a party. Paper cups and food wrappers lay strewn across the tables. I walked steadily, slowly, with everyone else across the floor to the top of the staircase. As I walked down the stairs Brian gave me some final words of advice, 'Speak slowly, keep your page low and look up from time to time.' We reached the bottom of the staircase and turned right to make our way towards the glass front doors, and as we did, a sea of flashlights lit up the dark night outside.

'Oh my God!' I carried on walking towards the flashing cameras. Brian continued giving me final words of advice and encouragement: 'Remember – project.' I queried what he meant by 'project' but I knew really. I smiled back at Brian as he gave me an explanation. I was just stalling, delaying the inevitable.

The Falconio family and I reached the front doors and walked through them into the hot Darwin air. Members of the media shouted for us to come closer to a rope barrier. Standing between Paul and Nick I lifted up my page and was about to read aloud but I stopped. I looked down and saw all the microphones and camera lenses pointing at me. In the past, Phil and I had often spoken of this moment; he considered this to be my time to stand tall. I paused and reminisced on all those difficult and emotional times leading up to the trial and the way Phil had supported me. I almost heard him tell me to just be myself. I felt proud of who I was and what I had done. I stood there and absorbed the moment.

Nick noticed my hesitation, perhaps interpreting it as nerves, and gentlemanly offered to read his statement out first. I replied firmly, 'No, I'll go first.' I took slow, deep breaths just as Libby had advised in her recent text message, just as she had advised four and a half years previously when I read out a media statement in Alice Springs.

Paul had his arm around my waist and my free arm was casually around his back. I appreciated his support. I held up the page and began reading out my statement; I proudly spoke Libby and Phil's names. When I reached the smiley face at the bottom of the page I looked up, spotted Lorelei among the crowd and gave her a wink. I remained on the steps between Paul and Nicholas as they each read out a short statement. Journalists began shouting out questions which Luciano politely answered. I had to stop myself from making a face when one journalist asked whether we could now have 'closure'. I hate that word. Another question was whether we thought that we would ever find Pete. Luciano replied, 'The Northern Territory – you know what it is.' That short sentence summed everything up for me. Anyone who has visited the Northern Territory will understand. The Northern Territory is more than fives times the size of the United Kingdom. It is a big space in which to keep a secret.

On that note I decided to leave. I felt that I had done enough to satisfy the media. Luciano was still answering their questions. I slowly released myself from Paul and told him that I was leaving. I stepped backwards feeling slightly disorientated, wondering which way would be best to leave. I heard Shaun call out my name. He gave me instructions to walk down the left-hand side of the steps to an awaiting car. I did as he said and climbed into the back of the familiar TRS car. There were two members of the TRS in the front and they asked me where I wanted to go. I hadn't previously thought about it. I decided I needed to change out of the courtroom clothes that I was wearing. I asked to be driven back to the Marrakai apartments. For a moment I thought that I didn't have a key to get into the apartment, as I had left my bag behind at the courthouse with someone and I couldn't even remember who with. I needn't have worried as someone had considerately put it in the car for me.

The TRS drove me to the apartments and parked outside. I thanked them and began opening the car door. One of them asked me whether I would like them to wait for me. I hadn't made any plans. I felt dizzy at the rapid speed with which everything seemed to be moving all of a sudden. The last few days had been long and drawn-out; and now suddenly everything was moving too fast, my life felt like a whirlwind. I told the TRS that if they were happy to wait I would rush and get changed and decide where I wanted to go. I knew that I wanted to be with the Falconio family.

As I entered my apartment I received a phone call from Superintendent Colleen Gwynne, she said that she and Shaun wanted to drop by, return my cameras to me, and have a celebratory drink with me.

They arrived quickly. Colleen handed over my cameras. They waited while I freshened up and were both sitting in the lounge area as I entered the room. They said that I'd just been on the TV news. I told them that it wasn't necessary for me to watch the news report, because I had been there.

I called Joan to see where she was, she told me that they were all in the bar at the Seville Hotel and to come and join them. Colleen, Shaun and I left to make our way there.

As I walked into the bar I saw the Falconio family sitting straight ahead at a table. Out of the corner of my eye I saw two sad, lone figures sitting at the bar with a bottle in an ice bucket placed on the bar between them. It was Algie and Twiggs. I was taken aback at first to see them, so I immediately asked the Falconio family if they felt comfortable. They didn't mind, after all they had been sharing the same hotel with Murdoch's defence team for the entire trial. I didn't care either. This was Darwin and I knew by now that your path inevitably crossed with everybody else's.

During the course of the night members of the prosecution team and the investigation team dropped by to join us for a drink. We talked and ordered drinks.

When everyone had a drink in their hand, Joan stood and proposed a toast.

'To Peter.'

20

Twenty-eight years

I woke up on the 15th of December 2005 and felt different. I felt a sense of freedom. I had almost finished the job that I had come to Darwin to do. I lay wide awake in bed staring up at the ceiling, thinking of the endless opportunities I had, of all the things that I wanted to achieve but had put off until the trial was over. I thought of all the conversations that I'd had over the years with my friends about how I could start living my life again, once the trial was over. There would be nothing to hold me back, no commitments in Australia. My mind was now clear to think of things other than Bradley John Murdoch and the trial. That time was only hours away. I felt happy and light. I sprang out of bed, excited. I could leave Darwin today. I could go to visit my friends in Sydney. I could go anywhere and do anything that I wanted to.

I showered and dressed for my final attendance in court. I'd dressed for court a great number of times during the past ten weeks but as I got ready this day I felt none of the anguish I'd felt on all the previous occasions. I had given Paul all of my court uniforms to take home to the UK, except for one skirt and one top. Looking into the empty wardrobe made me feel good. It verified the fact that today was the final day of this long, exhausting and emotional journey.

I was picked up and driven to the Supreme Court by Sergeant Megan Rowe. There were a lot of media congregated on the courthouse steps waiting to film and photograph me and other people. For a brief moment I thought about the time when my shoe had become stuck for a few seconds on a step. Normally incidents like that do not bother me, but when you've got an audience with cameras, it does make you feel more self-conscious. I voiced my concern to Megan and her response was light-hearted but perfect. If my shoe were to become stuck again, I should just simply take them off and leave them there.

I stepped out of the car and walked faultlessly up the steps, photographers and cameramen standing either side of me. I was immediately greeted by Nannette Hunter from Victim Support. She had in her hand what I believed was my victim impact statement. It required my signature before it could be presented to the court and read out by Rex Wild. I signed it and left to go upstairs to courtroom six for the very last time.

As I stepped into the hall on the first floor, I could instantly see Dallas and Lorelei's warm smiles. Dallas had kindly offered to sit with me during the sentencing. For many years I had dealt with things on my own, hiding my emotions, never asking for help, convincing myself that I didn't need any. I know that I can get through anything on my own, but all those weeks of the trial had taught me that I didn't have to cope alone and that it was a whole lot easier with the support of my friends and others. It was the little things: just to hold my hand, tell me a joke, to give me a hug, a smile, and to listen.

The judge, being aware of the media interest, had made the decision to allow one TV camera into the courtroom to film his sentencing remarks, the footage was to be pooled amongst all the media outlets.

Rex Wild started by reading out my victim impact statement. As soon as he began I suddenly felt shivery. I wrapped my arms around my body to warm myself and to conceal my trembling. As Rex continued to read I realised that he was reading an old draft copy. How had that happened? Nannette must have printed an old draft from her computer instead of using the latest original copy that I had handed to her the day before. I was disappointed because I thought that the media may misinterpret one or two sentences, but it had been read out now and there was nothing that I could do. In the scheme of things it wasn't such a big deal.

Here is what I had wanted to be heard:

VICTIM IMPACT STATEMENT
NAME OF VICTIM: JOANNE LEES
NAME OF DEFENDANT: BRADLEY JOHN MURDOCH
OFFENCE COMMITTED: 14 JULY 2001

Harm Suffered as a Result of the Crime

The magnitude of the impact that this crime has had on me, my relationships, family and friends is impossible to convey in this short statement.

On the night this crime occurred, I thought I was going to be raped and murdered. I was terrified and extremely distressed when I was hiding, as I thought I would never see my family again, and no one would know what happened to Pete and me. I also felt that

Pete was very close but that I couldn't do anything to help him. This made me feel helpless and guilty.

I have suffered the loss of the person who knew me the best and loved me the most. Pete was the person who encouraged me to achieve and to be strong and a better person. He was the one I was to travel the world with and share new experiences.

I was with Pete all of my adult life. I was 22 when I met him. We looked forward to visiting new places and sharing experiences with each other. In losing Pete, I have lost some of the opportunity to share family life with the Falconios such as shared Christmases and family dinners.

Pete was in the prime of his life: professionally successful, fit and healthy, loved and popular. This crime ended our dreams of travel, marriage, children – a future. I never imagined not being with him and not sharing my life with him.

Much of my life has been closed down since this crime happened. I have had to delay University studies because of the requirement to travel to Australia to give evidence on two occasions. This has involved me being absent from the UK for extended periods.

There have been related difficulties for me in terms of employment. I have been able only to take on employment which did not involve dealing with the public as people's curiosity has made my life very difficult. Prior to this, I had been working with an international travel agency but I could not maintain that employment because of the notoriety associated with this crime. I have also been unable to make long-term commitments to employment due to the need for me to travel to Australia. There have been substantial financial implications as well.

Some aspects of the investigative process were hurtful and insensitive, as well as causing me considerable anxiety at a time when I had been through an experience that can only be described as horrific.

The massive intrusion of the media into my life has had devastating effects. I have had to move house eight times. I have experienced being on the train and seeing pictures of my face on the front page of people's newspapers. It is all so invasive. I have been watched and followed.

My mother was very distressed with all the media coverage and the impact it had on her and me.

People have to be wary of becoming friends with me because they might find themselves in the paper. This makes forming new friendships and maintaining existing ones is a continuing challenge.

I have visible scars from the physical injuries I received on that night. They are fading with time. The emotional scars, however, remain.

I am stronger, wiser, less naive.

I am sceptical, untrusting, fearful and heartbroken.

It is lonely being me.

Immediately after Rex Wild had finished reading my statement he read out Joan's victim impact statement.

VICTIM IMPACT STATEMENT
NAME OF VICTIM: JOAN FALCONIO
NAME OF DEFENDANT: BRADLEY JOHN MURDOCH
OFFENCE COMMITTED: 14 JULY 2001

Peter was a very kind and caring person. He always had time to listen to people. He was popular and outgoing and made friends easily. He also had a wonderful sense of fun.

Peter was bright and intelligent and had worked hard for his university degree. He had worked in construction management in the south of England before leaving for Australia in November 2000.

I spoke to Peter for the last time on the 13th July 2001. We had a lovely talk together; he was laughing and joking – making plans as he always did. Joanne was beside him and I could hear her laughing. They sounded so happy.

Little more than twenty-four hours later our lives changed forever.

On the 15th July 2001 the telephone rang. Two English backpackers had been ambushed on the Stuart Highway just north of a place called Barrow Creek. A male of 28 and a female of 27. The female was safe, her boyfriend was missing.

I knew Peter and Joanne were on that road but didn't want to believe it was them. I prayed it wasn't.

Two hours later the phone rang again – *it was them*. Peter was gone. There was a pool of blood on the road. I fell to my knees.

I could never describe to you the depth of my feelings, and what I tell you next will only touch the surface.

The torment and *constant* physical pain never left my body for months. The images of what had happened to Peter were always in my head – the not knowing was unbearable.

I suffered the most awful panic and anxiety attacks. I never knew mental and physical pain could be so relentless.

Days merged into weeks; weeks into months. I honestly thought I would die and many times I wanted to.

I had to constantly see my sons or check on them that they were safe.

Our family was always a close one. But the pressure we were under was immense. At times we were torn apart. You walk on egg shells each not wanting to hurt or upset the other. Sometimes the tension was so great I thought our marriage would collapse.

The press were intrusive and invaded our privacy. They failed to focus and report the facts, preferring to print articles that were irrelevant and detracted from the crime itself.

Luciano, my sons and I came to Australia nearly ten weeks ago to see justice done for the murder of Peter.

The trial has been long and very harrowing.

We have listened to the evidence and have no doubt the jury have made the right decision.

We hope the sentence given to Murdoch will reflect the brutality of the crime he committed and of the life he took.

The pain will never go from me. I think of Peter every minute of every day.

He was only twenty-eight years old and had so much living left to do.

It was powerful, moving and heartfelt. I wanted to break down and cry. I took slow, deep breaths to stop myself.

The judge adjourned the court until 11.00 am, a break of half an hour. Dallas and I sat in the hall and after a while Dallas said that she was going outside on to the balcony for a cigarette. I told her I'd keep her company. I'd never been out on to the balcony before. It was positioned on the opposite side of the hall to where I had always waited. There were a few journalists standing smoking on the balcony and they looked surprised to see me walk past them. It felt good to get some fresh air and to feel the warm outside air. The airconditioning in the courtroom was fierce and I often felt cold.

We stood out there and discussed my departure. Dallas and her husband both worked for Qantas. I wanted to leave as soon as possible and Dallas agreed that it would be best if I left that day. She was concerned for my wellbeing but was also conscious that many flights out of Darwin were almost full – it was approaching Christmas and half the town were leaving for holidays. I didn't have a flight booked because I had not known when the verdict would be given and what day sentencing would take place. We decided that straight after the judge had finished his sentencing we would leave and enquire about a flight.

At 11.00 am we went back into the courtroom and listened to Chief Justice Brian Martin sentence Bradley John Murdoch.

Listening to Justice Martin address Murdoch had a profound effect on me.

JUSTICE MARTIN: Having mentioned the effects of your crime, I need to add something about the particular effects upon Ms Lees. From the calm and detached atmosphere of this courtroom it is difficult to imagine the true extent of the terror that you inflicted upon Ms Lees. Although Ms Lees did her best to describe those effects during the course of her evidence and in her victim impact statement, I doubt that any description is capable of fully conveying the true extent of the trauma and terror that you imposed upon her. It must have been close to the worst nightmare imaginable. Unlike you, Ms Lees displayed considerable courage.

For Ms Lees, the trauma did not end with her escape. The evidence at the trial and her victim impact statement have touched upon subsequent events, but again it is difficult to fully appreciate the stress associated with the subsequent investigation and the enormous media attention.

The extent and impact of that attention cannot be visited upon you because, ordinarily, such attention would not be expected as a consequence of the crimes you committed. However, the fact remains that the ordeal for Ms Lees has continued long after the events.

It cannot be left unsaid that the manner in which you have conducted your defence has been an aggravating factor for Ms Lees and the family of Peter Falconio. You explored with Ms Lees in the public forum of the preliminary examination events in Sydney that were utterly irrelevant and served no useful purpose except to embarrass Ms Lees by endeavouring to cast a shadow over her reputation.

At trial, in the face of a powerful Crown case, you endeavoured to darken that shadow to the point of suggesting to the jury that not only was Ms Lees an unreliable witness, but she was not telling the truth about the disappearance of Mr Falconio. You pursued the idea that Mr Falconio is still alive and the conduct of your defence was such as to convey the clear innuendo that Ms Lees was implicated in Mr Falconio's disappearance. By their verdicts, the jury rejected those assertions and suggestions. I, too, reject those suggestions.

These words, publicly spoken by a man for whom I have a great deal of respect and admiration, counteracted every negative article written about me.

I held my breath as Justice Martin declared Murdoch's sentence.

JUSTICE MARTIN: I am satisfied that by reason of the objective and subjective factors affecting the relative seriousness of your crime, a longer non-parole period than twenty years is warranted. In that situation the legislation provides that I may fix a longer non-parole period. In other words, my discretion to fix a longer non-parole period is enlivened. All of the factors to which I have referred must be weighed in determining whether to fix a longer non-parole period. In arriving at a period, I have borne in mind the advanced age at which you will become eligible for parole and the real prospect that you will die in gaol.

I fix a non-parole period of twenty-eight years, commencing on 10 November 2003.

Would you please remove the prisoner.

Twenty-eight years. That was the age Pete was when he was murdered.

The judge didn't look at Murdoch as he spoke these words. Nor did I. I was looking at the Chief Justice and replaying, 'Would you please remove the prisoner,' over and over. I liked the sound of that. In six short words it was all over. Swiftly and clinically, that man was removed from my life. Just like that. Gone. I used to hate him. Now I feel nothing and never have to think of him again.

* * *

Courtroom six emptied quickly, as did the Supreme Courthouse. All that was left for me to do was to walk down the courthouse steps, past the waiting photographers and film crews, for the final time.

As I stood in the hall with Joan, Luciano and Nick, members of the prosecution team each said goodbye. I'd had limited contact with them, they had always upheld professional boundaries. I am grateful to them for the part that they played in gaining a conviction against Bradley John Murdoch. I may never have fully expressed my gratitude to them, so I would like to now. I would also like to describe how I often felt they were doing their job in their chosen profession. Nearly everyone I met was being paid to do a job and that was why they were there. I'm well aware that careers could be enhanced in prosecuting Murdoch. I wasn't there through choice. I was there because a crime had been committed against Pete and me. It doesn't get much more personal than that. I'm very aware that the investigation and trial consumed so many people's lives, but it was their work. It is what they do. But this was my life. For me and the Falconio family this was something we had to do. The Falconios were there to find justice for Pete. So was I. But I also wanted it for myself.

I will not apologise for being a strong person. I have had to be, otherwise I would not be here. I will not apologise for being sceptical and guarded, for I have learnt to be. I just want you to understand, this was my life.

The courthouse was the emptiest that I had ever seen it. I was glad of the peace and quiet. I took my time before leaving. I wanted to look around the building one final time. I walked slowly down the steps from the first floor to the ground floor. I was about to leave the building when I remembered the warm, friendly ladies, Poppy and her mum, who worked in Rumpole's cafe. I had to say goodbye to them. I told Nannette where I was going and that I wouldn't be long. The cafe was empty and the two women were preparing to close. I walked down through the cafe with my camcorder filming (for my own personal memories) and they greeted me, as friendly as they always had been. I thanked them for all the lunches they'd provided me and my friends over the weeks. I cooed over Poppy's babies then said my final goodbye and left. I was keeping people waiting.

I caught up with Nannette and the others and we walked slowly through the building. I did some filming of the large mosaic floor, which I'd always admired, and apologised to the others for taking my time but told them that I was going to be a little while longer.

I realised that I didn't have to hurry for anyone. I was getting used to the thought of freedom.

As I approached the glass doors I shook hands with some of the security guards and court sheriffs who were standing lined up on the inside of the foyer. They wished me all the best for the future. One guard made a joke and told me to try not to lose my shoe again. I laughed.

I exited through the glass doors, down the steps, past all the cameramen and journalists. Questions were being thrown at me from all directions, but I ignored them and continued towards the car. Just as I was getting in the car I heard one cameraman shout out 'Smile, Joanne' and I did, not because I was asked, but because I felt like smiling.

Tribute to Phil

I was at a pretty low point when Phil Banton came into my life in June 2004. He had been appointed my family liaison officer by the UK police. I was immediately sceptical, and wondered what kind of support he could possibly provide me more than three years after the crime.

Those three years had been very traumatic for me. My world had been turned upside down, I'd become reclusive, untrusting and frightened. Phil was my first contact with any police from the UK. Up until that point, I had only ever dealt with police from the Northern Territory.

Quite simply, Phil restored my faith in humanity. He also restored my faith in the police service and the justice system.

Phil became my mentor, my rock of support. He was a true professional and became a significant person in my life. Our meetings started out as a monthly engagement but became more frequent as the trial approached.

He provided me with the kind of support and guidance I had been lacking, but more than that – he made me feel good about myself again. That is a gift I will always cherish.

He rebuilt my confidence and self-belief. The day before I was due to give evidence Phil gave me a simple piece of advice.

He told me to be myself.

I received a call from [Phil's wife] in Darwin on the morning of the verdict in December last year. She told me the devastating news that Phil had been diagnosed with cancer. We spent some time that morning crying and trying to come to terms with it all.

Late last week, I received the news that Phil had passed away. I haven't been able to stop crying since. Now, I've decided not to try. I am just being myself.

To [Phil's wife], family and friends, my thoughts and prayers are with you all today. I know in all the sadness there will be a sense of pride in what Phil achieved in his life. I feel very privileged to have been a small part of it and am forever in his debt.

Phil was the person that I wanted most to be proud of me. I am so proud of him.

Epilogue

While writing this book I have been living in the past and at times it has been difficult. A terrible thing happened to me, but I have been able to take some positive things away from what happened. I have met some inspirational people on this journey and I have found strengths in myself I never knew I had.

I hope after reading my book people will know me better. After sharing my journey I hope you will understand who I am and why I made the choices I did. I hope I have satisfied your curiosity.

I withdrew my letter of complaint after the court case. I felt too emotionally drained after the trial and I felt it more important to move forward. Hopefully there will be lessons learnt by the police and in the future there will be more focus on caring for victims of violent crime.

Some may feel sorry for me after reading my story, but please don't.

I am so glad to have had my Mum and Pete in my life. I have been lucky to have known such amazing people, people like Phil

Banton. I have also been touched by the loyalty and love I have received from my friends.

The title of my book says it all: No Turning Back. It is time to concentrate on my future.

So don't pity me. I am the lucky one.

'I am not a victim or a witness anymore.'

Acknowledgments

Diane Ward – I am honoured to call you my best friend. You give me strength, faith and make me smile.

AJ (Judith) – I've known you all my life, yet only in recent years have I begun to truly know you. I see a lot of you in myself. I want you to know how much you mean to me, I love you.

Sam – I will always be your big sister and I will always be here for you.

Martin Jaffier – Thank you for being a true, loyal and dependable friend. Also for the years of technology advice.

Carol Stead – I don't know what it is like to have a sister, but I can't imagine that it feels any different to what I feel for you. Thank you for listening, caring and always being there.

Keith Campbell – Your positivity and energy is infectious. I'm inspired by your passion. You remind me that if I work hard and believe in myself, I can achieve my ambitions.

Joan, Luciano, Nick and Paul Falconio – I regard you as family. Thank you for the love and support you have given me over the years.

Ali – Thank you for welcoming me into your home and family. We have a unique friendship, throughout the years and across the thousands of miles it has remained strong. In many, many ways you educate me, you inspire me, you encourage me. Most importantly you remind me what the important things in life are. It breaks my heart to think that I won't be seeing you every day. Thank you for sharing this journey with me, being with you was where I needed and wanted to be.

Kahu – Thank you for allowing another girl into your home and for giving me the opportunity to dive with sharks.

Jesse and Tess – Thank you for sharing some of the happiest times of mine and Pete's life.

Amanda Wealleans – You are my favourite Kiwi. Thank you for putting up with me twenty-four hours a day during the time I was living with you. For not judging me, for true friendship, loyalty, the fun times and putting up with me playing my music over and over again.

Lisa Gosling – It is wonderful to have someone to share my travelling memories with. Thank you for the trouble you went to in coming to Alice Springs to look after me.

Libby Andrew – You're a special person. Whenever I think that I can't carry on, that I've made it as far as I can possibly go, I think of you and I know that I can go the extra distance. Your compassion and insightfulness got me through my darkest days.

Megan Rowe – Thank you for your professionalism and dedication to the investigation. You give me faith and you inspire me. Thank you for your help with this book.

Nicola Hamilton – I love you, I love your family. Sometimes I think you know me better than I know myself. Thank you for always telling me what I need to hear and not what I want to hear.

Mark Sanders – BBM, I will be forever grateful to you for the love and support you gave me during the lowest times of my life. Maybe I never told you how much, I hope this acknowledgment in some small way makes up for that. Thank you for giving me a smile when I needed one the most.

Sharon Forbes – Thank you. You brought some much-needed light into my life during the trial in Darwin.

Brian Tyson – Thank you for your generosity, encouragement and wisdom. I will try to live up to your faith and 'supreme confidence' in me.

Lorelei Fong Lim and your entire family – Your efforts went far beyond the role you were given. Thank you for the hospitality you gave to me and my friends. We hope to return the favour one day.

Rosemary and Alan – Thank you for being valued members of my book club.

Noel – Thank you for being my first tennis coach, for all your support and contributions to the book.

Matthew Kelly – Thank you. You understood from the start.

Vanessa Radnidge – 'It's all good.'

Everyone at Hachette Livre – I made the right choice. Thank you for believing in my book and me. Thank you for giving me the opportunity to make this all possible. And for making me feel very welcome.

I am smiling and feel incredibly lucky. Jx